Communicating
Peace

COMMUNICATING
PEACE
Entertaining Angels
Unawares

Philip Lee
Editor

SOUTHBOUND
Penang

WACC

taking sides

Published by
Southbound Sdn. Bhd.
Suite 20F, Northam House, 55 Jalan Sultan Ahmad Shah, 10050 Penang, Malaysia.
Fax: 604-228 1758. Email: books@southbound.com.my
Website: http://www.southbound.com.my

Published in association with
World Association for Christian Communication
308 Main Street, Toronto, Ontario
Canada M4C 4X7
Website: http://www.waccglobal.org

Index by Kay Margaret Lyons
Typeset by Chin Kooi Hong
Cover design by Terence Goh, C-Square Sdn. Bhd.
Pre-press services by Eefar Lithographic Sdn. Bhd., Penang, Malaysia
Printed by Jutaprint, Penang, Malaysia.

Perpustakaan Negara Malaysia   Cataloguing-in-Publication Data

Communicating peace: entertaining angels unawares / editor Philip Lee.
  Includes index
  ISBN 978-983-9054-53-8
  1. Communication–Social aspects. 2. Mass media–Social aspects.
  3. Communication–Social aspects. I Lee, Philip.
  302.2

Contents

I   **Introduction** • PHILIP LEE • *1*

Part One

II   **The Media and Civil Society in Africa**
• ROBERT A. WHITE • *19*

III **The One-and-the-Many Problem in
Communication Ethics**
• CLIFFORD G. CHRISTIANS • *45*

IV **Cultivating Journalists for Peace**
• KAARLE NORDENSTRENG • *63*

V   **Publicity and the Public Sphere in the
Internet Era** • SLAVKO SPLICHAL • *81*

VI **Journalism in Africa: Modernity
versus Africanity** • FRANCIS B. NYAMNJOH • *97*

VII **Advertising against Racism: Reflections on
Consumer Culture and Social Activism**
• LIV SOVIK • *115*

VIII **Making a Difference: The Right to Information
Movement and Social Change**
• PRADIP N. THOMAS • *137*

IX   Communicating Peace: The Pity (and the
      Absurdity) of War • PHILIP LEE • *157*

Part II

X   The Holy Spirit and Communication (1990)
      • MICHAEL TRABER • *177*

XI   Communication as a Human Need and
      Human Right (1992) • MICHAEL TRABER • *193*

XII   Beyond Patriotism: Escaping the Ideological
      Prison (1995) • MICHAEL TRABER • *205*

XIII Towards the Democratisation of Public
      Communication: The Need to Reconsider the
      Criteria for News (1995)
      • MICHAEL TRABER • *219*

XIV   Communication Transforming Conflict (1998)
      • MICHAEL TRABER • *231*

XV   Communication is Inscribed in Human Nature:
      A Philosophical Enquiry into the Right to
      Communicate (1999) • MICHAEL TRABER • *243*

      Index • *259*

      About the authors • *267*

*This book is affectionately dedicated to the memory of
Mike Traber, inspirational colleague
and friend to so many.*

I

Introduction

PHILIP LEE

Part I

This book is a posthumous tribute to Fr Michael Traber (1929-2006), who for twenty years guided the study and action programmes of the World Association for Christian Communication. Inevitably, it is much more than a mere accolade. Sparse biographical details provide a background, but its chief aim is to memorialize the principles that Michael Traber stood for and the necessarily unfinished nature of the work of which he was a philosophical and theological guiding light. Mike could justifiably have claimed, 'I have fought a good fight, I have finished my course, I have kept the faith' (II Timothy 4:7). But with characteristic modesty he would not have done so, preferring instead to describe himself, in his last days, as a 'gift'. It is the inspirational nature of that gift that this book celebrates.

Michael Traber was born in Switzerland on 5 July 1929 where his secondary education took place during the years of the Second World War. In 1956 he was ordained as a Roman Catholic priest into the Bethlehem Mission Society from where he went to the USA (1956-60) to study sociology and mass communication at Fordham University and New York University (PhD in Philosophy). His doctoral thesis was called

'The Treatment of the Little Rock, Arkansas, School Integration Incident'. It studied the degree and focus of attention given by the daily press of South Africa, West Nigeria, and Ghana to what was one of the most dramatic racial conflicts in the USA of the 1950s. Journalism, racism, and Africa defined an intellectual territory that Mike vigorously pursued in subsequent years.

The Bethlehem Fathers' close ties with Southern Africa led Mike to work in Southern Rhodesia (now Zimbabwe) as Director of Mambo Press and Editor of the critical weekly newspaper *Moto* (1962-70). As well as producing audiovisuals, Mambo Press published books in English and Shona — a language that Mike took time to learn, especially its proverbs. In 1970 he founded and managed Imba Verlag, a book-publishing house in Fribourg, Switzerland, before returning to Africa as Senior Lecturer in journalism at the Africa Literature Centre, Kitwe, Zambia (1973-76). During those years he also did research in Ethiopia, Ghana, Malawi, Uganda, Tanzania, and Zambia.

Mike Traber joined the staff of the World Association for Christian Communication (WACC) in 1976 as Director of its fledgling Periodicals Development Programme and Editor of its quarterly journal *Media Development*. One of his first responsibilities at WACC was to find a way of using the press to support the anti-apartheid struggle in South Africa. In the 1970s a number of organizations in that country, and several church-related donor agencies, had been considering how to establish a newspaper that would be truly representative of black peoples. In early 1976 WACC convened a meeting of representatives of various organizations from South Africa to discuss different possibilities and from that meeting the Black Press Fund (BPF) was born.

It was agreed that the BPF would be used to support periodicals that most effectively critiqued the apartheid regime and its inhuman policy of segregation and discrimination. When the South African Council of Churches (SACC) set up a newspaper in Johannesburg, called *The Voice*, for which it sought financial aid, the BPF contributed to its operational costs as well as supporting *Grassroots*, a black community newspaper in Cape Town. Mike Traber was a consultant to both newspapers.

Communication rights in theory and practice

In 1976, in response to the call of many developing countries for the 'decolonisation of information', UNESCO undertook a review of communication in contemporary society against the background of technological progress and developments in international relations. It established the International Commission for the Study of Communication Problems under the presidency of Seán MacBride. The outcome, published in 1980, was *Many Voices, One World: Communication and Society Today and Tomorrow* with its slogan 'Towards a new more just and more efficient world information and communication order'. Under Mike's guidance, WACC became one of the earliest church-related and non-governmental organizations to support the New World Information and Communication Order (NWICO).

During the early 1980s international controversy over the call for this new order led to conflict between NWICO supporters (which included most Third World countries) and government and private sector interests in the North. One outcome was the withdrawal of the USA, Great Britain and Singapore from UNESCO. Another was reluctance on the part of UNESCO to promote *Many Voices, One World*, supplies of which by 1988 had run out. WACC sought and was given permission to republish it. In 1988 *Media Development* also devoted the first of several issues to the theme 'Communication is a human right'. Its editorial identified the still evolving third generation of human rights as 'solidarity rights', calling for international cooperation to implement them and for human interests to be placed above national interests. The editorial reaffirmed the need for a more just and more efficient world information and communication order:

As yet there is no definition of the right to communicate. But the
majority of thinkers want it to stress the equality of all partners in the
communication process. It should embrace a multi-cultural, multi-way
flow of information, including a passive as well as an active right to
communicate, while promoting the highest possible degree of
feedback, participation and access (Traber, 1988: 1).

In 1989 Mike Traber became a founding member of the
MacBride Round Table on Communication, which met for the
first time in Harare, Zimbabwe, continuing what was to become
a lifetime's unwavering support for the values inherent in the
MacBride Report and, later, the communication rights
movement.

Similarly, he put his intellectual weight behind the growing
call for a systematic study of the connections between theology
and communication, a WACC programme that began in the
early part of 1983. Six years later some 48 working papers, 59
course outlines for teaching communication in seminaries and
12 complete syllabi had been produced. A book on theology
and communication was published in Latin America and an
extensive study of courses in every major theological seminary
in North America was carried out. This pioneering work stood
Mike in good stead when he later joined the staff of United
Theological College, Bangalore, to teach doctoral students.

Mike Traber also worked closely with Dr Robert A. White,
at that time director of research at the Centre for the Study of
Communication and Culture (London), to edit a series of
monographs on 'Communication and Human Values'. The aim
of the series was to contribute to the development of social
philosophies of communication based on a general conception
of human rights and appropriate to particular cultural contexts.
The American publisher Longman brought out the first book
in 1983, *Cultural Autonomy in Global Communications* by Cees
J. Hamelink. However, for reasons unconnected with the series,
Longman withdrew and a second contract was signed with Sage.
From 1986 to the end of the series in 1997, some 30 titles had

appeared, including the first English translation of Jesús Martín-Barbero's *Communication, Culture and Hegemony* (1993), and culminating in *Communication Ethics and Universal Values* (1997), edited by Clifford G. Christians and Michael Traber.

WACC's Christian Principles of Communication

In 1984 at the suggestion of Dr Hans W. Florin, then WACC's General Secretary, Mike Traber drafted eight propositions on communication for discussion by its Central Committee. He argued that although information and communication were drastically changing the world, instead of establishing commonality and solidarity, they were tending to reinforce divisions, widen the gap between rich and poor, consolidate oppression, and distort reality. The effect was to maintain systems of domination and to subject the silenced masses to media manipulation.

Formally adopted in 1986, WACC's *Christian Principles of Communication* affirmed that genuine communication liberates, creates community, is participatory, supports and develops cultures, and is prophetic. This landmark in the political development of WACC provided the theological basis and rationale for its first international Congress (1989). It also laid the foundations for WACC's study and action programmes, in which Mike took the lead in elaborating six thematic areas: 'communication ethics'; 'the right to communicate'; 'communication and religion'; 'communication, culture and social change'; 'communication education'; and 'women's perspectives'.

Mike Traber retired from WACC — but not from communications — in 1995. A book on *The Democratization of Communication* was published in his honour, containing contributions from colleagues working in the field of mass communications. As the introduction emphasized, Michael Traber stood for: '...the universal values of humanism, above all peace, democracy, human rights, social progress and national liberation, while respecting the distinctive character, value and dignity of each culture, as well as the right of each people freely to choose and develop its political, social, economic and cultural systems.'

Until 2004 Mike continued to teach for one month each year at the Gregorian University, Rome, but his principal activity was to spend six months of every year in India, working with colleagues to build up a master's and later a doctoral degree course at United Theological College, Bangalore, where he combined his passions for journalism, theology and communication rights.

WACC conferred Honorary Life Membership on Mike Traber at a ceremony held in Switzerland on 11 March 2006. Owing to his illness, Mike was unable to speak – an irony not lost on one who had emphasized the importance of the *logos* throughout his life. His great friend and boyhood companion Fr Joe Elsener read out a statement on his behalf:

> I consider myself a gift of the Catholic Church to the ecumenical movement. By participating in this movement I was in effect — and happily — under the authority of Protestant Churches. One of my tasks has been to bear witness to the seamless and undivided garment of Christ, or to the ecumenical character of God's Reign. A second task was not only to bear witness among my Protestant friends but, equally so, among my fellow Catholics. In that sense, I am also a gift of the ecumenical movement to the Catholic Church. This double witness has occasionally caused confusion and misunderstandings, some of which were painful. But that pain has been wiped out by the enthusiasm of my Indian students, both Protestant and Catholic, in the last ten years. I learned early on in my life that public communication, at least in Africa and Asia, ought to be ecumenical in principle. I consider the churches' public communication not primarily as a service to the churches but, more comprehensively, as an action centred on furthering the Kingdom of God. The church, after all, does not exist for its own sake, but for the sake of the Kingdom. The values of God's Reign — such as equality, justice, reconciliation, freedom,

harmony, peace and love ('shalom') — have inspired my work May
these values guide me to the end of my days. In conclusion, I would
like to thank all those who have accompanied me in my life's journey.
In particular I would like to thank all of you, gathered here for an
honour I do not deserve, but for which I am grateful — for the sake of
the Kingdom.

Mike Traber died on 25 March 2006. He would have smiled
in gentle disbelief if the following maxim were to seem to refer
to him, but he would have wholeheartedly endorsed the values
of openness, communicative action, and shalom that it implies:
'Be not forgetful to entertain strangers: for thereby some have
entertained angels unawares' (Hebrews 13: 2).

Part II

There is a general consensus that a public sphere as a (possibly
idealized) theatre of communicative action is crucial to
democratic systems and good governance. This is the
philosophy of Jürgen Habermas and, among others, Amartya
Sen who, in the context of an exploration about the
'miniaturization of human beings', underlines the singular
importance of public reasoning in democracy: 'There is a strong
case for advancing widespread public discussion even when
there would remain many inescapable limitations and
weaknesses in the reach of the process' (Sen, 2006: 184).

Many would argue that there is no single public sphere, but
a multiplicity of public spheres, including 'alternative' spheres
that challenge the assumptions and specifics of more orthodox
or powerful ones. Public spheres are characterized by
communication in its broadest sense (face-to-face interaction
and exchange in public), spaces that people can enter and leave
without hindrance regardless of ethnicity, religion, gender or
economic status, and spaces that mediate between people who
are relatively powerless and institutions that are much more
powerful.

Public spheres must be inclusive spaces in which everyone can place their concerns on the public agenda and participate in decision-making; spaces that allow a process of transparent public deliberation in which all voices have equal weight, even if democratically taken decisions disappoint some sectors. It requires no great leap of the imagination to see that the mass media of communication ought to constitute a public sphere (a normative claim), one that inherently enhances democratic decision-making and contributes constructively to a culture of peace. Equally, it is clear that political and economic control of communications systems, especially the mass media, and/or monopolisation by governments and corporate interests, obstruct communication rights and can be detrimental to peace.

German philosopher and sociologist Jürgen Habermas developed his theories of communicative action and the public sphere in a series of books published from 1981 onwards. This is not the place to attempt to summarize or discuss complex theories about which a great deal has already been written. Yet, communicative action resonates profoundly with the principles underlying the concept of communication rights with their emphasis on justice, equality, participation and accessibility. Communicative action asserts that through systematic discussion, universal truths and codes of appropriate conduct can be uncovered in such a way that everyone involved can reach agreement and from which they can benefit equally. Communicative action rests on the ability of everyone to dialogue and to understand or temporarily adopt each other's individual perspectives and, from that starting point, to develop actions that have just consequences for everyone. Without taking into account the viewpoints of others, people risk acting out of ignorance or minimizing conditions that cause suffering to others:

> Mutual acceptance is always an essential precondition. In principle it
> can exclude no-one as a partner in communication, for basically its
> aim is an unrestricted community of communication. The moment I
> begin to speak I enter a universal dialogue. Rules of behaviour, that is,

ethical decisions, can only be founded on and, therefore, justified in terms of this unlimited community of communication. Universal solidarity is thus the basic principle of ethics and can be shown as the normative core of all human communication (Peukert, 1981: 10, quoted in Traber, 1990: 213)

Despite their apparent theoretical and practical complexity, universal solidarity, communicative action, and genuine dialogue are the watchwords of many of Michael Traber's writings collected here. They find an echo in Robert A. White's emphasis on the significance of community media in Africa, where notions of good citizenship and communication rights are being promoted in local situations in an effort to make controlling elites more accountable:

The people are much more aware of injustices, conflicts and problems and bad governance at the local community level. It is for this reason that community media, especially community radio, have been much more successful in confronting unjust treatment of and lack of services for women, poor farmers, school children, the sick, prisoners, and the tendency of the central government to exploit and exclude the community as a whole (p. 41).

Communicative action, the sacredness of life, truth-telling, and comparative communication ethics are foremost in the thinking of Clifford G. Christians, whose chapter explores how the moral imagination is rooted in what is universally human, not in self. He argues that universal solidarity is the normative core of all human communication and that globalization has to be re-interpreted through the lens of dialogic communication:

The dialogic ethics I propose is fed by the sacredness of our universal humanity as tacit knowledge. Dialogic ethics of all kinds are community-oriented, the relational by definition entails the communal. The dialogic rooted in the self and Other is conditioned always in terms of the protonorm — human solidarity around the sacredness of life. Shifting ethics from the self to a radical otherness

avoids the self-deception, self interest, and moral arrogance of
individualism... A commitment to universals does not eliminate
differences in what we think and believe. Normative ethics grounded
ontologically is pluralistic. The only question is whether our
community's values affirm the sacredness of life and ethnic diversity at
the same time (p. 60).

Professional ethics of journalism are crucial to the legitimate
functioning of the press and to responsibly fulfilling the role
that journalists can play in a democratic society. Since
independence and pluralism of the media lie at the heart of any
initiative aimed at promoting good governance and equitable
development, media freedom must be protected so that ethical
journalists and independent media can monitor and expose
poor governance and malpractice in public life. This watchdog
role of the media is essential to building public confidence in
the democratic administration of society, particularly where it
concerns open and inclusive processes of social development
and restraining public and private power. By the same token,
as the International Principles of Professional Ethics in
Journalism (1983) make clear, 'The journalist participates
actively in the social transformation towards democratic
betterment of society and contributes through dialogue to a
climate of confidence in international relations conducive to
peace and justice everywhere, to détente, disarmament and
national development.' However, Kaarle Nordenstreng goes
further in arguing that the ethical journalist has a professional
commitment to universal values such as peace, democracy,
human rights, social progress and denouncing violations of
human rights:

> Thus it becomes the professional responsibility of all journalists to
> pursue, not only truth in general, but the universal values of humanism
> as well. In other words, the definition of professionalism takes a great
> leap forward from the libertarian notion of a journalist whose task is
> merely to transmit facts and opinions by remaining independent and

neutral with regard to various socio-political interests and values
(p. 72).

Concepts of public sphere, citizens' participation in political life and 'cyber citizenship' underlie the application of new information and communication technologies (ICTs) to modern societies in all their complexity. Slavko Splichal argues that the problems of democratic political representation and participation have not been solved by the emergence of virtual communities and that what is needed is a redefinition of boundaries between public and private, real and virtual:

> Similar to former revolutionary technologies that have substantially
> contributed to economic growth and social change but not to the
> reduction of social inequalities, ICTs are not a 'classless' technology.
> They are shaping a new class structure separating the 'rich-and-wired'
> and 'poor-and-unconnected'. Since ICTs are becoming an
> indispensable infrastructure for both civil society and the public
> sphere, exclusion from these 'technological' structures has not only
> economic but much broader and fatal consequences for 'unconnected'
> individuals — they lead to exclusion from civil society and the public
> sphere, and from citizenship altogether (p. 89).

Francis B. Nyamnjoh explores what it means to be African in the context of modernity and globalization and caught up in contexts shaped by unique histories, unequal encounters, misrepresentations, and devalued humanity. Based on such a legacy, he questions the contribution that African journalists trained in Western models are making to democratic reform in Africa, at the expense of ignoring a deeply embedded sense of communalism that stresses African cultural values of sociality, interconnectedness, interdependence and conviviality:

> Regardless of the status of those involved in 'rights talk' and 'culture
> talk', they are all convinced of one thing: 'cultural citizenship' is as
> integral to democracy as political and economic citizenship. If African

philosophies of personhood and agency stress interdependence between the individual and the community, and between communities, and if journalists each identify with the many cultural communities seeking recognition and representation at local and national levels, they are bound to be torn between serving their communities and serving the 'imagined' rights-bearing, autonomous individual 'citizen' of the liberal democratic model. A democracy that stresses independence, in a situation where both the worldview and the material realities emphasize *inter*dependence, is bound to result only in dependence (p. 105).

An unusual 'take' on social activism is offered in Liv Sovik's chapter on aspects of global capitalism, corporate social responsibility, and the struggle against racism in Brazil. It is an attempt to revisit the production of advertising — characterized as having been 'naturalized' by the industry — in the context of NGOs, social movements, and corporations that take an interest in social responsibility. Framed by Jean Baudrillard's critique of the consumer society and by Gilles Deleuze's notions of symbolic power and control, she identifies a problematic inequality between advertising professionals or corporations developing social responsibility projects and social movements/ NGOs:

If advertising agencies are relatively weak in comparison to their major clients, much weaker are NGOs in relation to the specialized knowledge of the advertising industry and the money of large corporations. When companies provide financial support for projects, with promotional goals in mind, NGOs are the minority partners, though they provide the relevant specialized knowledge about social projects, community development, education among deprived groups or other issues. Decisions are made together, but the partnership is made difficult by more public and sometimes open-ended decision-making processes among NGOs and clear hierarchies of command within companies. While social organizations work in an open field and are committed to transparent accounting, much less is known about business strategies of advertising agencies or other companies (p. 133).

All the above themes are present explicitly or implicitly in Pradip N. Thomas' assessment of the right to information as an essential plank of communication for social change. His argument is that communication rights need to be articulated at the local level as well as at all intermediary levels. It is far easier to talk in terms of international declarations and treaties than to contextualize the implications of such calls in lived realities. If the World Summit on the Information Society (WSIS) led anywhere — and in some quarters its outcomes remain vague and inconsequential — it was to recognition that, while common and universal deficits exist in global communications, the solutions proposed — 'access', cultural and human rights, the strengthening of the public domain, etc. — do not take into account the diverse specificities of local communication needs:

> In other words, one can argue that in order for communication rights to really become a global policy discourse, it must relate to critical communication deficits in local contexts. There is a need for many local-specific understandings of communication rights rather than the one, universal framework that, however well-meaning, is not suitable to advancing the local cause of communication rights (p. 142).

Finally, the contribution that cinema can make to building a more peaceful society is explored in my own chapter, which contrasts two films – *All Quiet on the Western Front* (1930) and *Oh! What a Lovely War* (1969) – in an attempt to discern how film might raise serious questions about warmongering (in the first example) or about its tragic absurdities (in the second example). The civilizing influence of 'great art' has long been the subject of ethical discourse, but the role of 'popular culture' in forming or changing opinions and attitudes may be less well articulated. Of course:

It is unrealistic to expect films about war to prevent other wars. It is a well known paradox that the great achievements of civilisation – literature, music, art, cinema, the Universal Declaration of Human Rights – are not in themselves capable of civilising humanity. Yet there is still a case to be made for the role played by cinema in providing moral guidance and critical reasoning on the great issues of life and death that affect society. Cinema has always tried to do this, but it needs to be part of a larger configuration of public education... The key question is: can societies educate people to create and maintain an environment in which the ethical imperatives of coexistence and peace are implicitly and explicitly recognized? (p. 172)

Universal solidarity

Communication rights and the ever more urgent need to construct a culture of peace are central to a vision of a world in which universal human values displace the accumulated weight of history's tyrannies. Michael Traber believed that there is only one way of overcoming the political, economic, social, and cultural inequalities and violence that have marred and obstructed justice for all — and that is genuine communication. For him, building a culture of peace meant building a culture of communication. And one of the enterprises that lay closest to his heart was the project he shared with Clifford G. Christians to identify fundamental principles of communication ethics that respond both to the rapid globalization of communications and simultaneously to the reassertion of local socio-cultural identities. Their aim was to make a significant contribution to a more humane and more responsible code of values that societies everywhere could and should adopt:

Communicative freedom always implies solidarity, a solidarity that is universal, that is, extends to all people and peoples. The reason for this does not lie in the fact that the present generation understands the interconnections between peoples in one world. Here, the concept of universality is based on the fundamental equality of all human beings and their identical claims to freedom. In the context of specific socio-political conditions, the abstract concept of universal solidarity becomes quite concrete. It is, above all, solidarity with those whose freedom has been taken away, or seriously diminished, thus rendering them less than human. In these cases, solidarity becomes, as it were, operational, that is, transforms itself into concrete communicative actions (Traber, 1997: 335).

Michael Traber's published writings, of which 189 are listed in the bibliography published by the Missionsgesellschaft Bethlehem Immensee (see Frei, 2007), reveal an abiding concern for people the world over and their desire for peaceful coexistence. From his very first articles focusing on China and Japan (1953) to his last on India (2005) — which address questions of faith, mission, racism, literacy, the political engagement of the church, the role of the press in democracy, the new world information and communication order, theological reflections on communication, communication ethics, and communication rights — the underlying motif is that all people should be empowered to live together in genuine communication and, therefore, in peace.

References

Frei, Fritz (ed.) (2007). *Bibliographie Michael Traber SMB (1929-2006)*.

Peukert, Helmut (1981). 'Universal solidarity as goal of communication', in *Media Development* 4/1981.

Sen, Amartya (2006). *Identity and Violence. The Illusion of Destiny*. London: Penguin.

Traber, Michael (1988). *Media Development* 4/1988, Editorial.

Traber, Michael (1990). 'The Holy Spirit and Communication', in *The Ecumenical Review*, Volume 42, Nos. 3-4, July-October. Reprinted in this book.

Traber, Michael (1997). 'An Ethics of Communication Worthy of Human Beings', in *Communication Ethics and Universal Human Values*, edited by Clifford Christians and Michael Traber. Thousand Oaks: Sage Publications.

Part One

II

The Media and
Civil Society in Africa

ROBERT A. WHITE

There is consensus among socio-political analysts that African countries have developed the socio-cultural structure of other post-colonial societies, such as Latin America, with a great concentration of cultural, political and economic power in a small, self-perpetuating elite (Mbaku, 2004). This relatively small group has privileged access to high quality education, a wealth of communication and information sources, economic and financial means, contacts in countries of the north and, above all, control of political decision-making. The mass of rural and urban poor – especially the rural poor – live generation after generation without access to good education and other services, except for a lucky few who are able to make contacts that allow them to emerge from this cycle of poverty. The son of a peasant farmer will be a peasant farmer or at best a street hawker or labourer living in urban slums. What is most dismaying is that the 'governing elite' seem to be without any strong sense of responsibility and untouched by the pressures of accountability to the public. In a recent study of members of the national assembly of Tanzania, 50 per cent said their primary motive was the large salary, another 25 per cent added that the contacts for income and business are a motive. Most live in the national capital far from their constituency and with little sense of service to their constituency (Mukandala, 2004). Most African countries have been governed since independence by the same party or shifting members of an elite which can trace its ascent to access to education and administrative experience in the colonial period.

In virtually all African countries, there is almost daily protest in the press against the oppression and exploitation of the masses of rural and urban poor – and of many other sections of the population. There are headlines every day about the plundering of the national treasury, the blatant manipulation of elections, the disastrous mismanagement of government ministries, the waste of national resources on luxurious living and, on the other hand, the continual decline of health services, education, roads and virtually all other services. Every interview with entrepreneurs on the development of industry begins with the ritualistic complaint about the poor investment climate: the continual interruptions of electric power, the disintegration of public highways into a mass of potholes, the lack of good communications, the high taxes with no services, the lack of a well-trained labour force. Analysts speak of Africa being dominated by a 'rentier' class, which simply lives off the produce of the industries of petroleum, mining and tourism managed by the large multi-national corporations such as Shell or Anglo-American. The Nigerian press runs regular 'Sunday supplement' accounts of the antics of the 'glitterati', the luxurious life of the super-rich flitting between homes in London, New York and other parts of the world.

Everyone says 'something should be done about all this'. But almost in the next breath they comment that so-and-so has been silenced, threatened, bought off or been 'sent abroad'. Widespread popular organization does not seem to appear. The poor street vendors, for example, were shifted off into the back alleys in Tanzania recently with relatively little organized protest and little strong public support. The one institution which seems to speak out consistently and with some effectiveness is the press: the daily newspapers, the news magazines and, to some extent, the press of particular institutions such as the religious press, the newsletters of professional groups and the labour unions. The press councils of some countries such as Tanzania seem to be significant supports of press freedom. The central question I would like to pose in these pages is the following: to what extent has the institution of the press been able to influence public opinion to bring those in position of power and decision making to greater public accountability and better use of the national resources for the general welfare? The answers among African analysts have not been particularly conclusive or productive. I would at least like to begin to understand how to frame the question and develop a methodology for finding some answers. The focus is sub-Saharan Africa, excluding South Africa.

Lack of democratic accountability

Governing elites in Africa vary considerably in their degree of accountability and service to the people, but it would be fairly accurate to describe most as 'despotic' (Ihonvbere, 2004). In most countries the same political parties or same group of civil and military leaders have been governing continuously since independence. The independence movements became the single ruling party which has controlled the state apparatus in which have been concentrated virtually all public services. The introduction of a multi-party electoral system in the early 1990s has not brought significant increases in accountability to the public. All parties are using some form of manipulation of the apparatus of liberal democratic institutions such as elections, parliaments, the police and the judiciary to favour the interests of this governing elite and enable them to continue in power perpetually. The major claim to the legitimacy of their control is the need to preserve national unity and, in the name of their links with great founding personalities such as Nyerere, continue the great work of liberation and development.

In other historical eras and other geographical contexts, when a despotic governing system of leadership has abused its legitimacy, the 'people' or significant parts of the society have been able to wrest the control of the state and other major institutions such as education, the church, the arts and the communication system from this elite. One example is the movement in early modern Europe that created the liberal democratic societies and, to some extent, continually reformed them to increase greater popular participation and greater popular benefit from the national welfare. In the face of the self-perpetuating concentration of power in the hands of monarchies and nobility, the 'people' who had no particular title to authority gradually built legitimacy to their claim to the right to govern and their ability to provide good governance.

The concept of civil society as distinct from the state developed in the late eighteenth century among the philosophers of the Scottish Enlightenment and other political philosophers to describe the socio-political movement of citizens to wrest control from the despotic rulers of the era and to bring accountable governance (Bratton, 1994: 53). The term gained new popularity and use in the wake of the rejection of the socialist governments of Eastern Europe in the late 1980s, and many analysts of African politics began to use the term to describe the introduction of multi-party politics in most African countries in the early 1990s (Young, 1994). To what extent there exists a civil society in Africa, and in what form, is widely debated (Harbeson, 1994). Certainly, there is great scepticism that the concepts developed by the Enlightenment in Europe, what de Tocqueville describes in the early United States or even the Gramscian theories of democratization in the context of early twentieth century European industrialization can be directly applicable to explain a process in the African context.

What is different about the African context, I would argue, is the beginning of modern African societies in European colonialism. African societies are so deeply resistant to a culture of public service and accountability to the public because the socio-political and economic institutions are rooted in colonial social structures and governmental institutions (Havnevik, 1993). The logic of colonial occupation and government was obviously not accountability to the African people of the interior but to a global imperial system.

Origins of the African power structure in colonial governments

The European imperial powers established a colonial state in African countries for purposes of control of dissent largely through indirect rule in order to carry out a process of economic extraction for the benefit of the metropolis, and made little or no effort to develop the education, health, transportation, or communication in the interior of the country. There was virtually no significant representation of native peoples in governmental decisions, and the governors did not see their primary role to respond to the needs of the people with administrative services. The expatriates sent to control the colonial 'protectorates' lived in their own enclave of spacious homes, clubs and separate facilities and maintained the perception of the natives in the interior as essentially incapable of ever achieving the level of civilization of Europe. Most governors prepared natives for a lower level of the colonial administration, especially for direct dealings with the people of the interior, but the Europeans who got jobs in the colonial governments saw this as a source of their own financial advancement, not as a way to serve the people of the 'interior'.

Independence came far more rapidly than Europeans expected, accelerated mainly by the native colonial bureaucracies who were anxious to take over the privileges of the colonial governors. Although European powers conceded political independence they expected that they could continue their cultural influence by educating a native elite in the home country and, through control of cultural tastes and interests, maintain the economic market for their goods. Through the

Bretton Woods institutions (World Bank, IMF, etc.) the new governments would be effectively guided largely in terms of the metropolitan interests.

The independence movements gained power to offer the nation the reward of rapid modernization, to become like the European masters, and the major instrument for rapid modernization was the state. The welfare state model and socialist state system of enterprises appealed to the independence movements as a way to keep power and develop a rhetoric to gain the support of the masses. There may have been no alternative since few native African entrepreneurs had emerged and the only way to control non African institutions and relate to the international system was through the state apparatus that the independence parties could control.

The governance ideal is the corporatist state. Virtually all of the development efforts were initiated by the state and the state tended to absorb into itself control of all sectors of the society: entrepreneurial efforts through the parastatals, education, health services, transportation and communications, banking and finances and, of course, public security. Initially, at least, all broadcasting and newspapers were taken over by the state. Agriculture, mining and petroleum were the overwhelming economic activity and this also was controlled by the state through marketing boards, mining parastatals or through state-controlled contracting. The governing elite attempted to bring all civil society organizations under its umbrella – labour unions, NGOs, free associations of women, youth and students.

A key point of control by the elites through the state has been the control of the central financial institutions which put them in a close symbiotic relationship with the international financial and monetary system. Since virtually all of the African states were soon burdened by large debts and large annual national fiscal deficits, most of the African states were, in fact, dependent on the international financial institutions for all major decisions. A country such as Tanzania has almost 50 per cent of its annual expenditures covered by donor countries. This gives these various financial sources a significant control over national policies and actions.

One of the most devastating obstacles to development of the countries is the colonial legacy of stigma of the interior as 'native', 'backward', 'uncivilized' or simply 'un-European'. The ideal of every 'modernized' person is to move to the Europeanized city, usually the seat of the colonial government. All services are centrally controlled out of the metropolitan, governing city. For a teacher, doctor or administrator to be sent out to the towns and villages of the interior is a form of punishment, a stamp that one is inferior.

The postcolonial culture and social structure of Africa is not unique but is typical of virtually all colonized parts of the world, notably Latin America. One might argue that the postcolonial structure of Latin America, after four hundred years, is much more rigid and change resistant. Africa will probably always bear the imprint of its colonial origins, but there are certain unique factors which can bring about a culture of service and a governance of accountability and responsibility. The educational institutions and the passion for education in Africa, if further developed, are a first force for greater equality and culture of service. A second factor is the inability of the state to provide all services and the appearance of autonomous initiatives of grassroots, people-controlled organizations to fill the vacuum. Thirdly, the independent press and the culture of performance in drama, music, film and the indigenous imaginative poetry and fiction are a major area for undermining of the legitimacy of the hegemonic global culture and legitimating alternate sources of culture.

The important role of the educational systems

The avenue of entry into modernity for virtually all Africans has been access to education in Europe or in a European-oriented school. It is not by accident that getting a school diploma is burned into the African imagination as an absolute essential thing in life. Today, extended families will make enormous efforts to get their children through schooling to obtain the credentials of schooling. Although education is an induction into the mentality of control, extraction, and maintaining a superior Europeanized way of life, distanced from the village, it also brings with it a culture of professional service to the people, quite different from the colonizing mentality.

The European teachers who established the school system in Africa introduced a demanding discipline, but they respected the African students and found their personal satisfaction in the student's development of their talents. This was especially true of the religious schools, but the elite secular schools for Africans were designed to develop leadership following the tradition of the best public schools of Britain or good secondary schools of France. In the British colonies, the university colleges in Accra, Ibadan and Kampala were models of a university education that introduced a tradition of good professional training with exacting examinations and a degree of scholarly attainment that would match that of Europe at the time. While the colonial governments were paragons of injustice because they excluded Africans from entrepreneurial activities and higher positions in the colonial government, the educational system followed a system of strict reward for merit. While colonial government was interested primarily in power control and subjugation of the Africans, the schools and the university colleges were interested in developing a genuine sense of professional service. While the corruption, lack of a sense of accountability to the people, and lack of a real desire to develop the interior of the African nations find their origin in the colonial governments, a very different culture of appreciation of African personal development and professionalism finds its origin in the colonial educational system. This clash of cultures, I would suggest, is at the heart of the desire of the African people to wrest control of governance away from the present corrupt, despotic governing elite and to develop a governing class which is professionally competent.

Emerging grassroots community organizations

In the twenty years after independence, many African countries were able to obtain loans and subsidies to develop educational and health systems throughout the countries which were much improved over the conditions of the colonial period. However, with the rapid increase in population, growing inflation after the petroleum crisis of 1973 and the rampant corruption in governments, the public services began to decline in the 1980s. Often what services existed in rural communities and in poor urban areas disappeared or were curtailed (Mushi, 2001). A series of factors made the people less dependent on the government bureaucracies, more self-reliant and more interested in a system of governance that would serve their new interests. A number of what one might call 'people-controlled organizations' came into existence to fill the gap caused by the disappearance or non-functioning of the services of the state. Some analysts began to see this as the foundation of a 'civil society' in Africa (Guyer, 1994).

Many of the churches and large NGOs began to assist these communities in small projects. Thus, a second area of growth of independence from the governing elites is the efforts of community leaders organized in some form of community councils. What is particularly interesting is the experience of grassroots community leadership in local community government. This gives many people criteria for how services should be provided and how the central government which has been providing these services could and should be responding to people's needs. The formation of these community efforts is providing the foundation for a fundamentally different model of development, a model in which the central government (and the governing elites) do not command what the public is to do or how local communities are to work but, to the extent that government is able, respond to the initiatives of local communities. The success of community efforts depends on their organization, which seeks information and resources at the district and regional level and circulates this information within the community.

One of the immediate effects was that the possibility of employment with government dried up and most young people in a rapidly increasing population had to find their own employment in small-scale entrepreneurial activity. Migrants from rural villages and school graduates begin to start their own small businesses providing some form of professional services and non-governmental development agencies. Those with less education engaged in entrepreneurial activity ranging from street vending to small-scale retail stores. The common characteristic of all of these small entrepreneurs was that they did not have collateral which would enable them to get loans from the extremely cautious, conservative and badly managed banking system. They formed the so-called 'informal economy', which soon became the most dynamic area of economic growth in African countries. What is significant is that these small entrepreneurs receive no direct benefits from the government and are much less dependent on the governing elite. In fact they have every reason to be resentful and even hostile because they must live on their own efforts and ingenuity.

These small entrepreneurs have a special interest in channelling whatever resources they get into a good education for their children. While most of the large industries are controlled directly or indirectly by overseas companies or their licensing efforts with much of the profit going overseas, all of the profit of the small entrepreneurs is going into education, improved housing, better diets and gradual improvement of the very basics of every day life. Much of the support of secondary and university-level education occurring in Africa today is coming from the relatively meagre incomes of these small entrepreneurs.

One of the important characteristics of the informal, entrepreneurial economy is that their success much depends on their information networks regarding markets, reliable employees and availability of raw materials at the lowest cost.

They often become avid information seekers and, although most of the information comes through interpersonal contacts, this opens their attention to the media as a source of information.

Professional associations and commitment to service

The gradual expansion of the educational system, especially the specialized secondary schools and universities, is producing a large number of people who have some form of professional training. Professional groups and associations are a third major sector of civil society in Africa (Chazan, Lewis, Mortimer, Rothchild, Stedman, 1999: 85–86). At the heart of professional formation is a commitment of service to clients. They also become private entrepreneurs attempting to create a market by offering satisfying services. For various reasons many become deeply critical of the inefficient system of services of the government.

Many teachers, doctors and a host of other professionally trained people despair of the employment conditions in government schools, hospitals or other services. Payment of teachers is often months late. Parents also despair of the education in these schools. In this context, a group of teachers will come together to open their own private school where at least they can live up to their desire to teach as a teacher should and where payment of salaries, even when it is less than the poor salaries of government schools, is more certain. Throughout Africa the quality of education in private schools is surpassing that in government schools almost everywhere. In countries such as Nigeria where corruption of public services is widespread, parents are often willing to make every possible sacrifice to send their children to a private primary or secondary school.

The same logic is operating in the desire of medical doctors to open private clinics. In government hospitals, medical supplies often simply do not arrive. In countries such as Nigeria, public hospitals are often semi-deserted because they lack the most elemental facilities for providing adequate services. In this atmosphere, medical doctors begin to lose their sense of professional commitment.

Professional associations in Africa are now quite well developed, especially in the areas of the classical professions of law and medicine. It is in the interest of the medical establishment to make sure that hospital services recommended are reputable, that the medicines prescribed are genuine and effective, that medical doctors are interested in the health of patients not just in increasing their wealth. Likewise, it is in the interest of lawyers that the context of the judiciary where their profession is exercised is considered honest and just. The legal profession has exercised considerable pressure to improve the credibility of the judiciary.

A fourth type of people-controlled associations is those that organize to point out violations of human rights, the injustices and poor services of the government, the greed of the powerful and the suffering of the great mass of people. This is the civil society as such. All of the above associations at some point engage in civil society action. Because education is so central in the aspirations of African culture, the universities are constantly confronting the contradictions of those elected to serve the public but who are instead exploiting and abusing the public for their own benefit. In the long run the most effective civil society associations are the professional associations of lawyers, medical doctors, financial and business experts who are pressuring the government to provide orderly, rational services. Lawyers stand to gain if the judiciary system is honest. Medical doctors gain if the hospitals are well run. The professional business community benefits if the banking system is honest and soundly managed. All of these associations are foremost in steady reform of the governance system. Women's organizations, labour unions and youth organizations are all important in this process.

Professionalism of the press and the journalistic establishment

The press in Africa has made a strong claim to be a profession and to be essential for making public services accountable to the public. Part of the press's claim to be a profession is the attempt to root its accepted procedures in a code of ethics, in a professional ethos and, ultimately, in a public philosophy, that is, in the values of truth, freedom, social responsibility and citizen's rights. It is the role of the press to present a continuous account of how government and all other public services are functioning so that the citizens can make their claims in the act of voting and in other demands placed on elected representatives. To what extent is the press playing a significant role in establishing a moral and legal order in African societies?

Since the early 1990s when pressure was put on African governing elites by international donor agencies and other international bodies to allow multi-party politics, a more open civil society, respect for human rights and tolerance of a free and diverse media, the press has been much more open and objective in its account of government activities and more critical of bad governance. The generally critical stance of the commercial, non-governmental press is motivated in large part because its principle markets are the groups of the informal economy, the local community leadership, the educated professionals and the civil society organizations eagerly looking for information to justify their view that the bad governance is a major obstacle to national development and well-being. The press can count on these groups as allies in gathering information and supporting its views.

The institution of the press requires that it be objective, impartial and free of direct association with any particular political party or interest group. The media do not have direct coercive political or economic power or even power over strong value commitments such as religious institutions. The power of the media is essentially rhetorical, that is, the ability to construct the meaning of a situation in such a way that it appeals to the world view of a national community as the 'logical' thing to do or appeals to the national ethos as the 'action that any decent citizen would do'. The media are only one form of the circulation of information among opinion leaders. In the African context, the informal, interpersonal networks, especially since the advent of the cellular phone and the internet, are the most important factor in the flow of decisive information or definition of world-view situations. Little has been documented about the flow of information among the members of the fluid community that one can call the governing elite or those who are close to these circles such as the key economic leaders. At the very best moments of the media, key people in the most influential newspapers or television networks or outstanding journalists are aware of how opinion leaders are thinking and motivated and how communication is flowing in the interpersonal networks of important opinion leaders. Good journalism can help articulate this and marshal information which shows how a given course of action will be of maximum benefit to all the parties involved, especially those close to the heart of decision making. The media may help to create a definition of the situation which strengthens the resolve of the opposition, convinces the dominant power to go easy in its use of harsh measures or even lead to major concessions.

The media undoubtedly establish the mood of a country, especially where there is a more literate and educated citizenry and where the press has a tradition for relatively good, responsible journalism. What is gradually brought about is a certain consensus about what is a course of action in which 'everybody is going to win' and where the governing elites will serve their own interest, even their interest in enriching themselves. Given the importance of international aid agencies, the international financial institutions and the opinions of other African states, the press often prominently mentions their opinions. The press knows that the government and the business community close to the government are very concerned about this. A government also knows that it may have the power to force the people to accept a decision, but that governing an unwilling and subtly rebellious citizenry is very difficult. Gradually the conviction is created that a given course of action which respects the public will and will have credibility as a moral action comes into focus.

Appeal to the demand for legality of public action

The groups of governing elites that have held power in African countries since independence (in varying degrees, the same party or group) attempt to base their moral legitimacy on their upholding the law, the constitutions and, finally, peace and development. Many of the governments have been simply military take-overs using their arms to enrich themselves with the oil, diamonds or other natural resources important for the developed world, but most will attempt to justify their holding power in terms of defence of justice, of human rights and human compassion. This presupposes a respect for independent judiciary action, the capacity of the legal profession to discern the possible violations of law and the 'courage' of some groups to initiate legal action. I use the word 'courage' because underneath the surface of legality and civil order, governing groups are using enormous intimidation through threat of economic, social or even physical harm. All this is taking place in an atmosphere of confusion about what is really going on. Most citizens are hesitant to act because they don't really know what is going on and they are ready to give governing groups the benefit of the doubt.

A first important role of the media is to report accurately what the governments are actually doing and reveal the gap between what the law stipulates and what governing actions are doing. The press may certainly carry on investigations to show the violation of legality, but, in order to guarantee objectivity and impartiality (at least the maximum appearance of this) the institution of the press, as it has evolved in modern societies, agrees not to enter directly into political action. In the public journalism movement in the United States, the regional press went far in mobilizing communities to express their preferences so that this could be reported. It became clear that, although the press can work side by side with citizens groups that are taking political action in order to report them with great sympathy, the role remains that of reporting and expressing opinion. Often the editorial columns, taking an action position, and the views on the 'op-ed page' are of great importance because they are usually based on a great deal of information that the editors have gathered but cannot publish because it is too close to political action or still too conjectural. Many quality newspapers in Africa, such as the *Guardian* in Nigeria, bring in the opinions of people who have a reputation for disinterested moral integrity.   Another set of allies of the press in its appeal to the sense of legality are all the local African and international institutions that raise their own moral and legal profile by supporting legality in African politics and other areas of governance. When the government of Obasanjo in Nigeria rather openly falsified the presidential election returns in April 2007, the press eagerly published the intention of the European Union, the US government and many other national and international bodies to impose sanctions on the new government.

Appeal to national pride and identity

African nations are continually jostling among themselves in terms of their ratings on economic growth, rates of educational and health services, their ratings on press freedom, the status of their universities and host of other comparative indicators of the quality of governance and various other national development efforts. Recently, the press in Nigeria wrote stinging editorials showing that in the international rating of universities, even the best universities of Nigeria were rated far below universities in other African countries. When President Nkapa was finishing his term as president in Tanzania, a leading newspaper published a taunting cartoon of the presidents of Uganda and Kenya telling Nkapa that he still had time to rewrite the constitution and continue on indefinitely as president. Countries such as Nigeria or South Africa are making an open bid to be a 'political, moral and economic leader and kingmaker' in Africa. When Obasanjo was seeking to 'rewrite the constitution' to allow him to continue another term or even indefinitely, the press made it clear that this would be incongruous with Nigeria's bid for leadership for good governance in the Organization of African Union and other fora of African continental cooperation.

What the press is appealing to is the sense of moral commitment that may be present in governing elites, in international bodies (including governments), in human rights groups, in organizations with some degree of responsibility for moral education (such as the churches), in the professions within the country, and in the best moral traditions of the nation.

In its best moments, the press attempts steadily to build up evidence that a particular government is acting illegally or with a high degree of mismanagement so that the legitimacy of the action is in question. Gradually public opinion is brought to the point where the citizenry can begin seriously to put on pressure. One of the great mysteries is how the public in Africa or special interest groups put pressure on governments. Why should the governing elites, holding enormous power to coerce or banish those who do not agree with them, listen to public opinion? In Nigeria, when Obasanjo was seeking to get the senate to rewrite the constitution to allow him to seek a third term, the press was able to bring before the public the views of church leaders and leaders of public opinion such as Nobel Prize winner Wole Soyinka. Once church leadership such as the Catholic bishops conference had taken a position, the local religious press was able to take a position. Since Obasanjo is in some sense a religious person and Nigeria has a strong religious culture, the homily given by the president of the Nigerian Bishops Conference in the presence of President Obasanjo, asking him not to seek a third term, was widely noted. The annual statements of the Nigerian Bishops Conference are also a signal to the press and the diocesan press to comment.

Disastrous effects of bad governance

In virtually every daily newspaper in every African country there are articles about the disastrous effects of bad governance. This is juxtaposed with promises that the government is making or has made regarding the solution of these problems. A favourite rhetorical tactic is to take the occasion of the celebration of national independence day when the promises of the independence movement are set against the actual increases in poverty, unemployment, worsening educational situation and other desperate situations. Another rhetorical occasion is to juxtapose the periodical addresses of presidents regarding grandiose governmental objectives with the facts of economic and social stagnation.

The general impact of this rhetoric is to convince virtually all that government services are hopelessly inadequate and that the only answer, if one can afford it, is to seek private education, private hospitals or other private services. Those who work in government-run services will blame the bad management practices of their superiors, their low salaries and the lack of facilities to carry out their jobs well. They will point out that superiors are often people of inferior training who are simply holding on to their jobs because of their party loyalty and their need to protect their income until retirement. Top managers will lament the difficulty of finding effective personnel for middle-management positions. At times those who are occupying positions of middle management argue that they are just about to introduce new methods which will dramatically improve services.

When one follows up these promises with an evaluation of results, there is always a story of sudden change of policy, unforeseen obstacles, or the inadequacy of personnel. Often the person promising new methods suddenly moves on to a better job and begins doing something entirely different. Rarely does one find personnel seriously interested in how to improve the services and solve the problems of the clientele. Most are engrossed in how to improve their domestic economic well-being, especially for the education of their children (in private schools if at all possible). Satisfaction from interaction with a clientele that is benefiting significantly is not a high motivation.

The owners or top managers of private services – education, health, etc. – are constantly in a frantic search for adequate personnel, resources and clientele in competition with other similar private entrepreneurs. They are interested in how they can please their customers or at least draw in more paying customers – whether the problems of the clientele will be solved in any substantial way or not.

All managers, especially in private services, live in fear of bad publicity from the media and are ready to punish any disloyalty or hint of discussion of inadequate services even when it is internal and private. Although public relations offices designed to improve the publicity of the enterprise are increasingly common, many managers do not know how to use them and fear giving any honest information about the organization lest it be used against the organization in a moment of disgruntlement.

Most good newspaper editors have a fairly good analytic understanding of the problems of governance and management and have invented a genre of journalism which one might call 'the success story feature', a kind of life history of an individual who has succeeded in private enterprise or government management in spite of all of the obstacles that are part of daily life in developing countries. The account focuses on the key moves that avoided the failures of so many and invented ways to respond to the needs of the clientele. Variations of this genre

may focus more on the community, on the organization or on
a life of outstanding public service.

In almost every issue of major newspapers of different
African countries there is some revelation of specific problems
of gross mismanagement or significant corruption in some
department of government. Virtually all newspapers that the
author has followed in Nigeria and in Tanzania have mounted
significant campaigns against mismanagement and corruption.
Scandals of this type attract the attention of the public and sell
newspapers especially when this deals with a problem that is
causing major disruption in public life. A good example is the
campaign that the newspapers of Tanzania carried out against
the management of the Tanzanian electrical energy agency at a
time of major crisis of electrical power that lasted almost six
months and caused severe economic problems throughout the
nation. Although the campaign was spearheaded by *The Citizen*,
an Aga Khan newspaper with Kenyan financial backing and
Kenyan management, it was eventually taken up by all of the
commercial, non-government media in Tanzania. The
newspaper campaign was matched by significant pressure from
international financial agencies and representatives in the
economic sector. Whatever might have been the precise line of
causality, one concrete result was the changing of the ministry-
level manager and the assurance of the government that
planning for major investment had been introduced to avoid
similar major crises in the future.

Almost all major corruption scandals in government are
publicized in the press. A major source of information is
virtually always from the inside of the ministry or enterprise,
but at times the organization may reveal its own mistakes by
the inadequate or contradictory information that it supplies.
As in all good investigative journalism, there are multiple
sources of information with varying degrees of honest
transparency, one of which may reveal the lack of openness and
bring pressure for new revelations from a central source. Often
the international financial agencies have an interest in making

available information in a 'disinterested way' in order to pressure local agencies to be more efficient in their use of loans and subsidies. Virtually all African governments now have extensive anti-corruption laws and an 'anti-corruption bureau' and, if illegality can be proved, the guilty parties are subject to prosecution. Thus, the media campaign is usually partially an account of how courts and judges are handling the matter. The media can also keep the public aware of potential sanctions such as strikes, boycotts, and termination of international aid.

Part of the problem of mismanagement and corruption is the lack of a good sense of planning and a good entrepreneurial culture. Good planning involves clear, feasible goals and the ability to solve the problems preventing achievement of goals. There is a lack of analytical, problem solving capacity, and the reporting on governance often does not have the ability to get to the heart of the cause of the problem and suggest solutions. In part, there are few journalists who are specialists in major areas of public life, and there are still relatively few popular magazines where more specialized journalism can be published. All good investigative journalism must use information resources from specialist research institutes and it requires long-term follow up (Bennett and Serrin, 2007: 330-333). Countries such as Nigeria can support large newspapers which have regular specialized departments which dedicate a periodical ten to twenty page in-depth report to areas such as education or the media industry

Media support of civil rights movements

As many studies have shown the publicity goals of civil rights movements are to attract new recruits; sustain the commitment of members of the movement; demonstrate the injustice, immorality and illegality of the situation; create both specialist (as a basis for good legislation) and general understanding of the causes of the problem; generate media coverage to attract the 'will' for favourable policy and legislative action, demonstrate the wrongness of the opposition and, ultimately, shape public policy and state action (McAdam, 2007: 270-271). There are many social groups in Africa which suffer gross injustices: women, rural subsistence farmers, urban slum dwellers, prisoners waiting indefinitely for trial, etc. How successful they are in achieving more just treatment depends on how well organized and persistent the movements are (Widner, 1994: 209).

The most successful in relating to the media and in getting favourable support are the women's movements, especially on specific issues such as female genital mutilation (Tripp, 1994). The massive poverty and injustice suffered by the rural poor, however, has attracted very little favourable action. In part, this is due to the fact that there is no coherent movement among the rural poor and they are easily divided and bought off by the governing elite. Most movements have been successful in publicizing their plight when there is a sharp and dramatic reversal of their situation which gets the injustice of their situation on the agenda of political action. The civil rights movement among blacks in America was successful only after the welfare of the labouring class in general had improved and that of the black labouring class had not. In Africa, the denial of civil rights is so general and the unjust privilege of the small governing elite is so invisible that it is difficult for the media to highlight one specific group as worse off. The poor tend to see the solution to their problems in terms of good client relations with the rich and powerful, not in terms of policies and legislation bringing a more just distribution of resources.

It is evident that the civil society does not really exist in Africa in the sense of the 'people' being conscious of confronting a powerful elite in control of the state apparatus and desiring to obtain resources for individuals and interest groups. Rather the people perceive themselves as a community linked together in a client hierarchy that has one or more of its members at the apex participating in the rich and powerful coalition of the governing elite and able to get for the communalistic group some of the riches available to the elite. The people are content when they see one of 'their own people' as part of the governing elite. The criticism of the national media of the governing elite is aimed at the lack of efficiency in increasing national wealth and resources that would be available to channel down in the different client hierarchies.

The people are much more aware of injustices, conflicts and problems and bad governance at the local community level. It is for this reason that community media, especially community radio, have been much more successful in confronting unjust treatment of and lack of services for women, poor farmers, school children, the sick, prisoners, and the tendency of the central government to exploit and exclude the community as a whole (Alumuku, 2006). The 'people' find it difficult to imagine the problems of the nation as a whole, but they can more easily imagine local problems and mobilize to negotiate a solution to those problems.

Role of the media in civil society in Africa

I have argued that a service-oriented associational life – community organizations, the informal economy, professional associations and interest-organizations – have emerged to fill the vacuum of services left by the inability of the state to respond to the needs of the people. The people in this associational life are hungry for education and for information because this, rather than access to the state, is now a major source of their well-being. The organizational networks at local, district and regional level are still the most important source of information, but the local entrepreneurial and community media are becoming an increasingly important source of formal and non-formal education and information.

The media could be far more effective in supplying needed information if there were more studies of information-seeking processes and better training of media personnel on how to respond to this information seeking. The national, urban press is continually revealing the mismanagement and corruption of the governing elites, but there is little evidence that the media are significantly empowering the people to wrest control of the state apparatus from these elites. Rather, what seems to be happening is that the elites continue to control the benefits of the state for themselves, but that, as the people become better educated, more professional and more involved in associations to solve their own problems, the state apparatus and the client structures become increasingly less important for them. The people-initiated associational life becomes far more important in the life of the African nations. The state bureaucracies and state media become an increasingly less important source of information and the entrepreneurial and community media are more important. As local people-organized initiatives demand a greater response, both the private and the state services and information sources are becoming more efficient simply because there is a stronger associational base to use well what resources and information are available (Selee and Magno, 2004: 309).

References

Alumuku, Patrick (2006) *Community Radio for Development in Africa and in the World*. Nairobi: Paulines.

Bennett, W. Lance and William Serrin (2007). The Watchdog Role of the Press, 326–336, In Doris A. Graber (Ed.) *Media Power in Politics*. Washington: CQ Press.

Bratton, Michael (1994) Civil Society and Political Transitions in Africa, 51–82, in John Harbeson, Donald Rothchild and Naomi Chazan (Eds.). *Civil Society and the State in Africa*. Boulder: Lynne Rienner Publishers.

Chazan, Naomi, Peter Lewis, Robert Mortimer, Donald Rothchild and Stephen John Stedman (1999). *Politics and Society in Contemporary Africa*. Boulder: Lynne Rienner Publishers.

Guyer, Jane (1994) The Spatial Dimensions of Civil Society in Africa: An Anthropologist Looks at Nigeria, 215–230, in John Harbeson, Donald Rothchild and Naomi Chazan (Eds.). *Civil Society and the State in Africa*. Boulder: Lynne Rienner Publishers.

Harbeson, John W. (1994) Civil Society and Political Renaissance in Africa, 1–32, in John Harbeson, Donald Rothchild and Naomi Chazan (Eds.), *Civil Society and the State in Africa*. Boulder: Lynne Rienner Publishers.

Havnevik, Kjell (1993). *The Limits of Development from Above*. Uppsala: The Nordic African Institute.

Ihonvbere, Julius O. (2004) Reconstructing the State: Constitutionalism as Public Policy in Africa, 239–254, in Kelechi A. Kalu (Ed.). *Agenda Setting and Public Policy in Africa*. Aldershot, UK: Ashgate Publishing.

Mbaku, John Mukum (2004) The State, Macroeconomic Performance and Development in Africa, 45–68, in Kelechi A. Kalu (Ed.). *Agenda Setting and Public Policy in Africa*. Aldershot, UK: Ashgate Publishing. Nearly all of the essays in the collection of Kelechi A. Kalu focus on the concentration of power in a small elite as the fundamental problem in developing accountability, responsibility and good governance in Africa.

McAdam, Doug (2007) Strategies of the American Civil Rights Movement, 270–277, in Doris A Graber (Ed.). *Media Power in Politics*. Washington: CQ Press.

Mukandala, R.S.(2004) *People's Representatives: Theory and Practice of Parliamentary Democracy in Tanzania*. Kampala: Fountain Publishers.

Mushi, Samuel (2001) *Development and Democratization in Tanzania: A Study of Rural Grassroots Politics*. Kampala: Fountain Publishers.

Selee, Andrew D. and Francisco Magno (2004). Decentralization and Democratic Governance, 295–320, in Philip Oxhorn, Joseph S. Tulchin and Andrew D. Selee (Eds.) *Decentralization, Democratic Governance and Civil Society in Comparative Perspective: Africa, Asia, and Latin America*. Washington D.C.: Woodrow Wilson Center Press and Baltimore: The Johns Hopkins University Press.

Tripp, Ali Mari (1994) Rethinking Civil Society: Gender Implications in Contemporary Tanzania, 149–168, in John W.Harbeson, Donald Rothchild and Naomi Chazan (Eds.). *Civil Society and the State in Africa*. Boulder: Lynne Rienner Publishers.

Widner, Jennifer (1994) The Rise of Civic Associations Among Farmers in Cote d'Ivoire, 191–214, in John W. Harbeson, Donald Rothchild and Naomi Chazan (Eds.). *Civil Society and the State in Africa*. Boulder: Lynne Rienner Publishers.

Young, Crawford (1994) In Search of Civil Society, 33–50, in John Harbeson, Donald Rothchild, and Naomi Chazan (Eds.), *Civil Society and the State in Africa*. Boulder: Lynne Rienner Publishers.

III

The One-and-the-Many Problem in Communication Ethics

CLIFFORD G. CHRISTIANS

Michael Traber travelled the world. He worked with colleagues across the globe. He was fluent in several languages, and under his editorship *Media Development* became the most representative international and cross-cultural magazine in our field. His Ph.D. in Communications from New York University ensured that he knew the world-wide scope of the media as well.

Indeed, communication has facilitated world affairs. The Berlin wall fell and Gorbachev's *glasnost* took hold before a watching world. A new world information order among nations emerged when the Cold War's strategy of mutually assured destruction began to fade. Television, radio, and the internet rallied the United States on 9/11 and nurtured empathy across the globe. In electronic narrative, working-class rescue teams in New York became heroes of national strength and resiliency, even while the media constructed an identity for global terrorism. News coverage of Iraq and Afghanistan helps keep the military accountable, and ensures that the abuses at Abu Ghraib prison are inescapable. The Qatar-based Arab network,

Al-Jazeera, in the search for transnational credibility, has refused to promote any government's agenda. Because of the global media, we recognize that conquering a nation in war and winning the international mind are two different things, and the latter indispensable.

In this complicated age of technology on a worldwide scale, today's two most powerful tools are in fundamental contradiction. Information technologies have created international communication networks that potentially involve us all in one another's business. But their opposite, military technology, threatens the human race with annihilation. Our fragile planet has the technological sophistication dialectically to destroy humanity while binding all nations into a worldwide information system.

Global technology is built in counterpoint. The only two technologies with global reach are yoked together. As information increases, we presume to facilitate global understanding. When the nuclear arms race is successfully curbed, these two technologies are thought to follow their proper trajectory. Open information unfettered, and destructive technology restrained, is a working formula for sustaining the planet. However, the fundamental issue is not technological globalization per se, but globalization *and* multiculturalism. Michael Traber understood it clearly:

> Communication ethics faces a monumental challenge at present. It has to respond to both the rapid globalization of communications and the reassertion of local sociocultural identities. It is caught in the apparently contradictory trends of cultural homogenization and cultural resistance. Therefore, ethics must confront these critical questions: Can theoretical models be developed that are explicitly cross-cultural? Can moral principles be developed that are universal within the splendid variety of human life? Will a multicultural comparative ethics replace the dominant canons, most of them North American and patriarchal? As the field grows empirically and matures conceptually, a new axis is needed to replace the mono-cultural one (Christians and Traber, 1997: p. viii).

Indigenous languages and ethnicity have come into their own in the twenty-first century. Religious and ideological fundamentalists insist on recognition. Culture is more salient at present than countries. Muslim immigrants are the fastest-growing segment of the population in France, and long-standing policies of assimilation are no longer credible. Thirty thousand Navajos live in Los Angeles isolated from their home nation and culture. The nomadic Fulani search for pasture throughout the sub-Saharan West Africa, held together by clan fidelity but their political future hangs in the balance. 37 distinct languages survive in tiny Burkina Faso. More than 30 percent of the information technicians working for mammoth Microsoft in North America come from India. At the turn of the twentieth century, 80 percent of immigrants to the United States were from Europe. Since the 1960s, the majority has come from Asia, Latin America, the Middle East, and developing countries in Africa. And rather than the melting-pot Americanization of the last century, immigrants now insist on maintaining their own cultures, religions, and languages. Identity politics have become dominant in world affairs since the Cold War, and ethnic self-consciousness these days is considered essential to cultural vitality.

While burgeoning universalization has produced a resurgence of diversity and multiplied the particular, 'difference in globalization is largely a difference on the surface.' The bewildering variety of goods 'tends to fade into the one overriding imperative to consume.' Particulars are evacuated by the 'stifling homogeneity' of commodification. The process of globalization is 'a peculiar proliferation of the many, still ultimately absorbed into the one.... Everything is available but nothing matters' (Cavanaugh, 2001: 331–333).

Communication ethics at this juncture has to respond to both the rapid globalization of communications and the reassertion of local identities. It is caught in the apparently contradictory trends of cultural homogenization and cultural resistance. Transnationalism faces tribalism's ferocity. Thus, developing a credible approach to communication ethics faces external demands of Himalayan proportions. While bringing the theory and practice of prophetic communication into its own, we do so in a powerful media environment where personal communication is admired but secondary. And as a new axis for normative discourse is constructed, the perennial philosophical problem of the one-and-the-many must be resolved. Hence this chapter on metaethics.

The-one-and-the-many

Globalization and multiculturalism are not just sociologically interesting, but they signal fundamental shifts of historic importance. And as we theorize communication ethics, it is the integration of globalization and ethnicity that is today's extraordinary challenge. For communication ethics to be multicultural, we need to reorient ethnicity in global terms. For internationalists among us, where is the pandemonium of cultural recognition in our work?

All of us across the communications spectrum are in this together. Media communications has a major role, of course. But interpersonal communications of various venues is concerned with world citizenship too. Multiculturalism is big from rhetoric to mass communication. Proactivists in all areas of communication act locally but think globally. In stark and inescapable ways, the enduring philosophical problem of the-one-and-the-many is on our common agenda, and we need to confront it and learn from it, before our theorizing in communication ethics can move forward constructively.

Whether the world is one or many is among the oldest questions of philosophy. Is there an underlying unity behind the multiple ways in which the world appears to human observers, or are things really as varied as appearances suggest? In this conundrum, the one dominates the many, or either side is absorbed in the other, or the proliferation of the many destroys their particularity, or the concrete is evacuated of any universal significance. The logic of their relation dictates that one domain must be abstracted from the other or that either is made disposable (Cavanaugh, 2001).

The one-many problem has a long tradition in Eastern philosophy. The Hindu Vedas discuss its composition in the eighth century B.C. In the Vedas, truth is One but has many appellations. 'God' and 'the Buddha', for example, are only sign names pointing to the same ultimate reality. The Indian Upanishads, in the following centuries, debate one-many hotly, and fall on both sides of the problem. In East Asia, the Neo-Confucianists, Cheng Hao and Cheng Yi, contended there was a fundamental pattern – *li* – to the universe. Each thing has its own *li*, but also contains the *li* of all other things. Many in the Confucian tradition work from that argument even today.

The earliest Western breakdown of the One/Many problem is with the Greek Presocratics, at the end of the sixth century B.C. Parmenides was the classic defender of the Oneness side of the argument, but ultimately concluded that if so, everything must be static and unchanging, which contradicts common sense. Parmenides' contemporary, Heraclitus, is the original defender of the Many side, contending as he does that even in everyday experience we do not step in the same river twice. Plato in *The Republic* and Parmenides argued for the 'One-over-Many' solution. In Platonist realism, universals exist independently of things. Aristotle agreed with realism, but contradicted Plato by arguing that universals exist in things, but not independently of them.

Over against realism, Boethius of Rome in the late fifth century translated Aristotle's logical writings for the Latin West, with his Platonic sympathies formulating the one-many problem into nominal universals. Do genera and species actually subsist or are they found in the mind alone? For a thousand years to William of Ockham, some version of nominalism established the medieval debate, that is, universals are constituted only in the mind. Realism as its alternative believes that material objects and theoretical entities are more than the experiential content of our minds. For realists, universals are not reducible to the particulars of which those universals are true. But if real objects transcend experience, how is knowledge of reality possible?

Translated as it has been into the nominalism/realism dichotomy by thinkers generally across the globe, the philosophical debate over the one-and-many problem continues to reflect different dimensions of this dualism but has not fundamentally reconceived it.

Monism/relativism in ethical theory

In ethical theory, the one-many conundrum is translated into monism versus relativism. Monism is the view that there is one and only one reasonable system of values, the same for all human beings, always and everywhere. Human lives are good to the extent to which they conform to this system, and particular values are better or worse depending on their standing in the system.

Relativism in ethical theory represents the Many side of the equation. For relativists, 'ultimately all values are conventional....What values people accept depends on the context in which they are born, on their genetic inheritance and subsequent experiences, on the political, cultural, economic and religious influences on them' (Kekes, 1993: 8). In short, what they value depends on their subjective attitudes and not on the objective features of values. Moral principles are generally presumed to have no credibility outside the societies within which they are constituted.

As we work out a new diversified comparative ethics, we do so in an intellectual world where monism has been replaced by relativism. What makes a life good is ambiguous. 'Just as there is a profusion of conflicting values, so also there [are multiple] conceptions of the good life comprising these values. The plurality of good lives, therefore, is a plurality twice over' (Kekes, 1993: 11). There is still the general conviction now that witches should not be burned or children sacrificed to idols. And we take seriously matters toward which our predecessors were largely indifferent, such as ecology, animal experimentation, and affirmative action. But we do not articulate other significant moral issues that well: the increasing power of bureaucracy and corporations, the demands of patriotism, vivisection, starvation and torture in distant lands. We may repudiate racism, but still find it difficult to face-up to fundamental questions, such as the amount we are willing to sacrifice for equality; or what reparations, if any, do we owe to the descendents of people victimized by our ancestors.

In fact, 'the conflicts are so numerous, so varied, permeate so many different areas of our lives; the arguments about them are so hopelessly inconclusive, carry so little conviction; and the opponents are so deeply imbued with ... moral fervour, that the fact of basic moral change' to relativism is undeniable (Kekes, 1993: 5). 'What thinking person in our society can be satisfied with the morality of the compromises we have arrived at, after decades of haggling, about pornography, abortion, ... death row, the welfare system, or measures taken to ensure the honesty of politicians' (p. 7). We have lost a rational foundation for our moral convictions.

Certainly, on the concrete level, relativism seems to carry the day, but intellectually we're conflicted about it. Relativism is subject to the naturalistic fallacy, that is, 'ought' statements cannot be derived from 'is' statements since they represent different realms. What exists in a natural setting cannot itself yield normative guidelines. And relativism faces the longstanding contradiction articulated by Karl Mannheim: those insisting that all cultures are relative must rise above them, and in rising above them they have given it up.

Moving from traditional communication ethics to a comparative model is loaded with good intentions. But the complications are enormous. Philosophically the one-many predicament remains unresolved and sociologically ethnic recognition in our global era is unshakable. And meanwhile, though we need its resources more than ever, the idea of a rational canon has collapsed internally.

Theoretical model of comparative communication ethics

Walking through the landmines of this intellectual terrain, I am brash enough to introduce a theoretical model of comparative communication ethics, one that serves the larger goal of prophetic communication.

The one-and-the-many problem has generated some great work conceptually, but is still an enigma. Therefore, we could ask, why turn to it even though globalization and multiculturalism seem to make it unavoidable? The axiological question of whether values are one or many generates in ethical theory the monism/relativism controversy. Again the question, why reiterate it in theory-building for today's communication ethics?

The one-many dilemma need not be reconciled for us to proceed, but understanding the debate is irreplaceable. Ignorance of it leads to unsupportable conclusions. Knowing its broader intellectual history yields concepts for theory-building. Being schooled in it enables us to avoid relativism. Three principles from the one-many tradition are especially relevant.

1) First, insist on universals but reconceptualize their character. The oneness side of the argument explains the most. The one-over-many solution withstands criticism the best. That is, the argument that even if every snowflake is unique, they can still be described by one term. The most promising way of dealing with one-many has been to consider the many as passing away into the one. In epistemology, empiricism is a 'corrective to the devaluation of the particular' but rationalism overcomes the 'brute factitity of the particular by locating the deeper explanation of things in the realm of essence' (Cavanaugh, 2001: 338). Humans cannot function without generalization.

A theoretical model of comparative communication ethics needs transnational principles, but those of a specific type – universals that are protonorms. Proto means both *first* and *beneath* in Greek. In the word 'prototype', we think of firstness. Toyota Motor Company builds a prototype and this model is then reproduced as replicas on the assembly line. And this has been the style of categorical imperatives in the Enlightenment tradition.

But instead, we should think of proto as *beneath*, as presuppositions, or in other words as originating claims that are fundamental to ethical reasoning. As Aristotle made irrevocable, we need a place to begin or we go nowhere – infinite regression makes structure and meaning impossible.

For the idea of universal norms, we should turn to our everyday experience in natural reality. The rationale for human action is reverence for life on earth. Purpose is embedded in the animate world, evident in its own reproduction. Ontologically speaking, the natural order has a moral claim on us for its own sake and in its own right. Our duty to preserve life is primal, timeless, and non-negotiable. Nurturing life has a taken-for-granted character. Human responsibility regarding natural existence contributes the possibility of intrinsic imperatives to moral philosophy. There is at least one generality of universal scope underlying systematic ethics. The veneration of human life represents a universalism from the ground up.

In recognition of Michael Traber's extensive work in Africa, note is taken here of Albert Schweitzer (1875–1965), for whom the sacredness of life is his overarching belief about the world. This multi-gifted man was a musician, physician, philosopher and theologian, but perhaps most famously he founded the Lambaréné Hospital in Gabon, Africa. He received the Peace Prize in 1953 for his *Ehrfurcht vor dem Leben* which he described in his autobiography (*Out of My Life and Thought*) as his greatest single contribution to human civilization. For him, respect for every kind of life had to be restored or ethical principles would continue to decay.

2) The second principle for comparative ethics is understanding the-one-and-the-many in terms of philosophical anthropology. The one-many problem has settled into the

domain of metaphysics. Its rational/empirical application is epistemological, and its monism-relativism derivative is axiological.

But we ought to reconfigure one-many in fundamentally human terms. Humans are cultural beings. As creators, distributors, and users of culture, people live in a world of their own making. Humans are the one living species constituted by language. In traditional epistemology, all acts are monologic, though actions may be coordinated with others. However, when the lingual interpretation of ourselves and our experience constitutes who we are, human action is dialogic. Humans are interactive agents within a language community.

Our meaningful references to moral matters are social. We are at home in the communal. Such protonorms as reverence for life can only be recovered locally. Language situates them in history. Ethical principles such as human dignity are of a universal order – they reflect our common condition as a species. Yet we enter them through the immediate reality of geography and ethnicity.

Universals are worked out within the cultural inflection of the second order. We distinguish between the first and second orders as with a windowpane – knowing that there is a decisive break, yet both realms are transparent to each other as well. And necessarily these mental processes often occur simultaneously without being diluted; for example, one ordinarily considers activities of the local police force in terms of elementary principles of political justice.

The community is understood to be axiologically and ontologically prior to persons. We are born into a sociocultural universe where values, moral commitments, and existential meanings are both presumed and negotiated. Morally appropriate action intends community. That prevents the dichotomy of the one, and the totalizing many. Now community is irrevocably in between. There can be no longer a category called 'the many' without community as a definitive, explicit component.

3) And a third conclusion in our model building out of the one-many tradition is to reconstruct the character of theorizing. The one-many problem has been constrained by a narrow preoccupation with the systematic construction of philosophical thought. The Greek tradition is prejudiced to a conceptual Logos. Greek philosophy has shaped the course of Western intellectual history to privilege the theoretical or rational aspect of life. Philosophical proclivity toward reason – be it theoretical, methodological, or practical – presumes an objective, ahistorical foundation of knowledge. And this is a quest for certainty over wisdom. Science, instead of living, became philosophy's subject, and the rules of knowledge its centerpiece.

However, theories should be understood not as the laws of reality, but what is best for us to believe. Florian Znaniecki's influential conception of theory, called 'analytic induction', insists on generalizing from the data. This is grounded theory, emphasizing the integrative and interpretive character of theorizing without jettisoning natural settings. These are theories that yield meaningful portraits, and not statistically precise formulations derived from artificially fixed conditions. Theorizing is redefined not as examination of external events, but the power of the imagination to give us an inside perspective on reality. Thomas Kuhn calls this revolutionary science – the constructing of paradigms – rather than the normal science of verifying that propositions are internally and externally valid.

Theories are not ex nihilo. They are not conceptually immaculate, arising out of nothing. Theories are not abstract theorems, noncontingent and decontextual. Instead they are oppositional claims about the world. We identify niches and inconsistencies and conundrums over against existing conventions, and theorize how to start over intellectually. Einstein did not formulate $E=MC^2$ in purity, but in opposition to Newtonian physics. Chomsky's transformational linguistics is contrary to Skinner's behaviorism.

Therefore, as a dynamic model of revolutionary theorizing, grounded theory defines itself over against the sovereign decision-maker in traditional ethics. From the perspective of grounded theory, the philosophical debates over the-one-and-many hold deeply to the autonomy of human reason, and the locus of morals in individual choice. And the radical opposite of the autonomous self is universal human solidarity. The total reversal of individual autonomy is *Homo sapiens* as a species. Our moral imagination is rooted in the universally human, not in an innermost self. One does comparative communication ethics by starting with the universal. Universal solidarity is the normative core of all human communication.

But universal human oneness is not a foundational a priori. This universal, in fact, belongs to a different category, philosophically speaking, than that of objectivist absolutes. Cartesian rationalism and Kant's formalism presumed noncontingent starting points. Universal human bondedness does not. Nor does it flow from Platonism, that is, the finite participating in the infinite and receiving its essence from it.

This perspective embeds normative phenomena within culture and history. As an intellectual strategy, it shifts transcendental criteria from a metaphysical and vertical plane to horizons of community and being, but transcendental norms they remain nonetheless. Our common humanity is not inscribed, first of all, in politics or economics, or in overcoming national boundaries by transportation of data. We resonate cross-culturally in our spirit with the moral imagination of others. Our mutual humanness is actually an ethical commitment rooted in the moral domain all humans share.

Principled dialogic ethics

A semiotics of the one-many tradition provides us with three building blocks for theory – a protonorm (the sacredness of life), community as ontologically irreducible, and the universally human for orienting the moral imagination. With these components in place, fashioned out of the one-many debate, a principled dialogic ethics becomes the obvious model in an age of globalization and multiculturalism. In terms of ethical theory, dialogic ethics is an alternative to both monism and relativism.

A comparative communication ethics is dialogical. However, it is dialogic ethics of an unusual kind. We come to community from the universal. We are doing social ethics but entering it from the human race as a whole.

The protonorm, understood as universal solidarity, is an embodiment of what Michael Polanyi (1968) called tacit knowledge. The foundations of our knowing are deeply ,interiorized. As we integrate particulars, we do not understand them externally but make value judgments regarding them. All our knowledge cannot be formalized. Any series of explicit operations presupposes a fund of inexplicit beliefs.

In experiencing a conceptual system as valid, we also tacitly depend upon the ground on which the system rests. It is our reliance on this ultimate which makes comprehension possible. Our thinking begins with core beliefs, but human knowing is not thereby restricted. In fact, commitment to a presupposition is the very condition through which human cognition gains intelligibility.

The sacredness of human life universally is our ultimate commitment, the core belief of our tacit knowledge. Our common humanness cannot simply be believed; it must be expressed. Holding this protonorm in silence is meaningless. As Michael Traber lived it out dramatically, its content, validity and motivating power depend on the way it is communicated. Given that language recapitulates, the symbols we use create what we view as reality. Representational forms matter. Concepts cannot be isolated from their representation.

The sacredness of life is lingual, and by definition it is also communal. Social relations define our existence as persons. The sacredness of life must, therefore, be understood sociologically. Reverence for life comes into its own through our public language. Therefore, as a protonorm cross-culturally shared, the veneration of human life belongs first of all to the general morality. Through our everyday conversations and experience, human sacredness will either flourish or wither. Within the popular mind it can prosper at hospital bedsides; among citizen action groups; through people's radio; in churches, temples, mosques, and synagogues; on the school playground when the disabled are struggling to keep up; or among campesinos as they're learning to read.

For Michael Traber, the ethics of human sacredness worked out as a people's manifesto, gave him credibility in Africa, teaching in India, and editing in London. As a tribute to his faith commitment, it must be observed that his Catholicism provided him a special edge in integrating the universal and particular in such a vibrant manner. Only Christianity claims to solve the one-many problem satisfactorily: Christ is the concrete universal. Only in the Incarnation can an individual be universal and the universal be individual.... Christ remains immersed in history, yet, as God, all historical norms are subordinated to Christ....The norm for history comes not from above it, from the absolute laws of universal reason, but from within it....What makes the form of Christ attractive is the perfect harmony between finite form and infinite fullness, the particular and the individual (Cavanaugh, 2001: 339, 341).

This integration is radically different from the way globalization renders particulars dispensable. The divinity of Jesus in Christianity claims for it a distinctive resolution of the one-and-the-many enigma, but only in the best sense of affirming pluralism among religious worldviews. This integration inspired Michael Traber but never in triumphalist terms. He knew that exclusivism denied the very essence of the incarnation's one-many harmony.

Within dialogic ethics that holds the one-and-many in concert, as Michael Traber did personally, story-telling becomes the premier mode of communicating truth. Stories are symbolic frameworks that organize human experience. Narration gives order to social life by inducing others to participate with us in its meaning. Through stories, we constitute ways of living in common. Through stories, dialogic ethics is close to the ground where the moral life takes place.

Narratives are linguistic forms through which we think, argue, persuade, display convictions, and establish our identity. They contain in a nutshell the meaning of our theories and beliefs. As Renato Rosaldo (1989) points out, 'Not only men and women of affairs but also ordinary people tell themselves stories about who they are, what they care about, and how they hope to realize their aspirations' (129–30). 'I have learned from Zimbabwe and Zambia,' writes Michael Traber (1991), that storytelling is fundamental to human life and at the very heart of communication, both interpersonal and technically mediated. Descartes' dictum, 'Cogito, ergo sum,' would, in Africa, have to be changed to 'I am a storyteller and I sing and dance, therefore I am' (chapter 4, 1).

Storytelling cuts through abstractions and obscurities so we can think creatively and imaginatively about a disorderly world. In the process, storytelling transforms essentially private experience into a shared and therefore public reality. The stories of Nelson Mandela's twenty-six years in prison, the Selma march, the demolition of the Berlin wall, Kosovo's history, and the 'velvet revolution' in Czechoslovakia were fodder for political revolution. (Michael Traber [1991] calls them foundational stories.) Ethnic narratives are particularly meaningful for the displaced – Palestinians, Armenians, Kurds, and Misquito Indians, for example. Great storytellers probe deeply into our belief systems and shape the social landscape.

Narratives mediate our common understanding of good and evil, tragedy and deliverance. Stories stitch together the webs of culture that shape who we are, how we live, and how long we shall survive. Everyone has general views on the meaning of life and death, of happiness and of reward. People may be wrong about their deepest beliefs or may not articulate them imaginatively. But, as Newton (1995) points out, finding oneself addressed by the ethical demands of narrative, in effect, 'establishes one's place in regard to others as well as to one's own life; it locates, in a word, one's address' (299). Communities are constituted by a set of values that specify their members' roles and aspirations.

The dialogic ethics I propose is fed by the sacredness of our universal humanity as tacit knowledge. Dialogic ethics of all kinds are community-oriented, the relational by definition entails the communal. The dialogic rooted in the self and Other is conditioned always in terms of the protonorm – human solidarity around the sacredness of life. Shifting ethics from the self to a radical otherness avoids the self-deception, self-interest, and moral arrogance of individualism. Other-regarding care in its various inflections opens the pathway to intercultural representation, and the Many side of the one-many equation. But otherness that begins with individualism does not encompass globalism and oneness, except by extrapolation.

The theoretical opposite of autonomous individuals is not the community, nor a shift from individual rationalism to narrative ethics. These are only half-way measures. If ethicists move directly from the individual to the community, they still need a standard outside the group by which to assess their conclusions. Therefore, the dialogic communication ethics I propose starts over intellectually from the universal. While taking on flesh-and-blood in the communal arena, it avoids the monism-relativism polarity and works at the intersection of multiculturalism and globalization.

If we make the universal the ground of ethical theory, there is a frame of reference for interpreting and measuring communities. Standards are essential for forming the common good. Communities turn in on themselves. Not all communities are legitimate. The white supremacist World Church of the Creator and armed gangs are communities for condemnation.

A commitment to universals does not eliminate differences in what we think and believe. Normative ethics grounded ontologically is pluralistic. The only question is whether our community's values affirm the sacredness of life and ethnic diversity at the same time.

Conclusion

With a comparative dialogic ethics carved out of the one-many problematic, we can make our way constructively at the intersection of the global and multicultural. Globalization reconfigures space by abstracting human relations from their concrete embodiments in the local. It imbricates the particular into the transnational marketplace. While globalization renders the specific disposable, strident fundamentalisms that combat the universal are also wrong on the interplay of the-one-and-many. The placeless language of panaceas and instant fixes, of economic and technological discourse, disempower people and erode the efflorescence of everyday life. Noncaucasians generally come through as dependent, with minimal talent and unlimited capacity for self-determining democracy.

With a comparative communication ethics we not only critique the one-way imperialism of multinational media corporations, but celebrate indigenous resistance in the people's voice. Only by keeping the local and global together, will we go beyond monolithic abstractions, to represent the struggles for justice in children's theatre, aboriginal art, folk tales, local composers, poetry, and community radio. With its roots in language, culture, and relational identity, dialogic communication ethics meets Michael Traber's standard of speaking prophetically and living justly in a complicated world.

References

Cavanaugh, William T. (2001). 'Balthazar, Globalization, and the Problem of the One and the Many.' *Communio: International Catholic Review*, Summer, pp. 324–47.

Christians, Clifford and Michael Traber, eds. (1997). *Communication Ethics and Universal Values*. Thousand Oaks, CA: Sage.

Kekes, John (1993). *The Morality of Pluralism*. Princeton, NJ: Princeton University Press.

Newton, Adam (1995). Narrative Ethics. Cambridge, MA : Harvard University Press.

Paul, Ellen F. et al. (1994). *Cultural Pluralism and Moral Knowledge.* Cambridge, UK: Cambridge University Press.

Polanyi, Michael (1968). *The Tacit Dimension.* Garden City, NY: Doubleday.

Rosaldo, Renato (1989). *Culture and Truth: The Remaking of Social Analysis.* Boston, MA: Beacon.

Traber, Michael (1991). 'Narrativity and Community: A Cultural Studies Approach.' In *Proceedings of the Conference on Narrativity and Community*, ed. M. Casey, ch. 4, 1–24. Malibu, CA: Conference on Christianity and Community.

IV

Cultivating
Journalists for Peace

KAARLE NORDENSTRENG

P eace is not the first thing that comes to mind with
journalists and the sum total of their work, journalism.
Given the widely criticized role of media in the
contemporary world, journalism and journalists are typically
viewed as serving misunderstanding and hatred rather than
understanding and confidence between individuals, groups, and
nations. Of course there are exceptions, but in general it is safe
to say that peace on earth prevails despite – not because of –
media and journalism.

This statement is substantiated by all those studies on media
content which show how mainstream journalism strengthens
prejudices and stereotypes, instead of insight and empathy.
There is a lot of evidence to this effect, but unfortunately this
evidence regarding our cultural environment is not
systematically collated and summarized in the same exemplary
manner as are trends about the physical and socio-economic
environment in the *State of the World* reports of the
Worldwatch Institute. (For initiatives of global media
monitoring, see Nordenstreng 2003; Ramonet 2002.)

Individual journalists do not normally advocate or admit
such biases; they typically believe that they are just engaged in

honest and objective reporting about the world. Yet journalists come to serve as instruments in a machinery that typically has a negative impact on peaceful relations between people and nations. Here we shall not address the eternal question to what extent media have influence in society – the above general position is taken for granted. However, it is understood that journalists are not totally determined by structural conditions and that they do have some room for making a difference including in matters of war and peace. This leads us to ask what are the ethical values which direct the gatekeepers – what is the mindset of the journalists and how is it formed?

Codes of ethics

Journalists, like other professions, have canonized their proper conduct in codes of ethics, which typically are adopted by national associations of journalists after thorough discussion in search of consensus. These codes can be taken as a fairly representative reading of prevailing professional values and thinking – the doctrine of professional ethics in a country. Admittedly, the codes represent only the professional ideology and do not indicate how journalism is, in actual fact, practised. The latter aspect of dirty practice in contrast to ideal thinking is covered by innumerable case studies as well as the self-regulatory institutions of press councils, which monitor to what extent professional standards are honoured by the profession. Yet the codes of ethics as standard-setting instruments for the profession are a most valuable resource for research about values behind journalistic practice.

I began to examine these professional codes of journalism ethics in the 1970s when involved in UNESCO's standard-setting projects such as the Mass Media Declaration and the MacBride Report (Nordenstreng, 1984). My special interest was focused on what the codes prescribed regarding international relations (Nordenstreng & Alanen, 1981), while I also supervised students to make comparative inventories about the whole spectrum of topics contained in the codes (see Cooper, 1989; Laitila, 1995). An additional boost to this research activity came from my role as president of the International Organization of Journalists (IOJ), which gave me special access to both the history of the profession and contemporary codes in countries and languages which were not normally available, leading to books on the topic (Bruun, 1979; Kubka & Nordenstreng, 1986-88; Nordenstreng & Topuz, 1989).

In 1995 my academic base in Tampere became the site of a databank of all the codes of journalism ethics which we had accumulated in the European region from the Atlantic to the Urals, as translations in English (http://www.uta.fi/ethicnet/). This EthicNet databank was updated in late 2007 and it now includes 50 codes from 46 countries – from Albania to the UK (the latter with two codes). Thus EthicNet provides handy material for an overview of contemporary thinking among mainstream journalists in the region. (For a worldwide database of 'media accountability systems' including press councils and ethical codes, although not currently updated, see http://www .media-accountability.org/.)

A content analysis of this collection shows that truth figures as the most common standard in European professional ethics, present in each of the 50 contemporary codes. Almost all codes forbid discrimination on grounds of race, sex or religion. Also high on the list are demands to use fair means in gathering information and to be clear about the nature of information – to separate facts from opinions and editorial material from advertisements. Compared to the situation in 1995, when the collection included 31 codes, the standards have remained more or less the same. Accordingly, there is a well-established and solid ideal for journalistic ethics in Europe.

What is the status of peace in the European codes? It is minimal: only one code out of 50 mentions the word 'peace' as something that journalists should promote. The code of ethics adopted by the Latvian Union of Journalists in 1992 has the following paragraph in its last section 6 entitled 'Journalists and Society':

> A journalist should stand up for human values – peace, democracy, human rights, people's rights to self-determination.

Six other codes – by journalists' associations in Albania, Armenia, Montenegro, Poland, Slovakia and Slovenia – include indirect reference to peace by condemning propagation of wars or conflicts between nationalities. For example, the code of ethics adopted by the Slovak Syndicate of Journalists in 1990, ends with the following paragraph under the title 'The Journalist and the Public Interest':

> The journalist must not promote aggressive wars, violence and aggressiveness as the means of international conflicts solution, political, civic, racial, national, religious and other sorts of intolerance. The journalist shows due respect to other states, nations, to their democratic traditions and institutions, to their culture and morals.

In the early 1980s also the Union of Journalists in Finland adopted the following paragraph in the introduction of its code called 'Guidelines for good journalistic practice':

> The professional ethics of a journalist involves the respecting of basic human values, like human rights, democracy, peace and international understanding.

However, this paragraph was deleted from the Finnish code in its latest revision in 2005. Consequently, Finland can no longer be listed next to Latvia as a country where the word 'peace' appears in its codes of ethics. Moreover, Finland can no longer be quoted as a country in which professional ethics incorporates broader values beyond strictly journalistic issues related to truth, fairness, etc. In other words, the Finnish concept of journalistic ethics can now be characterized as technocratic – free from elements of universal idealism.

The Finnish move should not be taken as symptomatic of a wider movement towards technocratic professionalism in

Europe. As described above, journalistic values seem to be fairly stable throughout Europe, and there is no evidence of a fundamental change – except in Russia where journalists seem to become increasingly PR instruments (Pasti, 2007). As far as the perspective of peace and war is concerned, it has always been a marginal phenomenon in mainstream journalistic ethics.

Rich legacy

Although peace and war remain low on the agenda of journalistic ethics, this particular perspective figured quite high in the global media debate around UNESCO and the so-called New World Information and Communication Order (NWICO) in the 1970s and 1980s (see Gerbner, Mowlana & Nordenstreng 1993; Vincent, Nordenstreng & Traber, 1999). It is instructive to contrast the contemporary reality as reflected in the codes of ethics with documents such as the Mass Media Declaration of UNESCO (1978), the MacBride Report (1980) and the International Principles of Professional Ethics in Journalism (1983).

The Mass Media Declaration, adopted by acclamation by UNESCO's General Conference in 1978, already highlighted peace and war in its title: 'Declaration on Fundamental Principles concerning the Contribution of the Mass Media to Strengthening Peace and International Understanding, to the Promotion of Human Rights and to Countering Racialism, Apartheid and Incitement to War'. In its time, this document, together with the MacBride Report, signalled a turning point in international media policy from confrontation to consensus (Mansell & Nordenstreng, 2006: 22). Nevertheless, it is hardly remembered today even by experts in the field. UNESCO itself has done nothing to keep it alive; it has been wiped off the agenda by the political hurdles which replaced a Third World NWICO perspective with a Western emphasis on press freedom (Nordenstreng, 2007). Yet the UNESCO Declaration of 1978 is worth recalling, since it contains a lot of material which is relevant to contemporary debates – for example Article VIII:

> Professional organizations, and people who participate in the professional training of journalists and other agents of the mass media and who assist them in performing their functions in a responsible manner should attach special importance to the principles of this Declaration when drawing up and ensuring application of their codes of ethics.

The MacBride Report (1980) also included several passages which are worth recalling and revisiting today, although this landmark document has also been largely forgotten – even actively played down by UNESCO (Nordenstreng, 2007: 20-25). Among its 82 recommendations many are still topical proposals under headings such as 'Responsibility of journalists', 'Towards improved international reporting', and 'Towards international understanding' (MacBride, 1980: 261-271). And one of the seven issues requiring further study was 'International standards and instruments' including the following (*ibid.*: 274):

> 6. Studies should be undertaken to identify, if possible, principles generally recognised by the profession of journalism and which take into account the public interest. This could also encompass further consideration, by journalists' organisations themselves, of the concept of an international code of ethics. Some fundamental elements for this code might be found in the UNESCO Declaration on the mass media, as well as in provisions common to the majority of existing national and regional codes.

The International Principles (1983) did exactly what the MacBride Report proposed here (Nordenstreng, 1989: 279). Actually this document contains a lot of food for thought for contemporary journalism, but it is likewise practically forgotten (although still easy to find online). It was issued on behalf or eight international and regional associations of journalists, which since 1978 have held consultative meetings under the auspices of UNESCO. The coalition represented altogether 400,000 working journalists in about 100 countries, i.e. a majority of the organized profession in the world. Thus the document was already historical because of its mere existence: it was the first joint statement of principle which the international movement of journalists was able to make since it was divided by the Cold War in the late 1940s. The document was a unique attempt by the journalistic profession to define parameters for global ethics. It was not called a code because the debates around the MacBride Report and NWICO had made journalists wary of strict rules which would be applied everywhere. Yet there was a widely shared understanding of certain common ethical standards and therefore a search for universal values was not considered taboo but a vital project among journalists' organizations coming from different geopolitical regions.

Take from its ten principles the following two:

Principle VIII: Respect for Universal Values and
Diversity of Cultures

A true journalist stands for the universal values of humanism, above all peace, democracy, human rights, social progress and national liberation, while respecting the distinctive character, value and dignity of each culture, as well as the right of each people freely to choose and develop its political, social, economic and cultural systems. Thus the journalist participates actively in the social transformation towards democratic betterment of society and contributes through dialogue to a climate of confidence in international relations conducive to peace and justice everywhere, to détente, disarmament and national development. It belongs to the ethics of the profession that the journalist be aware of relevant provisions contained in international conventions, declarations and resolutions.

Principle IX: Elimination of War and Other Great Evils
Confronting Humanity

The ethical commitment to the universal values of humanism calls for the journalist to abstain from any justification for, or incitement to, wars of aggression, and the arms race, especially in nuclear weapons, and all other forms of violence, hatred or discrimination, especially racialism and apartheid, oppression by tyrannical regimes, colonialism and neo-colonialism, as well as other great evils which afflict humanity, such as poverty, malnutrition and diseases. By so doing, the journalist can help eliminate ignorance and misunderstanding among peoples, make nationals of a country sensitive to the needs and desires of others, ensure respect for the rights and dignity of all nations, all peoples.

Today, 25 years later, we may ask whether these principles are still current. One concept can be seen to be outdated: apartheid was abolished as a state system in South Africa in 1994 and in this respect also the UNESCO Declaration is outdated – fortunately. Also Principle X on promotion of NWICO refers to a global discourse that is passé, although the issues involved remain relevant (Padovani & Nordenstreng, 2005). But all other aspects, both positive values and socio-political evils, are current in the contemporary world. For example, the above quoted Principle IX, with the commitment of the journalist to poverty, etc., is in perfect accord with the UN Millennium Declaration's resolution 'to ensure the freedom of the media to perform their essential role...' (Nordenstreng, 2007: 26-27).

The last sentence of Principle VIII above concerning international conventions, declarations and resolutions is of particular importance. It determines that a truly professional journalist knows and understands the framework of international law, and therefore this subject should belong to the basic toolkit of a serious journalist. This is not a call for adhering to universal values of humanism as made in the preceding two sentences but simply a call to have a roadmap for navigating the delicate landscape of the conflict-ridden yet globalized world. Sounds reasonable, but looking around the community of journalists and their educators shows that this task has been largely neglected.

Committed journalism

The International Principles of 1983 deserve to be examined more closely as an authoritative – although by now forgotten – manifestation which prescribes journalism as a socially committed profession. The commitment originates from the people's right to acquire a truthful picture of reality, on the one hand, and from the universal values of humanism on the other. The commitment to truth is, in principle, the same as that held within the libertarian mainstream of journalism, although there are obvious differences between traditions as to how truth is understood. But the commitment to the universal values as established by the international community means a significant departure from the typical Western tradition and a move toward the notion of professionalism as it was generally understood in the socialist and developing countries of the time.

Accordingly, 'a true journalist', as defined by the Document, is not neutral with regard to the universal values of 'peace, democracy, human rights, social progress and national liberation' (Principle VIII). Neither is a journalist neutral with regard to violations of human rights such as 'justification for, or incitement to, wars of aggression, and the arms race, especially in nuclear weapons, and all other forms of violence, hatred or discrimination, especially racialism and apartheid, oppression by tyrannic regimes, colonialism and neo-colonialism' (Principle IX).

In fact, such an ethics of journalism implies two significant steps beyond what is typically held by the technocratic tradition with its passion to remain free from any socio-political obligations other than the pursuit of truth. First, there is an invitation for a journalist – as a proper citizen – to support a number of universally recognized ideals and to fight corresponding evils. This is a general social commitment, applying to all citizens in the same way. Beyond this, however, it calls for a particular professional commitment whereby the universal values in question are understood as vital constituents of journalism, along with the commitment to truth and other conventional characteristics of professionalism (integrity, etc.). Thus it becomes the professional responsibility of all journalists to pursue, not only truth in general, but the universal values of humanism as well. In other words, the definition of professionalism takes a great leap forward from the libertarian notion of a journalist whose task is merely to transmit facts and opinions by remaining independent and neutral with regard to various socio-political interests and values.

Obviously, not all journalists had really made the two-step social commitment an integral part of their professional ethics. For many, what was involved is no doubt as much fashionable lip service as a fundamental reorientation, especially with regard to the second type of commitment, which brings universal values to the core of professionalism. Yet it is obvious that a new, socially committed professional ethics was emerging at the time. Accordingly, while the Document did not suggest that all of the 400,000 professionals represented by the organizations concerned would have fully stood for the ten principles, it was an indication of a trend among professional journalists that was taking place along with the movement toward a new information order.

Those professionals who, under the influence of a libertarian way of thinking, were suspicious or afraid of committing themselves to the socio-political values in question, were referred to readings in international law and politics to find out that the journalist is not expected to follow haphazard political values, but that there is a specific set of ethical values that have gradually evolved in the international community. Advocates of the Document such as myself emphasized that there was little ground for fear or reluctance, once a person had realized that, instead of being 'politicized' in an unspecified way, he or she is invited to a commitment only to those values that have a legitimate status in international law and politics.

Given this awareness, one was supposed to see that the concepts of peace and war, democracy and tyranny, national liberation and colonialism, and the like are not simply political slogans subject to arbitrary interpretation according to tactical interests. Most of these concepts have a specific meaning under international law, and in cases such as war propaganda there are extensive applications to journalism. Naturally, there is room for interpretation and political disagreement around these universal values and principles, but so it is with any concepts that embrace human nature and behaviour. Scepticism regarding the validity of universal values typically is based on ignorance of the issues involved.

In this perspective, the new 'committed' professional ethics appears to be a less remarkable leap forward than was suggested above. After all, the journalist does no more than become openly committed to the values that constitute the foundation of international law and order. If this seems to be a radical step, it shows only how poorly the universal values have been recognized, often because of the dominance of parochial values which stand in opposition to those held by the international community. For example, if commitment to peace is perceived as a politically radical position, it exposes a poor knowledge of the concept of peace rather than a politically biased approach.

Thus committed journalism did not bring any particular 'politicization' into the field of media and journalism; it only provided a safeguard protecting values of peace, democracy, and so forth. It goes without saying that journalism is and will continue to be a highly political field – both overtly and covertly. In such a situation, any choice of professional ethics – old and new alike – represents a direct or indirect political position. The question is not which is political and which is apolitical; the question is what is the political orientation being advocated. In this respect, the new professional ethics of committed journalism had as 'impartial' a foundation as can be imagined: the universal values of the international community – something that could be called 'United Nations ideology'.

Committed journalism seems to have gained considerable support in the professional ethics of journalism around the world, and it has been boosted since the 1980s by environmental issues such as global warming. Accordingly, the Finnish code in its 1983 revision made a reference to environment, next to peace etc., quoted above. However, this commitment was also removed from the 2005 revision of the Finnish code, turning it into an instrument of the conventional libertarian version of journalism. As a Finnish journalism educator I am naturally sorry, even ashamed, to admit that my own professional association has turned from a progressive line towards a technocratic notion of professional ethics. However, as noted above, the Finnish case should be taken as an exception in the broader universal development. While the Finnish turn can be seen as a temporary departure from an intellectual vanguard, it presents a challenge for me and my colleagues in journalism education tò try harder in cultivating journalists.

Admittedly, the overall trend toward committed journalism is far from clear and contains many contradictory tendencies. This is a challenge for all to get involved in cultivating journalists – for ethical quality in general and peace in particular. And there is a lot of material to support addressing this challenge – not only the legacy of the past but also recent contributions from academic as well as professional camps.

Fresh material

Regarding journalism on topics of peace and war, a whole new academic specialization has emerged during the past few years, bringing along books (e.g. Nohrstedt & Ottosen, 2000) and journals (e.g. *Media, War & Conflict* http://mwc.sagepub.com). Also institutions for training programmes have been established, including 'Transcend Peace University', an online centre for peace studies founded by Johan Galtung (http://tpu .transcend.org/), a network of European, American and African centres ('Institute for War and Peace Reporting' http://www .iwpr.net/# as well as an Australian 'Centre for Peace and Conflict Studies' http://www.arts.usyd.edu.au/centres/cpacs/).

These provide a lot of case studies and general perspectives for the study of journalism and peace. In addition, the following are worth consulting: http://www.warandmedia.org/ and http://scs.bgsu.edu/mwcrConf/index.php.

Particularly valuable material is included in the electronic journal *conflict & communication online* (http://www.cco.regener-online.de/) theme issues of 'peace journalism' (2006 Vol. 5, No. 2 and 2007 Vol. 6, Nos. 1-2). There, both the advocates of this concept, such as Jake Lynch and Annabel McGoldrick (2005), and its critics from both journalistic practice (BBC TV journalist David Lyon) and academic research (German media scholar Thomas Hanitzsch) present well informed and most thoughtful interventions in the eternal debate about what is good journalism with a view to objectivity, responsibility, etc. With the editor's synthesis 'Peace journalism: A tightrope walk between advocacy journalism and constructive conflict coverage' (Kempf, 2007), this package is a unique contribution not only to the peace journalism controversy but to journalism studies in general.

In addition to these academic developments, peace and journalism also coincide among professional journalists – not only in their routine work in covering conflict areas around the world but also as more general reflections and initiatives regarding the quality of journalism. The most significant of these professional activities is the worldwide Ethical Journalism Initiative (2008) created by the International Federation of Journalists (IFJ) as 'a campaign and programme of activity developed by journalists and media professionals to restore values and mission to their profession... in a period of global turbulence, marked by war in the Middle East, fears over international terrorism and a resurgence of multicultural tension.' With a serious rationale about developments in the world in general and the media landscape in particular it 'raises awareness of how informed, accurate journalism and reporting in context helps create mutual understanding in the face of division, whether defined by language, culture, ethnicity or religious belief, and strengthens democracy.' The Initiative includes a programme of activities (prepared jointly with European broadcasters and publishers), a set of core values and principles, and some concrete guidelines for media. The core values, with a focus on truth, independence and professional social responsibility, are another version of international principles such as the 1983 document.

In short, there is a rich legacy of ideas and a lot of material for cultivating journalists for peace. By the same token we must admit that this topic is neglected in professional ethics of journalism as well as in the education of journalists. The question is the classic: What is to be done?

Action lines

There are two main directions in which action can realistically be taken: professional associations and academic institutions.

National associations of journalists should sustain continuous debate among their members on the values and practices of professional ethics – both in general and regarding peace in particular. A concrete and engaging way to do this is critically to examine the national codes of ethics and periodically to revise them. If properly conducted, such activities will probably result in better codes of ethics with peace occupying more than a marginal position.

Likewise, professional associations should be actively involved in monitoring and criticizing media performance. It would be unwise to let media criticism become the privilege of only political and intellectual groups outside the media; this would only turn journalists on the defensive and strengthen an unhealthy tendency of media people to create a fortress culture around them. Professionals should be in the forefront of constructive criticism of the media.

These national activities are supported by international professional associations with projects such as the exemplary Ethical Journalism Initiative of the IFJ. And although intergovernmental organizations have no formal role in the business of free journalism, they should provide platforms for professionals to promote journalism for peace and other universal ideals of the UN. In 2008, 60 years after the Universal Declaration of Human Rights, it is high time for UNESCO to return to the ideas of the MacBride Report which it has kept effectively 'on ice' since the early 1990s.

Academic institutions, for their part, should do more both conceptual and empirical research on issues of peace as an element of ethics and professionalism. A particular challenge is to introduce elements of international law to professional ethics. This aspect is badly neglected in journalism education and there is a burning need to produce textbook material on the topic. Questions of international conflict are more and more recognized due to cases such as the Mohammed cartoons, but they have not been properly established in the curricula of journalism education as demonstrated in the UNESCO-sponsored *Model Curricula* (2007).

Studies of media performance are a natural part of academic institutions. These studies should not be carried out in isolation from media practitioners but there should be close cooperation between the two camps. Monitoring and assessment of media performance jointly by academics and practitioners is also a stimulating way to promote media criticism – again both in general and regarding issues of peace in particular.

Furthermore, academic institutions have a challenge to promote media literacy and media education in schools. This is no longer addressed to journalists as such but rather to their future readers, listeners, viewers – and partners in tomorrow's blogosphere.

Some of these action lines are only remotely related to issues of peace and war. However, peace is not a particularistic topic but an integral part of social and international relations. Accordingly, the cultivation of journalists for peace should not be seen as a separate item but as an aspect of promoting universal values and international law – global ethics or, as suggested above, 'United Nations ideology'.

References

Bruun, Lars (ed.) (1979) *Professional Codes in Journalism*. Prague: International Organization of Journalists.

Cooper, Tom (1989) 'Global universals: In search of common ground'. In T. Cooper (ed.), *Communication Ethics and Global Change*. White Plains, NY: Longman, pp. 20-39.

Declaration on Fundamental Principles concerning the Contribution of the Mass Media to Strengthening Peace and International Understanding, to the Promotion of Human Rights and to Countering Racialism, Apartheid and Incitement to War (1978) Paris: UNESCO. Online http://portal. unesco.org/en/ev.php-URL_ID=13176&URL_DO=DO_PRINTPAGE &URL_SECTION=201.html Also at http://www.casi.org.nz/statements/ decmedia.htm and http://ics.leeds.ac.uk/papers/vf01.cfm?folder=193 &outfit=pmt

Ethical Journalism Initiative (2008) Brussels: International Federation of Journalists. Online http://www.ifj.org/assets/docs/133/202/f258585-de980ca.pdf

Gerbner, George, Mowlana, Hamid and Nordenstreng, Kaarle (eds.) (1993) *The Global Media Debate: Its Rise, Fall, and Renewal*. Norwood, NJ: Ablex, 1993.

International Principles of Professional Ethics in Journalism (1983) Prague: International Organization of Journalists. Online http://www.mediawise .org.uk/display_page.php?id=310 and http://www.ijnet.org/Director.aspx? P=Ethics&ID=8320&LID=1

Kempf, Wilhelm (2007) 'Peace journalism: A tightrope walk between advocacy journalism and constructive conflict coverage'. *conflict & communication online*, Vol 6, No. 2 http://www.cco.regener-online.de/2007_2/pdf/ kempf.pdf

Kubka, Jiri and Nordenstreng, Kaarle (1986-88) *Useful Recollections: Excursions into the History of the International Movement of Journalists*, Parts 1 & 2. Prague: International Organization of Journalists.

Laitila, Tiina (1995) 'Journalistic codes of ethics in Europe'. *European Journal of Communication*, Vol. 10, No. 4, pp. 527-544.

Lynch, Jake and McGoldrick, Annabel (2005) *Peace Journalism*. Stroud, UK: Hawthorn Press.

MacBride, Sean et al. (1980) *Many Voices – One World*. Paris: UNESCO. Reprinted in 2004 by Rowman & Littlefield.

Mansell, Robin and Nordenstreng, Kaarle (2006) 'Great media and communication debates: WSIS and the MacBride Report'. *Information Technologies and International Development,*

Vol. 3, No. 4, pp. 15-36. Online http://www.mitpressjournals.org/doi/pdf/ 10.1162/itid.2007.3.4.15

Model Curricula for Journalism Education for Developing Countries and Emerging Democracies (2008) Paris: UNESCO. Online http:// portal.unesco.org/ci/en/ev.php-URL_ID=24824&URL_DO=DO _TOPIC&URL_SECTION=201.html

Nohrstedt, Stig Arne and Ottosen, Rune (eds.) (2000) *Journalism and the New WorldOrder. Vol. 1: Gulf War, National News Discourses and Globalization.* Gothenburg: Nordicom.

Nordenstreng, Kaarle (1984) *The Mass Media Declaration of UNESCO.* Norwood, NJ: Ablex.

Nordenstreng, Kaarle (1989) 'Professionalism in transition: Journalistic ethics'. In T. Cooper (ed.), *Communication Ethics and Global Change*. White Plains, NY: Longman, pp. 277-283.

Nordenstreng, Kaarle (2003) 'Something to be done: Transnational media monitoring'. In K. Hafez (ed.), *Media Ethics in the Dialogue of Cultures. Journalistic Self-Regulation in Europe, the Arab World, and Muslim Asia*, Hamburg: Deutsches Orient-Institut, German Institute for Middle East Studies, pp. 215–227. Also as 'Afterword' in R.D. Berenger (ed.), *Global Media Go to War. Role of News and Entertainment Media During the 2003 Iraq War*, Spokane, WA: Marquette Books, 2004, pp. 343-352. Online http://www.uta.fi/jour/laitos/Nordenstreng_Media_Monitoring.pdf

Nordenstreng, Kaarle (2007) 'Myths about press freedom'. *Brazilian Journalism* Research, Vol. 3, No. 1, pp. 15–30. Online http://www.uta.fi/ laitokset/tiedotus/laitos/myths_about_press_freedom.pdf

Nordenstreng, Kaarle and Alanen, Antti (1981) 'Journalistic ethics and international relations'. *Communication*, Vol. 6, pp. 225-252.

Nordenstreng, Kaarle and Topuz, Hifzi (eds.) (1989) *Journalist: Status, Rights and Responsibilities*. Prague: International Organization of Journalists.

Padovani, Claudia and Nordenstreng, Kaarle (2005) 'From NWICO to WSIS: Another World Information and Communication Order?' *Global Media and Communication*, Vol. 1, No. 3, pp. 264-272. Online http://www.uta.fi/laitokset/tiedotus/laitos/From_NWICO_to_WSIS.pdf

Pasti, Svetlana (2007) *The Changing Profession of a Journalist in Russia*. Tampere: University of Tampere Press. Online http://acta.uta.fi/pdf/978-951-44-7101-8.pdf

Ramonet, Ignacio (2003) 'Set the media free.' *Le Monde diplomatique*, October 2003. Online http://mondediplo.com/2003/10/01media

Vincent, Richard, Nordenstreng, Kaarle and Traber, Michael (eds.) (1999) *Towards Equity in Global Communication: MacBride Update*. Cresskill, NJ: Hampton Press.

V

Publicity and the Public Sphere in the Internet Era

SLAVKO SPLICHAL

Despite intellectual diversity in conceptualizations of the public sphere, which is related to specific social-theoretical traditions in grasping the essence of the phenomenon and marked by the division between normative theories and sociological analyses, interest in the public sphere and other phenomena of publicity (the public, public opinion, public service) is primarily rooted in democratic (political) theory. In addition to democratic theories, I may list several approaches developed in communication and media studies, such as political communication tradition (closely related to democratic political theories), political economy (of the media) and cultural studies, and I could also add others, such as feminist theories. Last but not least, the growing popularity of the concept 'public sphere' was given strong impetus by the rapidly growing computer-mediated communication of the Internet in the 1990s, which created new puzzles with the concepts of publicity and the public sphere.

In the first place, however, I should refer to the founders of the modern concept of publicity, Jeremy Bentham and Immanuel Kant, who have 'disconcerted' the intellectual history of publicity since its very beginning with their antithetical conceptualizations of 'the principle of publicity'. Bentham favoured 'the public opinion tribunal' and free press as instruments for public control of government, in the interest of the general welfare. Kant favoured free public discussion as an instrument for the development and expression of autonomous rationality and publicity as the fundamental principle of democratic order, in which citizens must be convinced by reason in the exercise of public debate that public policies are just, lest the state lose its moral legitimacy.

Kant's and Bentham's concepts of publicity are strongly opposed to contemporary (mis)understandings of publicity as 'the activity of making certain that someone or something attracts a lot of interest or attention from many people' (*Cambridge International Dictionary of English*) or 'a type of public relations in the form of a news item or story which conveys information about a product, service, or idea in the media', as advertisers conceive of it. Deriving from the principle of publicity, the early concept of freedom of the press was instituted exclusively as a personal right and, thus, intrinsically associated with individual's access to the public sphere. Before the state of civility, individuals as human beings already enjoyed the *natural right* to communicate, which they could not alienate or else they would cease to exist as human beings. Thus the right to express opinion in public that was conceptualized as a *civil right* of citizens in the age of Enlightenment was a reappropriation of the human right that has existed for centuries only as a privilege of elite minorities.

The most important part of Kant's defence of the rights of subjects acting under the surveillance of government was their right of publication:

> Consequently, the *right* must be conceded to the citizen, and with the direct consent of the sovereign, that he shall be able to make his opinion publicly known regarding what appears to him to be a wrong committed against the commonwealth by the enactments and administration of the sovereign. For to assume that the sovereign

power can never err, or never be ignorant of anything, would amount to regarding that power as favoured with heavenly inspiration and as exalted above the reach of mankind, which is absurd. Hence *the freedom of pen* is the sole palladium of the rights of the people (Kant, 1793/1914: 40).

However, the realization of individuals' civil right to communicate in modern democratic societies requires a level of resources proportional to its increase in complexity since the time when it existed as a natural right, which makes full access to the media virtually impossible for large parts of citizens across the world. The right to communicate existed as an inalienable natural right of human beings only as long as the individual's ability to communicate was determined by sheer membership in a language community, when no external means were needed for communication, and all the people were able to use all (their natural) communication means.

Misconstruing the press in the public sphere

A radical change in the relationship of an individual to his or her oral language was first introduced with alphabetical codes. Writing not only made possible the recording of communication, but also divided the previously homogeneous collectivity into those capable of the new form of communication and those falling short of it. Like writing, all subsequent communication technologies developed down the centuries reveal that new forms of communication that imply a possible expansion of human powers to learn and to exchange ideas and experiences, can also easily be misused. It typically happened with the press.

Since the earliest conceptualizations of publicity, the press was considered constitutive of 'the public' and 'public opinion' in two senses: (1) as a means of information supply to the public which significantly influences the formation of public opinion; and (2) as the main 'expression means' or 'organ' of the public.

However, after the establishment of the constitutional guarantee for a free press in parliamentary democracies, discussions of freedom of the press were largely reduced to the pursuit of *freedom for the media*, thus neglecting the idea of publicity as the basis of democratic citizenship. Yet a free press embodied in the property rights of the owners of the press failed to achieve either Benthamite or Kantian goals. Discrimination in favour of the power/control function of the press clearly abstracted freedom of the press from the Kantian quest for the public use of reason and Benthamite quest for control exercised by the public opinion tribunal. In democratic societies where the people rather than different estates legitimize all the powers, the control dimension of publicity embodied in the corporate freedom of the press should be effectively supplemented by actions toward equalizing citizens' opportunities to participate in public debates.

The developed countries show an immense quantitative growth of political communication, but the aim of political communication is primarily to make others accept expressed views rather than to express themselves. As Habermas argues:

> the political public sphere is ... dominated by the kind of mediated communication that lacks the defining features of deliberation: ... (a) the lack of face-to-face interaction between present participants in a shared practice of collective decision making and (b) the lack of reciprocity between the roles of speakers and addressees in an egalitarian exchange of claims and opinions. Moreover, the dynamics of mass communication are driven by the power of the media to select, and shape the presentation of, messages and by the strategic use of political and social power to influence the agendas as well as the triggering and framing of public issues (Habermas, 2006: 414-5)

In contrast to 'mediated publicity' based on the operation of traditional, non-interactive press and broadcast media, the Internet and intranets offer such new opportunities for participatory communication. The Internet technology further expands the process of the transformation of an individual opinion into social opinion, which was based on public oral communication in an earlier period and on the press in modern times, 'but at all times and primarily, on private conversation' (Tarde, 1901: 41). With the new interactive virtual spaces it has created, the Internet substantially increased the feasibility of citizens' participation in public discourse thus stimulating tendencies and capacities of innovation and change. It had a constitutive role in the development of an informal global communication network of individuals, organizations and movements, which may help create an international civil society aspiring towards a genuinely cosmopolitan public. In this way it helped to develop an understanding of a deterritorialized public sphere not bound to a particular locality (state).

In its early period, the Internet was believed radically to challenge the hierarchical, top-down mass communication model typical of traditional media, and to democratize not only communication but also political relations in general, irrespective of all other (former) impediments. It was thought to offer new possibilities for political participation leading to a kind of direct democracy not only locally but even at the national level: a genuine or 'strong' electronic democracy was expected to oust populist democracy dominated by traditional mass media, particularly television. While there is no doubt that new types of engagement are made possible by new communication technologies and communication infrastructures (in developed societies), it is much more questionable if they stimulate and revive political participation and civic engagement.

Indeed, new forms of communication and network ('virtual') communities established with its help may not only help revitalize democracy, but they could also entice us into an attractively packaged surrogate for a democratically organized public sphere – the (hi)story well known from the past when the press and other 'big' media conceived as the pillars of democracy had largely lost their democratic responsibilities. Yet despite the disillusions about the Internet, it 'retains' several important advantages over other mass media regarding the level of reciprocity of communication and equality of communicating participants. In terms of C. W. Mills' classic differentiation between the mass and the public, the technology of computer mediated communication significantly reinvigorates 'communities of publics' characterized by discussion as 'the ascendant means of communication' – in contrast to the mass media which only 'enlarge and animate discussion, linking one *primary public* with the discussions of another', whereas 'the publics become mere *media markets*: all those exposed to the contents of given mass media' (Mills, 1956/2000: 304).

Cyber citizenship did not solve the problems of democratic political representation and (even less) participation. It is true that a large number of web communities were formed both locally (nationally) and globally, which are based on common interests and often imply a certain level of solidarity among participants. Yet the web communities do not significantly enhance democracy because they are just as narrowly defined as traditional public factions defined by racial, gender, age, ideological, or religious identities and interests. The democratic merit of computer mediated communication is mostly limited to the successful overturn of political suppression and censorship of authoritarian regimes that try to control and repress (mass) communication and public opinion. In some cases, they may have contributed to overcoming fragmented cultural and political interests, but they may also have deepened that fragmentation. The boom of millions of more or less specialized chat rooms and blogs across the world does not lead to an inter- or supra-national public sphere but rather to 'the fragmentation of large but politically focused mass audiences into a huge number of isolated issue publics' (Habermas, 2006: 423n).

There is something deeply solipsistic about the idea of every man with his web page. Because it can be done, we do it. A mirror makes a poor substitute for the politics of compassion and empathy. Private web pages also create a dangerous illusion of equality. My page and Disney's page equalize us! My 'portal' and Bill Gates' portal, what's the difference? The difference is of course that power lies not in the capacity to express yourself but in the ability to get others to listen. This depends in turn on resources, and in resources there is no real equality at all (Barber, 2002).

Internet challenges and problems

Perhaps the most significant difference between the Internet and traditional mass media is in the nature of social communication carried out by the users. On the whole, the new interactive technology provides individuals with a number of new tools and forms of interactive and non-interactive communication and generates new forms of human association. Being at variance with the media-centric conceptualizations of the public sphere, it calls for a redefinition of the boundaries not only between the private and the public, but also between the real and virtual, which are constitutive of any theorization of the public/ity. Thus it also calls for a new concept of publicity in which the nature of openness and visibility is radically transformed.

The Internet brought about a new form of publicity – mediated and dialogical at the same time – supplementary to the mediated publicity constructed by traditional mass media, which could also be considered *media-distorted* publicity. Whereas the mass media primarily extended the possibilities of passive *visibility* (i.e. of one being made visible by producers of media contents), the Internet is based on widespread active *participation*. In contrast to the Internet, traditional mass media favour and facilitate primarily reception and consumption through *imitation* owing to the market mechanisms and tendency of profit maximization that stimulate only publication of ideas and news stories that do not annoy or confuse their consumers. They often help block innovation, particularly when they are heralds of particular interests with powerful interest groups backing them. On the other hand, the Internet is pluralistic in terms of both producers and users, and diversified in terms of content by its very nature – due to its decentred structure. If the concept of public/ity has been determined by the internally confined model of a community gathering by the end of the twentieth century, as Bohman (1996: 106) suggests, the rise of the Internet definitely helped transcend this limitation.

The Internet is particularly appropriate to initiate processes of abandoning prejudices preventing relevant problems from appearing in the public sphere. However, the interactive potential of Internet technology not only makes individuals and groups more socially visible at their own will and facilitates interaction among different cultures, but also makes – as a kind of disciplinary technology – others' behaviour overt and widely visible *against* their will. It also increases the visibility of hate speech and other kinds of communication that violate citizens' rights.

The ideal of universal access to the Internet has failed. The personal right to communicate which originally dominated the Internet 'philosophy' was soon ousted by private property and privacy discourse, and most recently, by protection from terrorism. The Internet certainly expanded the sphere of communication but it also, and to a higher degree, expanded the sphere of capitalist economy. As 'the modern newspaper [became] a capitalistic enterprise' in the late nineteenth century (Bücher, 1893/1901: 242), the Internet of the late twentieth century became the main promoter of capitalism in general.

Although there are over one billion Internet users and twice as many mobile communication users worldwide, and most countries continue to make steady progress in terms of access to these technologies, the 'digital divide' – the gap between groups of individuals, social classes, countries and geographic areas with regard to the level of effective access to information and communication technologies (ICTs) and, specifically, to their use of the Internet – is far from being a matter of specific 'life style'. Rather, it reflects economic and political inequalities. A wide gap in the access to the Internet exists between developed and non-developed countries, and between rich and poor people within most countries. This gap between the 'haves' and 'have-nots' often correlates with religious, ethnic, gender, cultural and racial differences which hide substantial economic divisions within and between societies.

Similar to former revolutionary technologies that have substantially contributed to economic growth and social change but not to the reduction of social inequalities, ICTs are not a 'classless' technology. They are shaping a new class structure separating the 'rich-and-wired' and 'poor-and-unconnected'. Since ICTs are becoming an indispensable infrastructure for both civil society and the public sphere, exclusion from these 'technological' structures has not only economic but much broader and fatal consequences for 'unconnected' individuals – they lead to exclusion from civil society and the public sphere, and from citizenship altogether.

Such exclusion can have grave repercussions not only for individuals but for the whole of society. Participation in the production of 'hyperspiritual reality' as Emile Durkheim named it binds members of society together. The inability to interact with other members of society and to participate in the formation of consensus on fundamental values and beliefs not only significantly limits interaction and participation in common activities but also reduces the level of (value) integration and, consequently, increases 'deviant behaviour'. New communication technologies did not change this fundamental Durkheimian 'social fact'.

Obviously, the Internet has ambivalent capabilities. It proved essentially inaccessible to complete hierarchical control, but it can hardly perform the role of a watchdog or create moral obligations in a way similar to traditional media. Internet technology enables dialogical communication that can hardly be effectively restrained by external surveillance, but at the same time it can hardly assure any response. While the Internet presents new opportunities for social interaction, it also stimulates fragmentation. Nevertheless, the Internet is a perfect communicative environment that enables reflexive reasoning of participants – to detach themselves from the subjective personal conditions of their judgment and reflect on it from a universal standpoint, as Kant suggested two centuries ago.

Compared with the traditional corporate mass media, the Internet may help much more effectively by removing obstacles that prevent relevant problems from appearing in the public sphere. It is an obvious contribution of the Internet that the nature of discussions of public issues (which does not necessarily equate with 'public discussion') has changed and become less exposed to authoritative intervention, and the number of active participants in discussions has increased; but the outcome of these changes is much less satisfying. On the other hand, the Internet is less capable of digesting ideas and presenting them in a form that would influence the authorities to heed them. In fact, the contrary is the case: online and offline debates among web users come close to a form of a public only when they get together around the issues placed on the agenda by the traditional 'big' media.

Advancing publicity as the supreme ethical principle

In terms of Mills' 'mass-public' dichotomy, which specifies the empirical conditions necessary to facilitate deliberative political communication in the public sphere, new communication technologies can help 'solve' less than one half of the problem. They make possible that (1) 'virtually as many people express opinions as receive them', and that (2) 'Public communications are so organized that there is a chance immediately ... to answer back any opinion expressed in public'. Immediately perhaps, but not *effectively*, which was the second part of Mills' claim (who will find your reply on the website?). On the other hand, new technologies have no significant impact on two other dimensions Mills uses to differentiate between the mass and the public, i.e. (3) whether an opinion formed in discussion could materialize into an effective action, even against authorities, or this process is controlled by authorities; and (4) whether the public is autonomous from authoritative institutions or interfered with by them (Mills, 1956/2000: 303–4).

Mass media have central significance in the creation of an institutional (infra)structure that enables organization of the general interest both nationally and internationally. Without the 'traditional' mass media, the public sphere would lack the most effective channel correlating the public with power actors appearing before the public and deriving their legitimacy from it. This (am)bivalent relation between the public and the state mediated through and by the media is constitutive of the public sphere. If properly regulated, it is also the precondition necessary for the advancement of the principle of publicity as the supreme ethical and organizational principle, superior to property right and freedom of the press based on it. The present lack of such an effective communication structure and practical impediments to its creation should again become the central issue in the ongoing discussions on media democratization, as it was long ago.

Bentham's main concern with representative democracy was in securing that all transactions in the political assembly would be subject to surveillance by the 'Public Opinion Tribunal'. He *operationalized* the rule of publicity with 'the liberty of the press [which] operates as a check upon the conduct of the ruling few; and in that character constitutes a controlling power, indispensably necessary to the maintenance of good government' (1820). He saw the main tasks of the press in reporting on government activities and proceedings of the legislature in an accessible form to readers, and presenting opinions of the public to the authorities.

When François Guizot praised the representative political system of England in the mid-1800s, he did so almost exclusively for *communicative reasons*. The advantage of representative government over despotic governments was attributed by Guizot to its potential to assist citizens to 'seek after reason, justice, and truth', and delegitimizing absolute power '(1) by *discussion*, which compels existing powers to seek after truth in common; (2) by *publicity*, which places these powers when occupied in this search, under the eyes of the citizens; and (3) by the *liberty of the press*, which stimulates the citizens themselves to seek after truth, and to tell it to power' (Guizot, 1851/1861: 264; emphases added).

Tönnies (1922) identified *the* Public Opinion as the most substantiated opinion about a public issue rephrased by the most important metropolitan newspapers and approached beyond partisan bias. According to Tönnies, genuine public opinion has to be displayed in/by the media or else it does not exist. It is another thing altogether if such a (national) consensus can hardly be found except in states of emergency.

Regretfully, recent developments rarely assisted citizens to 'seek after reason, justice, and truth' but often brought them to the 'normal state of prison' as Mike Traber put it. His powerful allegory of prison – a modernized version of Plato's cave allegory – reveals the complexity of human alienation in the media-dominated world:

> Try to imagine yourself as an inmate in a prison. In fact you have been in prison all your life. You were born there and grew up there. You live there with many other prisoners. But neither they nor you really know why you are there. You catch glimpses of the outside world, and you wonder what it is like out there. But the fact that you really don't know does not worry you excessively. Because you consider the state of being a prisoner as normal, the prison is your natural habitat... This worldview from prison is a metaphor of our news culture. We see and hear very little of what is really going on in the world, and what we see and hear are unconnected fragments of an often distorted reality. The real tragedy of this situation is that we consider it normal, that, like life prisoners, we trust the media's intercom system... Fortunately there are

people and groups who from time to time are determined to break out
of this prison; they start digging tunnels so that they can escape
(Traber, 1995: 25).

We are facing a growing discrepancy between the generic
human ability and need to communicate and our inability to
use more and more complex, state and/or privately controlled
technical means of communication. The development of
communication technologies and organizations necessitated by
new technologies fosters not only greater communicative
power, but also more intensive alienation. The conditions under
which one enters the public sphere are more complex and
sharper than ever before. Not only the abilities to feel and reason
with others and to use various means of communication are
required but also access to appropriate communication. In
modern capitalist societies, 'access to' communication means
usually means *owning* them as one's own private, or as a part of
corporate, property. As Peter Doebler (1971: 75) emphasized,
'the right of free speech must include access to the technology
of reproduction and dissemination which the printers [...]
control. To deny someone access to printing techniques is
directly analogous to denying them access to the telephone or
airwaves.'

There is a lot of (pretended) ignorance about the idea of
creating opportunities for public expression in the media age.
As Abbie Hoffman argues in the introduction to his book, *Steal
this Book*, 'To make the claim that the right to print your own
book means freedom of the press is to completely
misunderstand the nature of mass society. It is like making the
claim that any one with a pushcart can challenge Safeway
supermarkets or that any child can grow up to be president'
(1971, vii). In fact, only the elite minorities of media owners
and advertisers (and media professionals to some degree) are
nowadays in the position to manage and control mass media
as a part of private (corporate) economy while for the rest of
the citizens the cost of access to the privately owned media is

prohibitively high. This is in sharp contrast to the inalienable human ability to communicate.

However, there is no need to see citizens and the media as adversaries in the battle for free expression despite conflicting theories on this issue, one – advocating the right to communicate – suggesting that freedom of the press should grant rights to the citizen and protect the media to the extent that those rights can be realized, and the other considering the media specific and primary addressees of press freedom and individual citizens only the ultimate beneficiaries of media freedom. As Jerome Barron (2003: 12) argues in an article on the rights of access and reply to the media in the United States, 'freedom of speech and of the press need not be exclusive of any single party in the communication process. These freedoms extend directly to the people as well as the media. The media can be both free and fair.'

The quintessential question is whether we believe that the mass media should be *primarily* (not exclusively) means of human communication that cannot be privately appropriated – or things and commodities with no specific inherent purpose, and thus they may be appropriated according to the private property right. The decision to take one alternative or the other answers the question of the appropriate kind of regulation. The authentic idea of freedom of the press to enable personal freedom of expression is based on the former assumption. Consequently, the main function attributed to the 'public serviceable' media is to enable associations, groups and individual members of civil society to make their politically relevant opinions and actions publicly available and, thus, at least potentially politically influential – in contrast to the prevailing practice that media, old and new, are used primarily as tools of political control or a business opportunity rather than as citizens' self-expression and political participation.

New communication technologies not only broaden temporal and spatial horizons and reduce the temporal and spatial distance between those communicating, but also require more specific communication capacities, skills and means, and eventually even ownership of some communication means in order to use them. To make the classical concept of freedom of expression applicable to modern complex societies and to make it functional in terms of citizens' participation in political life, it should be rethought and expanded in correlation with the increase of technological progress, productivity and affluence. In fact, the demand to broaden the concept of the personal right to communicate due to new communication technologies and opportunities correlates with the extension of the property right, which has been de facto broadened – i.e. more and more property has been privately accumulated – as a consequence of the colonization of new territories in times past and the development of new production technologies today.

References

Barber, Benjamin R. 2002. The Ambiguous Effects of Digital Technology on Democracy in a Globalizing World. In Heinrich-Böll-Stiftung (ed.), Gut zu Wissen, Westfälisches Dampfboot. <http://www.wissensgesellschaft.org/themen/demokratie/democratic.pdf>

Barron, Jerome B. 2003. Rights of Access and Reply to the Media in the United States Today. *Communications and the Law*, April, 1–12.

Bentham, Jeremy. 1791/1994. Of Publicity. *Public Culture*, 6, 3:581-595.

Bentham, Jeremy. 1820. On the Liberty of the Press and Public Discussion. <http://www.la.utexas.edu/research/poltheory/bentham/bsp/index.html>

Bohman, James. 1996. Die Öffentlichkeit des Weltbürgers: Über Kants "negatives Surrogat." In M. Lutz-Bachmann and J. Bohman (eds.), *Frieden durch Recht: Kants Friedensidee und das Problem einer neue Weltordnung*, 87–113. Frankfurt: Suhrkamp.

Bücher, Karl. 1893/1901. *Industrial Revolution*. New York: Henry Holt.

Doebler, Peter D. 1971. The Printer and Censorship. *Newsletter on Intellectual Freedom*, May.

Guizot, François. 1851. *History of the Origin of Representative Government in Europe*. London: H. G. Bohn.

Habermas, Jürgen. 2006. Political Communication in Media Society: Does Democracy Still Enjoy an Epistemic Dimension? The Impact of Normative Theory on Empirical Research. *Communication Theory* 16, 411–426.

Hoffman, Abbie. 1971. *Steal this Book*. New York: Perate Editions.

Kant, Immanuel. 1793/1914. The Principles of Political Right. In *Immanuel Kant, Eternal Peace and other International Essays*, 27–54. Boston: The World Peace Foundation.

Kant, Immanuel. 1795/1983. To Perpetual Peace. In *Immanuel Kant: Perpetual Peace and Other Essays*, 107–144. Cambridge, Ind.: Hackett.

Mills, C. Wright. 1956/2000. *The Power Elite*. Oxford: Oxford University Press.

Tarde, Gabriel. 1901. *L'opinion et la foule*. Paris: Felix Alcan.

Tönnies, Ferdinand. 1922. *Kritik der öffentlichen Meinung*. Berlin: Julius Springer.

Traber, Michael. 1995. Beyond Patriotism: Escaping from an Ideological Prison. *Javnost-The Public* 2, 2, 19–26.

VI

Journalism in Africa: Modernity versus Africanity

Francis B. Nyamnjoh

My experience with Journalism in Africa and Africa in Journalism (JAAJ) is primarily as a consumer of journalistic production and also as an observer of journalists and journalism at work. As a little boy, crumpled newspapers were always the bearers of good news, as I would watch in anticipation as my mother unwrapped them to reveal their contents of akara beans, puff balls, bread, groundnuts or whatever other consumer goodies she had bought from the market woman, shopkeeper or street vendor. At that time, unsold newspapers were simply worth their weight in gold, even though I couldn't quite read them, and, of course, they contained interesting pictures.

I grew up appreciating newspapers in other ways too. I remember making clippings of newspapers that had brought me good news, such as when they published the results of the various examinations in which I had succeeded, including in 1986 when I obtained a Cameroonian government scholarship to pursue a doctoral degree in media and communication studies. I proceeded to the Centre for Mass Communication Research at the University of Leicester, where consuming JAAJ became a scholarly compulsion, and observing journalists a professional impulse.

Back in Cameroon in the early 1990s and unemployed, when the winds of democratization were rustling the baobabs of dictatorship, I was able to sustain my appetite for the multiplicity of newspapers that proliferated the newsstands with colourful and screaming headlines, only thanks to the fact I could pick them up a few days later at almost no cost from market women and storekeepers who were used to buying the unsold in devalued bulk, determined to put them to better use.

As for the broadcast media, I grew up listening to national radio on shortwave band, which was as liberating as it was dictatorial. I recall how state functionaries used to be hired and fired, promoted and demoted mainly through the radio, which faithfully and regularly broadcast the thunderous outbursts of The Great Dictator or his dogs of war against freedoms. Civil Servants would breakfast, lunch and dine glued to their radio in a mixture of expectation, uncertainty and foreboding, as radio could make them eat with joyous relish, just as it could make them lose their appetite, throw up or faint. Television, which came much later in the mid 1980s to crown the reign of Face Powder Democracy with coloured vision, simply enshrined the dictatorship of the radio, as functionaries could know no better in real terms. Not to mention the masses swimming at the margins of freedom and opportunity.

Behind every newspaper, radio or television, behind every kind of journalism, African or otherwise, is The Journalist. Often, I have wished I were a journalist, but when I watch African journalists at work, when I scrutinize the challenges facing them daily and fathom the compromises they have to make, I thank God I am only a journalist to be.

African Journalism is like swimming upstream most of the time, given all the hurdles journalists and the media face in our various countries. A lot of media freedom advocacy groups, journalists and media scholars, myself included, have catalogued the daily economic, political, institutional and professional constraints confronting African journalists. Among these are the tendency by African governments towards excessive centralization, bureaucratization and politicization of state-owned media institutions, making it very difficult for state-employed journalists to reconcile the government's expectations with their professional beliefs, or with the expectations of the public.

Also stifling, especially for the critical non-government media and journalists, are the legal frameworks regulating the press in many an African country. The craving by most states to control leaves little doubt about how the lawmakers see journalists as potential troublemakers who must be policed. In some countries, even when certain draconian aspects of the press laws of the one-party era have been replaced with new provisions that are relatively more tolerant of opposition views and of criticism, often the selective application of the law, together with the use of extra-legal measures, have been to the detriment of the critical private press, and have made it very difficult for this press to have the professional independence it needs.

Other factors adversely affecting African Journalism include widespread job insecurity, poor salaries and the poor working conditions of most journalists. Financial difficulties, lack of personnel and inadequate specialization or professionalization, ignorance of the market, and the uncertainties of life in the age of flexible mobility and its paradoxes, have only compounded the predicaments of African Journalism. However, these are not the challenges that concern me in this chapter. Of concern here are the basic assumptions that underpin African Journalism and their consequences.

What is Africanity?

What does it mean to be African? Who qualifies to claim Africa? Is being African or claiming Africa an attribute of race and skin colour (black, white, yellow), birth (umbilical cord, birth certificates, identity cards, passports), geography (physical spaces, home village), history (encounters), culture (prescriptive specificities), economics (availability and affordability, wealth and deprivation), sociology (social configurations and action, inclusion and exclusion), psychology (mind sets), philosophy (world views), politics (power relations), collective memory (shared experiences and aspirations), or a category through which a world that is not rigidly geographical, racial or cultural is constructed, to name just a few of the many possibilities that present themselves? These are questions which have deep roots in debates on citizenship and identity – and, therefore, in the definition of rights, entitlement, duties, and responsibilities.

The questions are, of course, not uniquely African – indeed, similar issues have been posed and debated with considerable passion in other parts of the world both historically and currently, and contestations around them have also often been played out in violent communal confrontations, civil wars, and inter-state conflicts. And while they may seem straightforward to answer, the questions have been rendered much more complex by the dynamic interplay of race, ethnicity, gender and religion in the structuring and exercise of power and opportunity. Precisely for this reason, they are not questions that can be addressed in the abstract.

How one answers the questions that are generated by any attempt at grappling with Africanity is not only determined by situation, but is also a function of how selective one is with regard to the various indicators available. Some individuals and communities on the continent and elsewhere might claim Africanity or have it imposed upon them for various personal, collective, historical and political reasons. But it is not always straightforward to say which of these claims may be legitimate and why, especially as identity is not only how one sees oneself, but also how one is seen and categorized by others, particularly where the absorption of new populations is involved. This is all the more so as identities are themselves always in mutation, shaped as they are by changing historical contexts and circumstances, such as internal and international migrations, and shifts in social power relations.

It is, however, safe to say that to most ordinary people in Africa, Africanity is more than just a birth certificate, an identity card, or a passport – documents that many of them may not have, even as others coming from elsewhere and waving the flag of Africanity may have all of these documents and more. For the ordinary person, to be African is not simply to be labelled or merely defined as such. It is to be a social actor/ actress enmeshed in a particular context that has been and continues to be shaped by a unique history that, among others, is marked by unequal encounters and misrepresentations often informed by the arrogance and ignorance of the economically and politically powerful who take the liberty also to abrogate a cultural superiority to themselves. For the masses of Africans, Africa is above all a lived reality, one that is constantly shaped and reshaped by their toil and sweat as subjected and devalued humanity, even as they struggle to live in dignity and to transform their societies progressively. For these people, the fact of their Africanity is neither in question nor a question. And the least they would expect from concerned journalists is to refrain from adding onto their burdens in the name of a type of journalism which, in being ahistorical, also trivialises their collective experiences and memories (Olukoshi & Nyamnjoh 2004).

Problematic assumptions in African Journalism

The basic assumptions underpinning African Journalism in definition and practice are not informed by the fact that ordinary Africans are busy Africanizing their modernity and modernizing their Africanity in ways often too complex for simplistic dichotomies to capture. The precepts of journalism that apply currently in Africa are largely at variance with dominant ideas of personhood and agency (and by extension society, culture and democracy) shared by communities across the continent, as it assumes that there is One-Best-Way of being and doing to which Africans must aspire and be converted in the name of modernity and civilization.

This dichotomy is at the heart of some of the professional and ethical dilemmas that haunt journalism in and on Africa, a journalism whose tendency is to debase and caricature African humanity, creativity and realities. It is a constraint that renders African Journalism a journalism of 'bandwagonism', where mimicry is the order of the day, as emphasis is less on thinking than on doing, less on leading than on being led. African Journalism lacks both the power of self-definition and the power to shape the universals that are deaf-and-dumb to the particularities of journalism in and on Africa.

Because journalism has tended to be treated as an attribute of so-called 'modern' societies or of 'superior' ones, it is only proper, so the reasoning goes, that African Journalism and the societies it serves, are taught the principles and professional practices by those who 'know' what it means to be civilized and to be relevant to civilization. Aspiring journalists in Africa must, like containers, be cleansed of the mud and dirt of culture as tradition and custom, and refilled with the tested sparklers of culture as modernity and civilization. African journalists are thus called upon to operate in a world where everything has been predefined for them by others, where they are meant to implement and hardly ever to think or rethink, where what is expected of them is respect for canons, not to question how or why canons are forged, or the extent to which canons are inclusive of the creative diversity of the universe that is purportedly of interest to the journalism of the One-Best-Way (Nyamnjoh 2005a: 25-99).

How well journalism is relevant to Africa and Africans depends on what value such journalism gives African humanity and creativity. If journalism is such that privileges a hierarchy of humanity and human creativity, and if such journalism believes that African humanity and creativity are at the abyss of that hierarchy, it is bound to be prescriptive, condescending, contrived, caricatured and hardly in tune with the quest by Africans for equality of humanity and for recognition and representation. And if African journalists were, wittingly or unwittingly, to buy into that hierarchy, they would in effect be working against the interests of the very African communities they claim to serve with their journalism.

A closer look at democracy in Africa is a good indicator of how journalism has tended to articulate and appreciate African realities through the prescriptive lenses of those who believe their ideas of humanity and creativity to be sufficiently rich and practiced for uncritical adoption by 'emerging' others. In Europe and North America, liberal democracy is said to guarantee journalism the best environment it needs to foster freedom and progress. Liberal democracy's colossal investment in the making of the independent individual is projected as the model to be promoted and defended by journalism in and on Africa. Yet the more African Journalism strives to implant liberal democracy, the fewer successes it has had to report.

'Barbie Doll' democracy

Even the most optimistic of African journalists would hesitate to describe liberal democracy and Africa as good bedfellows. If African journalists were even minimally to scrutinize the democratization projects with which they have been involved since the early 1990s, for example, they would agree that implementing liberal democracy in Africa has been like trying to force onto the body of a full-figured person, rich in all the cultural indicators of health Africans are familiar with, a dress made to fit the slim, fleshless, Hollywood consumer model of a Barbie doll-type entertainment icon. They would also agree that together with others, instead of blaming the tiny dress or its designer, the tradition among journalists has been to fault the popular body or the popular ideal of beauty, for emphasizing too much bulk, for parading the wrong sizes, for just not being the right thing.

African journalists have rarely questioned the experience and expertise of the liberal democracy designer or dressmaker, nor his/her audacity in assuming that the parochial cultural palates that inform his/her peculiar sense of beauty should play God in the lives of Africa and African cultures. In Africa, the history of difficulty at implementing liberal democracy and the role journalism plays attest to this clash of values and attempts to ignore African cultural realities that might well have enriched and domesticated liberal democracy in terms of greater relevance. By overstressing individual rights and underplaying the rights of communities (cultural, religious and otherwise), African Journalism and the liberal democracy it has uncritically endorsed, have tended to be more a liability than an asset to the aspirations for recognition and for a voice by the very Africans and communities they target.

Yet, given the fact that Africans (journalists included) in their daily lives continue to emphasize relationships and solidarities over the illusion of autonomy, it is difficult to imagine the future direction of democracy outside a marriage or conviviality between individual aspirations and community interests. Thus, for democracy and journalism to succeed in the present context, it must recognize the fact that most Africans (and indeed everyone else) are primarily attached to their home village (region, province, ethnic, cultural community, etc), to which state and country in the postcolonial sense are only secondary. It is in acknowledging and providing for the reality of individuals who straddle different forms of identity and belonging, and who are willing or forced to be both 'citizens' and 'subjects', that democracy stands its greatest chance in Africa, and that journalism can best be relevant to Africa and Africans (Nyamnjoh 2005a: 231-253).

Citizens and subjects

Despite the tendency to distinguish between citizen and subjects in scholarly circles (Mamdani 1996), in Africa, we find individuals who are both citizens and subjects, who straddle 'cultural' and 'civic' citizenships, but who would not accept sacrificing either permanently. Sometimes they are more the one than the other and sometimes more the other than the one, but certainly not reducible to either. They appropriate both in the most creative and fascinating ways. A democracy or journalism that focuses too narrowly on the individual and is insensitive to the centrality of group and community interests is likely to impair and frustrate the very recognition and representation it celebrates.

Regardless of the status of those involved in 'rights talk' and 'culture talk', they are all convinced of one thing: 'cultural citizenship' is as integral to democracy as political and economic citizenship. If African philosophies of personhood and agency stress interdependence between the individual and the community, and between communities, and if journalists each identify with the many cultural communities seeking recognition and representation at local and national levels, they are bound to be torn between serving their communities and serving the 'imagined' rights-bearing, autonomous individual 'citizen' of the liberal democratic model. A democracy that stresses independence, in a situation where both the worldview and the material realities emphasize interdependence, is bound to result only in dependence.

The liberal democratic rhetoric of rights dominated by a narrow neo-liberal focus on *The Individual*, does not reflect the whole reality of personhood and agency in Africa, which is a lot more complex than provided for in liberal democratic notions of rights and empowerment. Instead of working for a creative mix with indigenous forms of politics and government, liberal democracy has sought to replace them, posing as the One-Best-Way of modern democratic political organisation, the right way of conducting modern politics. So, also, has the journalism it inspires stayed narrow and asphyxiating to alternative outlooks and practices of sharing news and information, and of entertaining and educating.

In the use of language alone, few African journalists have dared to write the way Chinua Achebe suggests is a popular mode of communication among the Igbo, where proverbs are the palm oil with which words are eaten. Fewer still have dared to contemplate using English, French, Portuguese or Spanish in the creative ways that ordinary Africans whom they purportedly target with their journalism do. While journalists mark time with linguistic orthodoxy, African communities have been busy creolizing inherited European languages by promoting intercourse with African languages, and in turn enriching local languages through borrowings. And everywhere the spoken word has also perfected its intermarriage with the unspoken through body language and other nonverbal forms.

When African journalists begin to reflect such popular creativity among Africans, and without a sense of guilt that they are violating journalistic taboos, they will be helping towards a democracy and journalism of relevance to, in and on Africa. In this, there is much in how Africans relate to their cultures and home village to inspire African journalists. African Journalism must recognize and provide for the fact that the home village in Africa has retained its appeal both for those who have been disappointed by the town, as well as for those who have found success in the town.

Recognizing indigenous African forms should not be mistaken for throwing the baby of adaptability out with the bathwater. African popular musicians, for example, have evolved and continue to develop musical idioms that capture ongoing processes by Africans aimed at modernizing their cultures and traditionalizing their modernities. Indeed, the mechanisms developed by Africans in response to the above scenarios are complex, fascinating and informed by ideas of personhood and agency that simply refuse to be confined to the logic of, dichotomies, essentialism, the market and profitability, as the rich personal account of one of Africa's leading contemporary musicians, Manu Dibango, demonstrates (Dibango 1994). As an African musician who has lived the best part of his professional life in Paris and whose music has been enriched by various encounters, Manu Dibango describes himself as 'Négropolitain', 'a man between two cultures, two environments', whose music cannot simply be reduced to either, without losing part of his creative self (Dibango 1994:88-130).

It appears that no one is too cosmopolitan to be local as well. Faced with the temporality or transience of personal success in the context of African modernities, even the most achieving and cosmopolitan of individuals hesitates to sever their rural connections entirely. The city and the 'world out there' are perceived as hunting grounds; the home village is the place to return at the end of the day. Investing in one's home village is generally seen as the best insurance policy and a sign of ultimate success, for it guarantees survival even when one has lost everything in the city, and secures and makes manifest a realisation of success through satisfying obligations and fulfilling requests.

Thus, although successful urbanites may not permanently return or retire to the rural area as such, most remain in constant interaction with their home village through all sorts of ways. Some leave express instructions with kin to be buried or re-buried in their home village. Prescriptive journalism that denounces this reality instead of understanding, adapting and relating to it, is bound to be a liability to Africans and their ways of life. Narrow insistence on individual rights and freedoms has thus impaired understanding of the interconnectedness of peoples, cultures and societies through individuals as products, melting-pots and creative manipulators or jugglers of multiple identities.

Discussing democracy and journalism in Africa calls for scrutiny of the importance of cultural identities in the lives of individuals and groups. This argument challenges reductionist views of democracy and journalism, acknowledges the fact that democracy and journalism may take different forms, and most particularly, that they are construed and constructed differently in different societies, informed by history, culture and economic factors.

Enriched realities

The way forward is in recognising the creative ways in which Africans merge their traditions with exogenous influences to create realities that are not reducible to either but enriched by both. The implication of this argument is that how we understand the role of African Journalism depends on what democratic model we draw on. Under liberal democracy where the individual is perceived and treated as an autonomous agent, and where primary solidarities and cultural identities are discouraged in favour of a national citizenship and culture, journalism is expected to be disinterested, objective, balanced and fair in gathering, processing and disseminating news and information. The assumption is that since all individuals have equal rights as citizens, there can be no justification for bias among journalists.

But under popular notions of democracy where emphasis is on interdependence and competing cultural solidarities are a reality, journalists and the media are under constant internal and external pressure to promote the interests of the various groups competing for recognition and representation. The tensions and pressures are even greater in situations where states and governments purport to pursue liberal democracy in principle, while in reality they continue to be highhanded and repressive to their populations. When this happens, journalists are at risk of employing double-standards as well, by claiming one thing and doing the opposite, or by straddling various identity margins, without always being honest about it, especially if their very survival depends on it.

To democratize means to question basic monolithic assumptions, conventional wisdom about democracy, journalism, government, power myths and accepted personality cults, and to suggest and work for the demystification of the state, custom and society. To democratize African Journalism is to provide the missing cultural link to current efforts, links informed by respect for African humanity and creativity, and by popular ideas of personhood and domesticated agency. It is to negotiate conviviality between competing ideas of how best to provide for the humanity and dignity of all. Above all, it is to observe and draw on the predicaments of ordinary Africans forced by culture, history and material realities to live their lives as 'subjects' rather than as 'citizens', even as liberal democratic rhetoric claims otherwise. The mere call for an exploration of alternatives in African Journalism, is bound to be perceived as a threat and a challenge.

In particular, such a call will receive a hostile hearing from those who have championed the cause of one-dimensionalism nationally and internationally – that is, those who benefit from the maintenance of the status quo, and who stand to lose from any changes in African Journalism. They cannot withstand the challenge, stimulation and provocation that a more democratic (as the celebration of difference and diversity) journalism promises. They want life to go on without disturbance or fundamental change. And they are well placed to ensure this, thanks to their power to regulate journalism, the power to accord or to deny a voice to individuals and communities. Only well-articulated policies informed by public interest broadly defined to include individual and community expectations, and scrupulously respected, would offer any guarantee against such abuse and misuse of office and privilege.

The future of democracy and the relevance of journalism to Africans and their predicaments will depend very much on how well Africans are able to negotiate recognition and representation for their humanity and creativity beyond the tokenism of the prevalent, politically correct rhetoric about equality of humanity and opportunity.

Creative appropriation of ICTs:
Lessons for African Journalism

Such a future for democracy and the relevance of journalism therein would have much to learn from the creative ways in which Africans are currently relating to innovations in information and communication technologies (ICTs). The same popular creativity that has been largely ignored by conventional journalism in the past is remarkable today all over Africa and among Africans in the Diaspora. The body of literature informed by empirical research is considerable and suggests that they must seek to harness, within the limits of the structural constraints facing them, whatever possibilities are available to contest exclusion and to seek inclusion. This is especially the case in the context of the ICT innovations that fuel globalization. True, ICTs are not free from the logic of domination and appropriation typical of neoliberalism, but they clearly offer marginalized voices an opportunity for real alternatives, as Miller and Slater have demonstrated in their ethnographic study of how the Internet shapes and is shaped by individuals and communities in Trinidad (Miller and Slater 2000), and as is increasingly the case with the cell phone in Africa (Nyamnjoh 2005b).

The Internet for example, far from being 'a monolithic or placeless "cyberspace", is, like numerous new technologies, used by diverse people, in diverse real-world locations', and therefore cannot be fully understood outside of how it is being harnessed and assimilated under differential political, economic, cultural and social circumstances of individuals and communities (Miller and Slater 2000:1–25). Thus, although Internet connectivity in Africa is lowest compared to other areas of the world, Africa's cultural values of sociality, interconnectedness, interdependence and conviviality make it possible for others to access the Internet and its opportunities without necessarily being connected themselves. In many situations, it suffices for a single individual to be connected for whole groups and communities to benefit. The individual in question acts as a point of presence or communication node, linking other individuals and communities in a myriad of ways and bringing hope to others who would otherwise be dismissed as not belonging by capital and its excessive emphasis on the autonomous individual consumer.

In parts of the continent where resident telephone lines are grossly inadequate and defective at best, and where Internet connections are difficult and expensive, literate and illiterate people eager to stay in touch with relations, friends and to seize opportunities in the Diaspora, flood the few Internet points with messages to be typed and emailed on their behalf. Replies to their emails are printed out, addressed and pigeonholed for them. What is noteworthy, however, is that the high charges do not seem to temper the determination of those involved to stay in touch with the outside world.

Through such connections, people are able to exchange news on family, projects, events and developments of a personal and general nature. They are also able to exchange news on different cultural products and to arrange how to acquire such products for one another. It is mainly through this means that many Africans abroad or in the Diaspora do not miss out on local music releases, publications, satirical humour, artefacts and fashion. Each visit to the home village is armed with a long list of cultural products to take back for oneself, friends and relations. Many unmarried young men and women in the Diaspora would have given up hope of marrying someone from their home village or country and doing so in accordance with local customs and traditions, had email not been there to facilitate contacts and negotiations with parents and potential families-in-law.

In addition, the cosmopolitan identities of Africans in the Diaspora personally and through websites serve as itinerant billboards or as evangelists seeking converts for the cultures of their home villages. Thanks to such advertisements and websites, *marabouts, sangomas, ngangas* have been drawn to the West and other centres of modern accumulation where growing interest in the occult is creating demand and opportunities for their *muti* or magic from Africa. The increasing need for magical interpretations of material realities under millennial capitalism has meant creating space at the margins for marginalized cultures and solutions. This would explain the back-street shops and dealers in African cultural products, ranging from foods to charms and amulets. It also explains the fact that not all the customers visiting these shops and markets are Diaspora Africans. The Diaspora and the rest of the world are thus connected to the local, and both can work actively to ensure continuity for cultures and communities marginalized at the national and global levels by the big players.

The same creativity displayed in relation to the Internet is true of the cell phone as well. Africa has the fastest growth rate in the world for cell phones. The latest technology to be domesticated is the cell phone, which almost everywhere on the continent is being used creatively by poor urban dwellers and Diaspora Africans to stay in touch with relatives back home and through them maintain healthy communication with their ancestors. Under the current structural adjustment programmes, most African states have restructured and privatized parts of their telecommunication facilities, providing for cellular networks that have transformed telecommunication. Although privatisation has largely benefited Western companies financially, the result has been a huge cultural benefit to Africans. Prior to privatisation and the cell phone explosion, owning a telephone was a luxury only a few could afford in the major cities, and telephoning was often too cryptic for the decorum and respect expected of exchanges in local cultures. Today, thanks to the cell phone and its proliferation, even those who cannot afford one stand to benefit thanks to the sociality and solidarity of the local cultures of which they are a part.

Most cell phone owners in West Africa tend to serve as points of presence for their community, with others paying or simply passing through them to make calls to relatives, friends and contacts within or outside the country. Thus for example, although Nigerians might actually own fewer phones than most countries in the West, it has been noted to generate higher average revenue per user (ARPU) per month. The ARPU of a cell-phone user in Nigeria, with a GDP per capita of US$ 363, is US$ 91, which is five times that of South Africa which has six times Nigeria's GDP per capita, and almost twice the United States, with close to 1000 times Nigeria's GDP per capita. For a country with a low level of economic activity relative to G8 countries, Nigeria has a high level of minutes of use (MOU) of 200, compared to 154 in France, 88 in Germany, 149 in Japan, 118 in Italy, 249 in Canada, 120 in UK and 364 in the US (cf. Merrill Lynch Investment Bank 2002).

Such statistics could be explained by Nigerians receiving more calls than they make, and also by the reality of single-owner-multi-user (SOMU) communities. This suggests that the economic and social value (ESV) of a cell phone in countries like Nigeria and Cameroon with a higher volume of SOMU communities is much higher than the ESV of a cell phone in countries with single-owner-single-user (SOSU) communities. Contrary to popular opinion, sociality, interdependence and conviviality are not always an obstacle to profitability (Nyamnjoh 2005b: 16-17). The lessons for African journalism of such creative appropriation processes underway are obvious.

The future may well be bright

The challenges of connectivity notwithstanding, Africans, on the continent and in the Diaspora, are harnessing ICTs (digital video, digital photography, Internet, cell-phones, reporting, SMSing and blogging) in ways indicative of what has been termed 'citizen journalism'. Indeed, thanks to innovations in ICTs, the structure and content of the big media are being challenged and compelled to be more sensitive to cultural diversity. The very same innovations facilitate new media cultures and practices through the possibilities they offer radical, alternative, small independent, local and community media. Through the capacity for flexibility and accessibility of ICTs that make possible new media, cultural communities hitherto marginalized are better catered for even within the framework of dominance by the global cultural industries. The current advantage being taken of ICTs by cultural communities the world over who are seeking recognition and representation should be seen in this light, and above all, as an example from which conventional journalism can draw.

References

Dibango, M. (in collaboration with Danielle Rouard) (1994), *Three Kilos of Coffee: An Autobiography*, Chicago: The University of Chicago Press.

Mamdani, M., (1996), *Citizen and Subject: Contemporary Africa and the Legacy of Late Capitalism*, Cape Town: David Philip.

Miller, D. and Slater, D. (2000), *The Internet : An Ethnographic Approach*, Oxford : Berg.

Nyamnjoh, F.B., (2005a), *Africa's Media, Democracy and the Politics of Belonging*, London: Zed Books.

Nyamnjoh, F.B., (2005b), 'Images of Nyongo amongst Bamenda Grassfielders in Whiteman Kontri', *Citizenship Studies*, Vol.9(3):241–269.

Olukoshi, A. and Nyamnjoh, F.B., (2004), 'Editorial', *CODESRIA Bulletin*, No.1&2 2004.

VII

Advertising against Racism: Reflections on Consumer Culture and Social Activism

LIV SOVIK

Historically, black activists have sustained the struggle against racism in Brazil. Public awareness of racism tends to exempt non-blacks: opinion polls show the overwhelming majority of the population thinks society is racist but that they, individually, are not. After successful cooperation in preparation for the UN World Conference against Racism, Racial Discrimination, Xenophobia and Related Intolerance, held in Durban in September 2001, a number of Brazilian non-governmental organizations (NGOs) decided to continue a multiracial engagement with the issue. Thus, members of black and non-black NGOs came together periodically to discuss how they could continue to do work together, calling their meetings 'Dialogues Against Racism'.[1] The first three meetings, in July and November 2001 and September 2002, generated a report that speaks of the need for unity and awareness-building and, too, of the difficulty of arriving at a decision on priorities. It proposes a wide variety of actions, from the search for public consensus on affirmative action (which has been the focus of controversy since 2001) and lobbying for a government committee to be set up to monitor compliance with the

International Convention on the Elimination of Racism, to the idea of an institute to work against racist dynamics within NGOs.

Given the Dialogues' focus on social consensus and the need to persuade government and peers to engage in the struggle for racial equality, it was perhaps logical that priority was given to a media campaign aimed at the general public, to spread wider the dynamics of those discussions. An agency was commissioned to design it and at the fourth session of the Dialogues, in November 2003, a proposal for a series of television public service spots was presented by Nádia Rebouças of Rebouças & Associados. Rebouças is a specialist in strategic planning, with considerable experience working for large corporations, and was chosen because of her leading role in the Citizens' Action Against Hunger, initiated by the charismatic Herbet de Souza, known as Betinho, in 1993.[2] Over the last decade and a half, Nádia Rebouças has come to concentrate on 'communication for change', mostly in the field of corporate social responsibility. Her concept for the campaign was unanimously approved at the fourth session of Dialogues and the campaign was launched in December 2004.

To evade the standard reaction ('society is racist, but I am not'), the campaign centres on a question, instead of a slogan or the use of role models and opinion leaders. The question – 'Where do you keep your racism?' – presupposes individual prejudice and engages the viewer in answering for it. The spots, available for download from the internet,[3] are of short responses to this question by members of the public. They were shown on the powerful Globo network, both its open access and cable channels, on public and congressional cable television and in a chain of cinemas. The spots were supplemented by billboards, posters, leaflets, radio spots and a website, with campaign materials and information that could sustain an argument about policy issues, including definitions of racism, discrimination, whiteness in the Brazilian context, affirmative action and the basic tenets of anti-racist legislation. During this phase of the campaign, according to the Dialogues website, 85,000 leaflets, 10,000 buttons, 5,000 posters were distributed, and 50 busdoor ads and 50 billboards were put up; the website received 64,000 visits. A second phase, of testimonials by black people about racism in everyday situations, was launched in May 2006.

A case study could be written about this national campaign, whose success is recognizable in the high quality of the public service spots and their strategic distribution through the dominant Brazilian television network, Globo, together with other supporting channels. The Dialogues Against Racism campaign generates considerable enthusiasm on the part of many of its proponents and, apparently, the many other people who downloaded and distributed materials. It could be thought of as a model for engaging NGOs and their constituencies, business leaders, broadcasters and some advertising professionals, at a time when actual social mobilization is low. The 'why did it fail?' question, with its attendant concerns about distribution, quality of production, back-up materials, personnel or major disagreements between the sponsoring parties and those who actually make the programmes, does not come to mind. However, perhaps there is yet room for a discussion of its limitations in combating racism. What is the special place of broadcast advertising, in the original sense of sowing words on fertile and rocky ground?

The question implies a whole theory of communication, in which advertising is seen as an extension of publicity or of *divulgação*, understood as the unleashing of information on a receptive audience. But advertising is usually seen in a different context, as one of a host of related activities, such as public relations, sponsorship, direct marketing, point of purchase, participation in exhibitions and fairs, personal selling, interactive marketing. The components of this list, taken from a manual on marketing (Smith, 1998: 2), are quite easily adapted to social concerns, with Social Forums and other major conferences serving as fairs and exhibitions, listservs as direct marketing, small meetings and consultations as personal selling and so on, but this shift from amplified publicity to active salesmanship is a substantial one.

Even so, these techniques of persuasion are increasingly used in the milieu of social movements and organizations, where advertising is most commonly seen as an enhanced or more potent version of the natural impulse to communicate. This version naturalizes the entire field of production of advertising, in which different actors and power relations are at work and the market-centred model dominant. These reflections try to undo the naturalization of advertising and see it anew in the context of its operation by social activists. This chapter's focus on racism as a central contemporary political problem and on re-politicising the theories of communication that are put into practice by social organizations is a small homage to Mike Traber's life and work and his impact on my thinking when I was still in my early twenties.

Corporate advertisers and advertising professionals assume advertising is successful, to the extent that it sells products, services and brand images. For this same reason, it is accused of changing social values. Some report that its power has been harnessed in undesirable ways, so that, for example, universities 'see themselves as competing in a marketplace, and have thus adopted the practices that are directed towards that end even though the objectives of the organisation are thereby hampered' (Lury and Warde, 1997: 101). In questions of social justice and social action, as in those of business, the dynamics of capitalist globalization are the main frame of reference. Indeed, the process by which social questions take on the shape of marketing is not strongest among NGOs or social movements, but among corporations that take an interest in social responsibility. In Brazil, the foremost actor in this movement is Instituto Ethos, whose members have in common an 'interest in establishing ethical standards for relations with employees, clients, vendors, the community, stockholders, public authorities and the environment.'[4]

The 1230 members of the institute, which is based in São Paulo, produce 35 percent of Brazilian GDP, but employ only two million workers of an economically active population of more than 92 million in 2004. In other words, Instituto Ethos represents the most advanced, high tech companies in Brazil, meaning, too, that they are the ones that do the most outsourcing. The institute promotes a common ethical vision of sustainable development and social justice, generates information, participates in public policy discussions and supports movements and social projects. Members enact policies that improve their companies' public image and respond to moral pressures from the society of which they are a part. This is also profitable; for example, it can reduce shoplifting or vandalism or, through policies favouring a diverse workforce, create loyalty among employees who have suffered discrimination. In sum, businesses involved in social responsibility discussions and action are often in the vanguard both of profit-making technologies and of the promotion of equal opportunity and diversity, which they recognize can be good business as well as ethically satisfying.

The broadly declared objectives of work for social justice are often to affect the dynamics of capitalist globalization, which thus form the main economic and political frame of reference. The most established Brazilian NGOs and movements were founded by people whose formative political experience in the 1960s, 1970s and 1980s was in the militant Left and are resistant to what was once called, in shorthand, 'capitalism' and is now more commonly known as neoliberalism. But if big business has come over to the side of the social, NGOs have also seen the light on marketing techniques. The Citizens' Action Against Hunger of 1993 can be seen as a key victory over prejudices against the use the powerful instruments of mass media and marketing, as they were put to use for democratic and popular purposes. The campaign showed how, with the help of the same tools that companies use – public relations 'events' to get on the media's agenda and the good will generated by images and testimonials by celebrities – it was possible to create interest in the general public, that then demanded access to the 'product', which was citizens' organized action against hunger.

Three million people became involved in committees and donations were made by groups and individuals, supermarkets and restaurants. Government agencies became involved, even though the campaign continued to be led by social organizations. The campaign was enormously successful in raising awareness and redistributing surpluses and it considerably reduced hunger, at least in urban areas. It eventually ran into problems, the most important of which may have been that it began to speak of unemployment and of hunger's causes, such as concentration of land tenure, issues that are much more difficult than hunger to explain and run into organized political resistance.

After prejudice against communication through marketing techniques diminished came the demand for them. Large NGOs that provide consultancy services and mediate funds, as well as some smaller ones, now understand publicity about their work to be an essential condition to survival and effectiveness. They are pressured to become more visible to the general public and to raise funds in Brazil. This pressure comes from international donor agencies, which in their turn are obliged to spread the word about their work and to promote it, competing among themselves for attention from their institutional or population constituencies. Now, it is practically obligatory for major players on the development project 'market' to produce an institutional discourse with advertising objectives. They must create prestige and increase visibility, move people and motivate them to provide money.

Two responses to this pressure are common, among non-governmental organizations and social movements. There can be resistance in principle to the techniques and tools of marketing as foreign to the values of NGOs and social movements and an understanding that promotional activities absorb more energy than they are worth, distracting from the central purpose of the organization. Among larger NGOs in urban centres, on the other hand, this yes-or-no policy discussion may not exist or affect action, as promotional activities come in through the back door of information campaigns and anti-globalization networking. In this second approach, marketing technologies are accepted pragmatically as being able to contribute to the effectiveness, efficiency and self-support of social organizations, and to social mobilization around important issues. There ensue technical discussions of campaigns: what looks best, what has bad connotations, what is persuasive or not. The audience and the message are at centre stage and marketing technologies are understood as communications tools, their origin in product promotion and in the advertising industry is taken for granted, if not forgotten.

Discourse and social change

A review of some recent ideas on the subject of advertising and marketing may be useful in carving out a space for discussion, beyond the minutiae of creating and operating campaigns, or a value judgment of such campaigns as a (perhaps necessary) detour on the path to more important priorities. One important contemporary critic of consumer society and its handmaiden, advertising, was Jean Baudrillard. He criticised views of consumption as alienation, views that try:

> to demonstrate that *people's relation to objects, and their relation to themselves is falsified*, mystified, and manipulated, consuming this myth at the same time as the object. Once having stated the universal postulate of the free and conscious subject (in order to make it remerge at the end of history as a happy ending), they are forced to attribute all the 'dysfunctions' they have uncovered to a diabolic power – in this case to the technostructure, armed with advertising, public relations, and motivation research (Baudrillard, 1988: 42).

Baudrillard suggests an alternative to this moralizing view and its preconceived notion of a consumer's autonomous selection of products from a range of choices. He understands that there is a system of needs, produced by the system of production. 'As a system, needs are also radically different from pleasure and satisfaction. They are produced *as elements of a system* and not *as a relation between an individual and an object* (1988: 42). Baudrillard then interprets the system of needs, or of consumption, as a language, in which each object has meaning in relation to each other term within the system. Thus, increases in the sale of Nike shoes are not a result of convincing people of something false, an inflated symbolic value of the shoes, but a response to a whole series of signs of belonging and exchange by which the wearer assigns him or herself a place in society, with peer relationships and alliances.

The difference may seem slight, in practice, but conceptually it is not. It means that the problem raised by the marketing of social values is not whether NGOs and social movements have surrendered to the enemy, by using promotion techniques, but what social activism advertising campaigns are actually saying. What do people 'buy' when they use campaign materials, when they affix a button to their clothes or distribute leaflets at a meeting? What alliances are they forming or marriages are they contracting, within which kinship system (another of Baudrillard's analogies) are they placing themselves? It is well known that racism has an institutional and a violent face. If general acceptance of a campaign can be measured by the number of people who adopt its signs and symbols, what does this imply for their action in institutions and in the face of violence? What is the role of good will? How do confrontation and resistance fit into a campaign's design, what is confronted, what resistance encouraged?

For Baudrillard, in consumer society there is a surge in 'altruistic ideology', resulting from the current impossibility of the belief in 'individual salvation for the community of all Christians, and in individual rights limited only by the rights of others.' Now, 'the exacerbations of multiple individualisms' are only constrained by the State, which at the same time stimulates consumer society. From this contradiction, Baudrillard says, arises the solution of 'an increase in altruistic ideology (which is itself bureaucratized), a "social lubrication" through concern, social reform, the gift, the handout, welfare propaganda and human relations' (1988: 53). Thus, Baudrillard delivers his usual package: the ineffectuality of any agency in a world dominated by appearances and surfaces, rather than essences and individuality, and the hopelessness of any collective cause. Though Baudrillard's warnings may not lead to the way out, it may well be worth remembering his caution about 'altruistic ideology' as palliative and conformist, when analysing campaigns

Naomi Klein, in her well known exposé of the dynamics of branding and global capitalist development, on the dynamics of Baudrillard's 'monopolistic, state and bureaucratic' system in which governments and business are intertwined, discusses precisely the contrast between general altruism and workers' interests. In her concluding chapter, she recalls Filipino activists saying that regulation in factories is of value when it results from worker action and not from codes imposed from outside. Then, she notes that action is possible on a global scale, today, and that in 1998 activists shot down the Multilateral Agreement on Investment, an initiative in the OECD to protect investors against the vagaries of national and labour interests. *No Logo* begins as a book about branding and the strong economic influence of symbolic production – brands and corporate images that float above and beyond the material production process – and ends as a paean to global internet and activism. The symbolic power of brands is combated in the battlefields of coordinated communication, not with counter-branding by social movements and the political interests they represent. For her, the symbolic power of brand and image find a limit in global (and local) activism, not to be confused with the altruistic ideology that Baudrillard scorns so heartily.

Klein dates the current ascendancy of brand and image, of advertising over production, to April 2, 1993, when Marlboro discounted its cigarettes to compete with house brands, stock markets momentarily lost confidence in branding as a money-making strategy and companies that relied on it dropped considerably in value. But there is a longer prehistory to the current moment, as shown by the prescience of the Baudrillard book quoted here, *The Consumer Society*, published in 1970. In Brazil, the prehistory can be traced to the explosion of the media industries in the 1960s, which coincided with the advent of the military regime. Sérgio Ricardo, a pop musician dedicated to making music with political overtones, expressed a common feeling of the time when he wrote in his memoirs about a shock of civilizations. Backstage at televised pop music competitions, he saw a nice man who floated 'as if the soles of his shoes didn't touch ground, subtly demonstrating that he came from a different world. The business world' (Ricardo, 1991: 60). Ricardo speaks of the censorship, after the 1968 'coup within the coup' that sharpened military rule and put regulation in the hands of the State, of the ascent of television, increasing popularity of foreign recorded programmes and music under the general rule of commercial concerns. Thus, Klein's 'Marlboro Friday' finds another explanation, beyond corporate strategies, in the increasing reliance on media as a tool of governability.

In 'Postscript on Control Societies', the French philosopher Gilles Deleuze (1995) wrote a denouncement similar to Sérgio Ricardo's businessmen 'in floating shoes' (Ricardo, 1991: 61), that mentions the 'arrogant breed who are our masters' (Deleuze, 1995: 182). But Deleuze provides a perspective that is more productive than any of those quoted so far, in defining the strategic and political problems that the advertising imperative places before social activists. Where Baudrillard speaks of administrative power blocs (corporate, government, bureaucratic), Klein of internet opinion formation and coordinated symbolic action in a parallel world to the hype of logos, and Sérgio Ricardo of economic and political contexts in which the media industries and their commercial strategies take the forefront, Deleuze speaks of contemporary regimes of symbolic power and control.

He starts from Foucault's descriptions of discipline as a system of supervision, regimentation and especially confinement. Now, Deleuze writes, companies control employees by motivating them to rivalry, while schools are 'being replaced by continuing education and exams by continuous assessment' (1995: 179). Flexibility and fragmentation are the rule in environments previously marked by discipline, whether school, barracks, hospital or prison. The factory system worked to find 'an equilibrium between the highest possible production and the lowest possible wages; but in a control society businesses take over from factories, and a business is like a soul, a gas' (1995: 179), defined by internal rules, numbers, profit centres and balance sheets – whose emblem is a brand.

Deleuze attends to marketing at two points, first, when he discusses the new logic of control, as opposed to discipline:

> ... the only people left are administrators. Even art has moved away from closed sites and into the open circuits of banking. Markets are won by taking control rather than by establishing a discipline, by fixing rates rather than by reducing costs, by transforming products rather than by specializing production. Corruption here takes on a new power. The sales department becomes a business centre or 'soul'. We're told businesses have souls, which is surely the most terrifying news in the world. Marketing is now the instrument of social control and produces the arrogant breed who are our masters. Control is short-term and rapidly shifting, but at the same time continuous and unbounded, whereas discipline was long-term, infinite and discontinuous. A man is no longer a man confined but a man in debt. One thing, it's true, hasn't changed – capitalism still keeps three quarters of humanity in extreme poverty, too poor to have debts and too numerous to be confined: control will have to deal not only with vanishing frontiers, but with the explosion of shantytowns and ghettos (1995: 181).[5]

Marketing is the mainspring of contemporary enterprise and the model of social control, while the sales paradigm dictates the mode of production, and the whole scheme yields very little for the poor majorities. In the conclusion to his short essay, Deleuze suggests a programme: 'We ought to establish the basic sociotechnological principles of control mechanisms as their age dawns, and describe in these terms what is already taking the place of the disciplinary sites of confinement that everyone says are breaking down.' He also predicts more direct and violent control over bodies, witnessed in recent years in the policing of shantytowns and favelas: 'It may be that older means of control, borrowed from the old sovereign societies, will come back into play' (1995: 182).

Finally, Deleuze turns to social resistance to control. Old forms of struggle against the new means of control may no longer work, for him, resistance to domination has itself become elusive, hard to identify:

> One of the most important questions is whether trade unions still have any role: linked throughout their history to the struggle against disciplines, in sites of confinement, can they adapt, or will they give way to new forms of resistance against control societies? Can one already glimpse the outlines of these future forms of resistance, capable of assailing the joys of marketing? Many young people demand strangely to be 'motivated', they're always asking for special courses and continuing education; it's their job to discover whose purpose these serve, just as older people discovered, with considerable pain and effort, the ends of disciplines (1995: 182).

Deleuze wrote in 1990, when the age of the internet was dawning. Trade unions and social activists, generally, have to some extent found an answer to flexible control in the internet as a cheap, efficient and instantaneous medium of communication against the control of globalized capital. But again, even as this occurs, the joys of marketing continue to take up considerable time and effort, and are extremely difficult to question. According to Deleuze, this is inevitable because of the nature of the new regime of social control. 'It's not a question of asking whether the old or new system is harsher or more bearable, because there's a conflict in each between the ways they free us up and subject us' (1995: 178).

This implies that it is a false problem that the Citizens' Campaign Against Hunger found promotion techniques useful and opened the floodgates of promotion onto the plain of NGOs and social movements: those floodgates were already open to all the citizens who participated in it. The real problem is that the specific nature of advertising discourse, its claim to 'change hearts and minds', must be examined not only as a problem of effectiveness, as if such discourse were a disembodied, omnipotent voice, but in the context of its own self-affirmation and relations of production.

Trying to reach hearts and minds

If publicity is a matter of survival for NGOs and their causes, how can it be used without naively promoting the idea that those who 'buy into' campaigns are somehow on the side of right and good, as if saying so made a difference? Maybe we face here the Church's old debate: truth through proselytism and conversion, or mission and action. Certainly, the transition from a discussion of possible action to a project of opening up to the public and trying to reach hearts and minds is one possible interpretation of the process by which Dialogues Against Racism slowly began to concentrate its energies on a media campaign, moving away from the encounters behind closed doors and the various proposals published in the report on its first three meetings. This transition was perhaps a necessary one to open up the Dialogues to new people beyond the first group, linked by close working relationships. It led towards valuing discourse as such, to a focus on what the campaign said, which is perhaps what advertising tends to do.

Celia Lury and Alan Warde, in what they call a sceptical account of advertising, raise the hypothesis that consumer behaviour is impossible to forecast and put forward six hypotheses about what the advertising industry or 'advertisers' do. The six can be summed up as follows: advertisers reassure uncertain producers that their products will sell; they formulate information about consumers and infuse this knowledge with an aura of specialization, thus legitimizing the work of advertisers – a legitimization that is necessary because they are highly dependent on their clients; and, in this way, 'the practitioners of the special knowledges are able to sell their divinations to the worried producers' (1997: 90). The joys of marketing are the sensation of participating in the world of power and knowledge that circulates among purveyors of goods, services and brands, the world of capital. By this sceptical view, the signs of the Dialogues campaign's success are its high professional quality and the pleasure in watching the spots, access to prominent commercial advertising sites like billboards and the sides of buses, broadcast on the Globo television networks, government funded television, and radio, more than the not unrelated, but quite separate, work of social organizations that used the campaign's materials in face-to-face discussions.

Again we come to a bifurcating interpretation of advertising's usefulness to social causes. On the one hand, it appears to value discourse for discourse's sake. Differences are constituted in culture, in consciousness, says advertising as did culturalism, a movement in the social sciences that superseded racial or biological explanations of difference. When culture constitutes an obstacle to adherence to a beneficial innovation, like a new agricultural technology or practice of hygiene, then culture must be changed, often by media campaigns: this is what culturalist development experts used to say. Here we find the first limitation of advertising discourse for social activism: it returns to the logic of the diffusion of innovations, aiming to reduce resistance to messages.

In Paulo Freire's critique of banking methods in education, it deposits information in people's heads. Advertising does require reflection, but it is about how to stage manage audience reactions, about planning and meeting expectations. Hence, although a great deal of thought goes into campaigns, the way people are meant to think and act on receiving the campaign is already formulated. Advertising professionals require knowledge of a population group's predispositions, how it reacts to certain messages. Ideally, focus groups are used to understand how to diminish resistance to a message, by understanding – as culturalists sought to – the emotional dynamics of collective life and, on that basis, working on people's values and awareness. When effectiveness is questioned, the advertiser carries out audience research and determines whether, in fact, focus groups think along the lines intended by the campaign.

Curiously enough, this expensive process is where advertising produces a pale imitation of the knowledge available to effective NGOs. One example of such knowledge is an impact study report of 158 project grants made over a period of 20 years to groups in the semi-arid Sisal Region of the state of Bahia, Brazil, by the Coordenadoria Ecumênica de Serviço (CESE), an ecumenical body that channels small grants to grass roots projects, mainly in the North and Northeast of the country. The report publishes a table showing:

> a preponderance of support for activities classified here as *campaigns/ mobilization* and *political education*, during both periods [1983–1992 and 1993–2002]. As seen below, campaigns and mobilization are the main forms of struggle of workers in the region and involve action oriented to specific groups (sisal amputees, youth and women, for example) or demonstrations involving a number of categories of people (May 1st, marches for citizenship and against hunger, etc.). The increase in *technical training* activities, from 7.9% in the first period to 20.0% in the second, is paralleled by a decrease in support for activities classified as political education, which went from 41.3% to 28.4%.

Apparently, local organizations and movements went through a period mainly centered on political leadership training to a later stage marked by an increasing concern with experimentation and proposing alternatives for regional development (Padrão and Pinheiro, 2004: 10).

The emphasis on campaigns and mobilization is positively valued in the report's conclusions:

> At least two of CESE's small project policy options for the region[6] deserve consideration. On the one hand, there was substantial support for campaigns and mobilization, activities that represent a third of the project grants. Information collected for the study demonstrates the importance of this support to enabling specific social groups to organize, establish common principles and strategies through networks, and get involved in the national political agenda. Campaigns and mobilization gave rise to the most important organizations that currently exist in the region (Padrão and Pinheiro, 2004: 43).

These campaigns brought people together around demands, they helped constitute a new social and organizational web that became institutionalized in rural workers' cooperatives and unions, currently so well developed that one cooperative exports finished sisal goods to Europe. The campaigns gathered interested parties around a proposal for change that is not thematic (what logic can be found in the list of affected groups above?), but the priorities of the poor represented by 'sisal amputees, women and youth', May 1st marches and so on. In other words, the campaigns did not seek out the average citizen with an idea, but used campaigns to gather the citizenry around the possibility of improving their economic and political conditions.

One could argue that a poor rural area in the 1980s and 1990s is far from the advertising culture that is central, today, to urban environments. The campaigns that helped the Sisal Region make a leap forward were produced within a set of social relations that were related to work, neighbourhood and at least the potential for solidarity. A broadcast-led campaign would simply be out of place in the Sisal Region, where even unequal social relationships would be personal. On the other hand, in today's urban areas, popular mobilization tactics of marches, campaigns and training are no longer as effective as they once were, so advertising and its joys may seem to provide a way forward.

The differences between these examples – broadcast campaigns as a starting point or campaigns as social mobilization – are not only sociological but epistemological; they have different presuppositions about social belonging and about the value of people's knowledge. Common to social activism in both rural and urban areas is the idea that the exceptional may be symptomatic of something important. Communication for social change, before changing people and their values, understands that the unique or exceptional may point to a value that has been repressed by conservative common sense or by the weight of the *status quo*. Working for social change means knowing how to recognize and formulate emerging demands, put pressure on the authorities, private enterprise, or social consensus.

It also means understanding that small scale consensus may be of little use against the power of such hegemonies. An anecdote comes to mind. In the second phase of the 'Where do you keep your racism?' campaign, television spots were made of testimonies by people who had experienced racial discrimination. When a long time participant in the Dialogues commented that, when she used this material in a group setting, it made her uneasy that one response was of pity. 'The poor things!' exclaimed one viewer. The answer from the advertising team was to point out that this could easily be a one-off, marginal response. The important thing is that the bulk of the audience understands the spots as intended, that it takes them in as information generating solidarity. If advertising seeks to turn positive values to its advantage and 'put in the best light' what are seen as a product's weaknesses, it is far less interested in what the minority or weak side has to say. It is not just a problem of advertising communication having difficulty communicating complex meanings. Advertising only values the emergent, the marginal, the repressed that occupy the attention of a great many social activists when they have become – often through political changes – a kind of vanguard or, like disabled fashion models or the United Colors of Benetton ads, an interesting exception.

A problematic inequality remains

Sometimes, as noted, promotional communication is part of movements and organizations' everyday activities, as they seek to survive in a very competitive information environment, unleashing their particular brand or take on the world on a waiting audience. In these cases, regular staff are most often charged with the duties of advertising professionals and house journalists. There are also moments in which there is a direct relationship between the social activist sector and corporations interested in promoting their names and with advertising agencies too. The Dialogues campaign entered a contractual relationship with an agency, though it may not have been a conventional one. A need was formulated, a briefing was made, a proposal delivered and embraced. Rede Globo and other firms joined in.

If, as Baudrillard would have it, the need for an antiracist public discourse was part of the system of needs, the advertisements in some way connected parties who identified with the message and 'bought' the idea. A series of activities and products supported the advertising campaign, in the effort to make its effects more concrete and effective, and these were centred especially on the website and in group discussions, two areas where NGOs and social movements have a constituency and expertise. Perhaps the reading of the campaign's success should be reversed or at least modified to put at centre stage these actors, the NGOs and social activists that brought it into specific contexts and personal discussions.

Society has come to be understood as consumer society, today, and individuals and groups are obliged to find a market niche. In this context, marketing brings 'joys' that are related to power and control. Deleuze remarks that the new situation, in which marketing is central, can be freeing and also exercise control. Advertising brings the freedom to raise social demands in a very public arena, to announce their importance to the world. The 'Where do you keep your racism?' campaign did this very well, in a context in which concern about the issue is growing. Based on some direct participation in discussions of the campaign, as well as some readings,[7] I have tried to point to where the option for advertising and promotion by social movements may need yet to be wrestled with. One issue still untouched is the problematic inequality between those who run advertising campaigns – whether advertising professionals or corporations developing social responsibility projects – and social movements and NGOs.

If advertising agencies are relatively weak in comparison to their major clients, much weaker are NGOs in relation to the specialized knowledge of the advertising industry and the money of large corporations. When companies provide financial support for projects, with promotional goals in mind, NGOs are the minority partners, though they provide the relevant specialized knowledge about social projects, community development, education among deprived groups or other issues. Decisions are made together, but the partnership is made difficult by more public and sometimes open-ended decision-making processes among NGOs and clear hierarchies of command within companies. While social organizations work in an open field and are committed to transparent accounting, much less is known about business strategies of advertising agencies or other companies.

What motivates their choices, in the field of corporate social responsibility, besides the social consciences of their employees and managers? What are the opportunities, compensations and risks for major advertising agencies and broadcasting organizations that produce and publicise campaigns for charities and public causes? What is the state of the advertising market and the relative importance of social responsibility work in it? What precisely are the considerations that lead a given corporation to adopt social responsibility policies?

If the questions are still large and relatively untouched, it is partly because criticism of these new socially aware actors seems crass, the product of a naïve denial of capitalism and all its works and all its ways. It is also because the language for such critiques has yet to be found and voices raised from within the world in which advantages and disadvantages of advertising and promotion are played out.

References

Baudrillard, Jean. *Selected Writings*. (Mark Poster, ed.) London: Polity, 1988.

Deleuze, Gilles. *Negotiations: 1972–1990*. (Trans. by Martin Joughin) New York: Columbia UP, 1995 (1990).

Ibase. *Sonhar o futuro, mudar o presente: Dialogues contra o racismo, por uma estratégia de inclusão racial no Brasil*. Rio de Janeiro: Ibase, n/d. (Report on the first three Dialogues Against Racism).

Klein, Naomi. *No Logo*. London: HarperCollins, 2001.

Lury, Celia and Warde, Alan. 'Investments in the Imaginary Consumer: Conjectures regarding power, knowledge and advertising.' In: Mica Nava, Andrew Blake, Iain MacRury, Barry Richards (eds.). *Buy This Book: studies in advertising and consumption*. London: Routledge, 1997, pp.87–102.

Padrão, Luciano Nunes and Pinheiro, Maria Lúcia Bellicanta. *Estudo sobre o impacto do Programa de Pequenos Projetos da CESE na Região do Sisal no Estado da Bahia*. Salvador: CESE, September 2004. (available in English)

Ricardo, Sérgio. *Quem quebrou meu violão*. Rio de Janeiro: Record, 1991.

Smith, P.A. 'Marketing and Integrated Communications Mix'. *Marketing Communications: an integrated approach*. London: Kogan Page, 1998.

Notes

1. The organizations at the origin of the initiative were: IBASE, Instituto
   Brasileiro de Análises Sociais e Econômicas; Articulação de Mulheres
   Brasileiras, a women's movement network; Articulação de Organizações
   de Mulheres Negras Brasileiras, a network of Black women's
   organizations; CEPIA, a human rights NGO working from the perspective
   of gender; Centro de Estudos Afro-Brasileiros and Cesec, two research
   departments of the Universidade Candido Mendes, in Rio de Janeiro, the
   latter being a research center on violence and security; Cfemea, a feminist
   lobby group based in Brasília; the Brazilian Bahá'í Community; Criola and
   Geledés, important Black women's organizations in Brazil. (Ibase, n/d) It
   continues to be backed by most of the founders and, too, by FASE, the
   Federation of Social and Educational Support organizations, focusing
   mainly on rights and with a history of local development initiatives;
   INESC, a civil society lobby group in Brasília; Instituto Patrícia Galvão, a
   feminist organization working in media and communication; Redeh, a
   feminist organization working on racial, ethnic and gender equality; and
   the Dawn Network in Brazil. Observatório da Cidadania, a Social Watch
   national group; ABONG – the Brazilian Association of NGOs. A number
   of foundations, including Heinrich Böll and Ford, have contributed to the
   project. For more information, see the website. www.dialogoscontra
   oraismo.org.br
2. For more information, see the website: www.acaodacidadania.org.br
3. Available at www.ibase.br/modules.php?name=Conteudo&pid=39
4. Instituto Ethos website. www.ethos.org.br. Accessed on 22 August 2007.
5. Some adjustments for accuracy have been made of the English translation,
   which rendered the *explosions* of the ghettos as their 'mushrooming', the
   joies of marketing as 'blandishments'.
6. The second option mentioned here is related to CESE's focus on rural
   projects, in the 1980s and 1990s, which the evaluators considered
   appropriate, while recommending a greater urban-rural mix in future.
7. I participated in the fourth session of the Dialogues, where the campaign
   was first presented, and was a co-author with Nilza Iraci, of Geledés, of a
   handbook on different issues related to the race debate in Brazil. As part
   of a rota, I responded to messages to the website and discussed the spots

and ongoing activities as part of a broad group of interested people. The centrality of the advertising campaign to the Dialogues has been the object of some discussion in this group, in the last year or two, because it has absorbed so much of the group's attention.

VIII

Making a Difference: The Right to Information Movement and Social Change

Pradip N. Thomas

The discourse of communication rights is currently going through a renewal and resurrection of sorts. Of sorts, because it is not undergoing a thorough, root and branch, renewal, but it is subject to patch-work repairs by concerned academics and communication activists who are committed to clarifying its meaning, mapping its conceptual framework and elucidating the links between its theory and practice. The re-publication in 2003 of the classic text on communication rights, *Many Voices, One World* is one indication of interest in this area. After the academic and policy initiatives immediately prior to and after the publication of the MacBride Commission's final report submitted to the UNESCO in 1980, and following that institution's volte face on communication rights, there were relatively few flag-bearers for this project, with the exception of the ecumenical organisation the World Association for Christian Communication (WACC) and the efforts of numerous scholars like Michael Traber, Kaarle Nordenstreng, Herb Schiller, Colleen Roach, Cees Hamelink, among others. While the MacBride Roundtable that was set up by concerned academics to take the discussion on communication rights forward did function for a while as a forum, the regularity of this gathering was affected by resourcing constraints and, in hindsight, contributed at best to bringing the faithful together every so often in order to discuss issues of concern.

It was in the 1990s, in the aftermath of the privatization of global media and the institutionalization of de-regulation and media liberalization, that there were a number of belated attempts at contesting the dominant media policy/environment order. Firstly George Gerbner's *Cultural Environment Movement* (1995), followed by Cees Hamelink's *People's Communication Charter* (1996), the setting up of the *Platform for the Democratisation of Communication* (1997) and, perhaps most notably, the *Communication Rights in the Information Society* (CRIS) Campaign (2001–) created in response to the UN's call for a *World Summit on the Information Society* (WSIS). Each of these initiatives offered opportunities to interrogate and strengthen the concept of communication rights, contextualize, hone, define its boundaries and eliminate the fuzziness and vagueness that accompanied the concept from its very beginnings.

It is arguable whether we have finally come to a universally acceptable working definition of communication rights despite all these initiatives. The CRIS campaign's *Assessing Communication Rights: A Handbook* (2005) provides the clearest evidence of movement in the field based on practical examples of the fit between theory, policy and practice, although the framework consisting of the four pillars of communication rights outlined on pages 40–44 (Communicating in the Public Sphere, Communicating Knowledge, Civil Rights in Communication, and Cultural Rights in Communication) seems to cover all the world's macro communication deficits in the tradition of *Many Voices, One World* but without sufficient recognition of the need to have diverse, context-based, understandings of communication rights. A number of media scholars including Marc Raboy, Philip Lee, Claudia Padovani, Seán Ó Siochrú and Robert Hackett among others have deepened reflection on communication rights for the 21st century.

The *National Conference for Media Reform* organized by Free Press, Robert McChesney and others (January 12–14, 2007, Memphis) in the USA, the *OurMedia* conferences (April 9–13, 2007, Sydney), the *Global Media Policy* working group at the IAMCR, and other groupings at AMARC and WACC conferences have also provided opportunities and venues for deepening understanding of communication rights. The application of social movement theory to an understanding of media reform movements is one example of new thinking in the field and critique on the discourse of communication rights (see Carol & Hackett, 2006; Thomas, 2006).

The CRIS campaign and numerous initiatives directly or indirectly related to that campaign have provided opportunities for a deepening and strengthening of the discourse of communication rights, a broadening of its base and its greater recognition in UN circles and among NGOs such as Article IX (which was initially sceptical about this project). However, I would argue that the current approach to communication rights, while well-intentioned, is flawed primarily because it is founded on discourses that by and large are European responses to the challenges of modernity and post-modernity. While there certainly are common and universal deficits in global communication that need addressing, the preferred universal solutions to these problems – 'access', cultural and human rights, the strengthening of the public domain, etc. – are a response to a mainly Anglo-European script that does not recognize the diverse specificities of local communication deficits.

Even CRIS's Global Governance Project that was intentionally built on a dialogue with the local is problematic primarily because the local itself consisting of NGOs, their institutional frameworks, objectives, priorities, etc., in their workings are responding primarily to the script of transnationality, rather than to locality. While the lack of a media law and a proper copyright regime in Kenya (*Assessing*, 2005: 45–49) certainly can be considered a drawback, it is not clear whether such deficits are the most critical communication rights issues facing ordinary Kenyans in the face of poverty and other fundamental survival challenges.

This leads to another vexing question – to what extent do contemporary NGOs involved in communication/information projects represent local as opposed to transnational interests given their binding links with donor-driven development strategies? As Seira Tamang (2003: 1) has observed in a critical article on civil society in Nepal:

> ....this constant reiteration that civil society is the solution to all of Nepal's ills does little to clarify the nature and potential of democratic space in Nepal. Instead, civil society and other associated terms in donor liturgy – 'democracy', 'development', 'empowerment', 'gender' – are deployed in simplified, sanitized and circumscribed forms... shorn of their particular political and economic histories, these privileged discourses are circulated as transparent and free-floating normative orders.

This critique of civil society from Nepal needs to be treated with all the respect that it deserves because that country, despite its attractiveness to a variety of international donors, foreign funds and technological transfers, continues to have major problems with poverty and is, of course, home to a successful Maoist movement.

The issue of 'how "local" is the local?' is of particular importance in the light of the de-centralization of international NGOs such as PANOS, AMARC, APC, and others. One can argue that the globalisation of civil society – institutions, movements, ideologies, against a strict hierarchy of funding that reinforces the North-South divide – has merely led to the cloning of these organisations, to the universalization of a specific form of networking based on expectations, correspondences, rhetoric, and to the reinforcement of a hierarchy – with funding organisations calling the shots. As Jude Howell (2002: 3) has observed '...in turning civil society into a technical project, donors not only impose a normative vision of civil society which is deeply embedded in the historical context of Western Europe and North America, but also empty it of its political content and potential.' So a valid question that needs to be posed is whether the global media reform movement as it currently stands is an obstacle rather than a solution to current communication deficits?

So what are some of the deficits in the contemporary tradition of communication rights? I would like to identify two inter-related deficits – an epistemological short-coming, that in turn is responsible for a limited practice.

1) The epistemological tradition of the discourse is located in a framework that is largely founded on the conceptual vigour provided by European scholars such as Jürgen Habermas (public sphere), Chantal Mouffe (radical democracy), Alberto Melucci (new social movements), Arturo Escobar (post-development) who are undoubtedly suited to understanding the changing nature of societies in Europe and perhaps in North America but not elsewhere. While we ought to acknowledge the contributions made by Habermas, Mouffe, Melucci, Escobar and others, it is also important that we take on board the numerous critiques that have been made of both structuralist and post-structuralist scholars – Calhoun (1993), Fraser (2003), Kiely (1999), Kapoor (2002), Pieterse (1998) – on the notion of the 'public sphere', the experience of difference and radical democracy, identity-based struggles and post-development. It is also necessary that we recognize the existence of multiple social imaginaries, societal and cultural formations and traditions of hope that are built on another set of expectations.

I am certainly not advocating a return to parochial theorising based on the all-sufficiency of 'Asian Values', pan-Africanist discourses and the like, although I would like to think that the valuation given to grand projects such as democracy, freedom, identity, need to be reality-checked against the persistence, even deepening, of poverty and struggles related to basic wants. Charles Taylor identifies the problem as the inability of Western theorists to think of traditions and solutions to modernity outside of a single, universal framework. 'Is there a single phenomenon here, or do we need to speak of *multiple* modernities, the plural reflecting the fact that non-Western cultures have modernized in their own ways and cannot be properly understood if we try to grasp them in a general theory that was originally designed with the Western case in mind?' (Taylor, 2002: 91). While the existence of identity politics can certainly not be denied in India, who can say that struggles over identity are more critical than struggles over basic needs? Or that identity politics in the context of the South can be separated from struggles over basic needs? What does the tradition of communication rights have to say to the deepening morass of politics in the Middle East and the many failed states that have found it impossible to deliver democracy and rights? Is there anything that the tradition of communication rights can contribute to making the situation in Iraq more bearable?

2) Universal understandings of communication rights offer few opportunities to contextualize 'practice'. While media ownership is a global and local problem and needs to be dealt with, it is not the primary communication rights issue in every context around the world. In other words, one can argue that in order for communication rights really to become a global policy discourse, it must relate to critical communication deficits in local contexts. There is a need for many local-specific understandings of communication rights rather than the one, universal framework that, however well-meaning, is not suitable to advancing the local cause of communication rights. The communication activist Nalaka Gunawardena (2005), in an article that was written just prior to the Tunis phase of the World Summit on the Information Society, points to the multi-faceted nature of communication deficits and its local specificity, in this case, in Sri Lanka:

The information needs – and wants – of the poor are as wide and varied as everybody else's. Sarvodaya, Sri Lanka's largest development organisation, once surveyed the information needs of poor people in rural and semi-urban areas. It was found they wanted information on health and nutrition, as well as details of bank loans, foreign jobs and insurance policies. There was also considerable interest in world affairs, new books and movies, national politics, and questions being asked in parliament.

In other words, the right to know, to information was considered the most significant communication right.

The Report 'State of Democracy in South Asia' (2006), that was brought out by the Delhi-based Centre for the Study of Developing Societies reiterates the very different nature of experiences and expectations of democracy in South Asia:

The most common association citizens have with the idea of democracy is 'freedom'. A closer look, however, brings out the differences between the dominant understandings of democracy as freedom. For one, the language of freedom is not used equally by all sections of society: the elite, the more educated and the better off tend to be more enthusiastic about 'freedom' than those at the lower end of the social hierarchy. Also, while people associate democracy with freedom, they do not necessarily emphasize freedom over democracy's other attributes. When forced to choose the most salient feature of democracy, only six percent of respondents region-wide picked up the classical virtue of freedom of expression. But most significantly, those who did mention freedom rarely understood it in the classical, negative sense of the absence of constraints imposed by the state or society. They would rather the state play a greater role in the provision of public goods than view it as a source of threat to their liberty. Freedom is understood by ordinary citizens in a wider and positive sense that includes political freedom but extends to freedom from want.

The issue of 'identity' which has been a key concept in cultural studies and new social movement theory is not, in the light of the findings from the study in South Asia, the most vexing problem in South Asia. Freedom from want is. By not locating our discourses in both macro and micro issues of concern, the discourse of communication rights runs the risk of aiding and abetting the 'manufacture of civil society from the outside' (Howell: 2002) and being unable to deal with the complexities of the global that do not necessarily stem from the informationalization of life processes in the 21st century or for that matter the politics of identity, but rather from the persistence, even deepening of structural inequalities.

In the context of the globalization of poverty, the right to information can become an extraordinarily powerful tool in human development as the case in India clearly shows. Such instances of communication rights articulated by local people – an instance of what one could call 'micro communication rights' is as important as the larger struggles over 'macro communication rights' – over media ownership and control, intellectual property and the reform of global media institutions. Ideally of course, there needs to be close correspondences between micro and macro struggles, each feeding off and strengthening the other.

The Right to Information Movement in India

Interestingly enough, legislations related to the right to information have only been enacted in the recent past by the world's major democracies. An extraordinary oversight given that public access to information is a requisite for functioning democracies. Twenty-six national governments have enacted right to information policies in the recent past. Thomas Blanton (2002: 50) writing in the journal *Foreign Policy* has observed that the enactment of right to information legislations has been accompanied by great public interest

26 countries – from Japan to Bulgaria, Ireland to South Africa, and Thailand to Great Britain - enacted formal statutes guaranteeing their citizens' right of access to government information. In the first week

after the Japanese access law went into effect in 2001, citizens filed more than 4,000 requests. More than half a million Thais utilized the Official Information Act in its first three years. The U.S. Freedom of Information Act (FOIA) ranks as the most heavily invoked access law in the world. In 2000, the U.S. federal government received more than two million FOIA requests from citizens, corporations, and foreigners (the law is open to 'any person'), and it spent about $1 per U.S. citizen ($253 million) to administer the law.

In other words it is clear that RTI legislations have allowed ordinary people throughout the world to access and use information to counter deficits that they have faced.

The right to information movement is today one of the most significant social movement success stories in India. The movement evolved against the background of endemic corruption at all levels of government. The Indian state has been involved in the subsidisation of national development ever since Independence. In a little more than fifty years, this state development apparatus has become gargantuan in scope and is involved in multi-sectoral development – in rural poverty alleviation, health, education, the provision of employment, rural infrastructure, food security among very many other national development projects. Food security is ensured through support for the Public Distribution System (PDS) that enables the average Indian to buy subsidized grains, essential oils and other commodities from 'ration' shops scattered along the length and breadth of the country, a project that is worth billions of dollars.

However, it has been widely known that the institutionalization of corruption has led to the 'leakage' of grain from these shops and funds allocated for the many national and state-level public development projects. In fact it is common knowledge that only a fraction of funds allocated for rural development ends up being spent for rural development. The rest is skimmed off by government officials in a chain that stretches from the various headquarters of rural development to the last rung on the bureaucratic ladder – the village official.

Politicians of all hues are also involved in such scams. It is little wonder that the international monitoring organisation Transparency International's annual audit of global corruption has consistently placed India at the top of its list.

In an infamous 'sting' operation carried out by investigative journalists belonging to the online newspaper *tehelka.com*, who posed as defence product dealers, they covertly filmed footage and exposed government ministers, prominent politicians belonging to the then ruling government party, the BJP, defence personnel and others accepting bribes in return for preferential deals related to the procurement of defence equipment including night vision goggles. This scam led to embarrassment for the government although, while some heads did roll including the then defence minister, George Fernandes, the government chose to focus on what it termed the 'illegal' methods used by the journalists to entice the unwary, but corrupt. In fact the journalists involved, the organization and one of its founders, Tarun Tejpal, became the target for a witch-hunt that nearly bankrupted this organization. In this context it is worth mentioning that the right to information movement has opted for that phrase rather than 'freedom of information' which, as has been argued, merely prohibits government interference in the process of acquiring information.

The right to information makes it a mandatory requirement for the Government of India to proactively disseminate information to the people. Two key advocates for the right to information movement in India, Mander & Joshi (no date: 2-3) describe the expected outcomes of this movement thus:

> The right to information is expected to improve the quality of decision making by public authorities, in both policy and administrative matters, by removing unnecessary secrecy surrounding the decision making process. It would enable groups and individuals to be kept informed to know the kinds of criteria that are to be applied by government agencies in making these decisions. It is hoped that this would enhance the quality of participatory political democracy by

giving all citizens further opportunity to participate in a more full and informed way in the political process.

The Mazdoor Kisan Shakti Sangathan (MKSS)

From a citizen's perspective, it is remarkable that the key impetus for a struggle that eventually led to the enactment of a national RTI legislation, and numerous state-level legislations, began at a grassroots level, specifically via a peasant's movement in the state of Rajasthan, the Mazdoor Kisan Shakti Sangathan (MKSS), a movement committed to land, livelihood and wage rights. The MKSS was officially formed in 1990 by local activists including Aruna Roy, Nikhil Dey, and Shankar Singh in Devdungri, a village in the state of Rajasthan. Initially, their advocacy focused on struggles for minimum wages, land and women's rights mainly with landless labourers, and initiatives related to making the Public Distribution System, accountable. Their own Spartan lifestyles, their life lived with people and their refusal to accept international or government funding for their work placed them in a different category from the average NGO employee in India who is, for the most part, beholden and captive to the exigencies of foreign or state funding. Very early on in this work, they realised that the key obstacle to development at village level was the lack of information on a variety of entitlements to rural people, in the area of employment, rural infrastructure such as dispensaries, clinics, schools, roads, irrigation along with information on the many government initiatives related to poverty alleviation.

Together they launched a campaign based on consultation, street-based discussions, popular theatre performances throughout the state. In 1994, and in the face of official recalcitrance and unwillingness to cooperate with people's demands, the MKSS decided to organize public hearings (*jan sunwais*). These hearings took the form of an audit of local level development projects, especially the social audit of 'employment muster rolls' and expenses related to public works and wages paid to workers. This led to the demand for all copies of documents related to public works to be made public. However, local government officials were not, in the beginning, cooperative, and, in fact, launched their own counter-campaigns against the right to information movement. The hearings however, took on a life of their own. As more and people throughout the state began to hear the literally hundreds of stories of corruption, they became empowered to act on this information. In district after district, these hearings exposed the vast gaps between official expenditures on development projects and the actual expenditures. The hearings unearthed evidence of widespread corruption and systemic links between local officials and politicians who were also involved in a variety of scams.

The evidence discussed at the public hearings led to non-violent civic actions, boycotts and sit-ins at government offices, that were systematically used to wear down the opposition and elicit a response from the government. These local resistances reinforced what the public already knew, the fact that there was gross misappropriation of funds – wages paid to fictitious people, even to workers who had died years back, recorded in local employment registers, incomplete public works projects such as roads and buildings that that were listed as complete when they were either partially complete, abandoned, non-existent and often made from sub-standard building materials. In a public hearing held in Janawad panchayat in Rajsamand District on documented public works worth Rs 65 lakhs (US$ 144,444) in November 2000, it was '....established that no less than Rs. 45 lakhs (US$100,000) of this sum had gone into fictitious, untraceable projects' (Muralidharan: 2001).

In 1997 after many protests and hearings, the state government in Rajasthan announced the right of all people to demand and receive photocopies of all public works projects undertaken by local development authorities (the *panchayat*). An additional focus was on the Public Distribution System that is mandated to provide subsidized 'rations' including grains and oils, the provision of which has notoriously been based on 'leakages' – the selling of subsidized grain on the 'black' market, non-availability when in actual fact these products were being hoarded, and the substitution of inferior grain and dubious types of cooking oil that were hazardous to local health. This movement spread to other districts in Rajasthan and spilled over into neighbouring states. While corruption was among the initial issues exposed, the need for transparency, accountability, and openness led to the scrutiny of higher levels of government funding, policies supportive of secrecy and to the demand that institutions that were previously outside the purview of public inspection, be open to such social audits.

In 1997, after an epic 52-day, sit-in (*dharna*) at the capital city of Jaipur, the then deputy chief minister announced that all local village local government institutions were required to give access to information on expenditures, muster rolls, and other documents. This eventually led to the Rajasthan government passing a right to information law in 2000. However, most importantly, the success of this movement in Rajasthan and the enormous benefits that it generated became the basis for a national movement focused on pressurising the government to enact a national Right to Information law. In 1997, the National Campaign for the People's Right to Information was established. In 2002, the then central government introduced the Freedom of Information Act. This was amended by the present government to become the Right to Information Bill (2004). One of the consequences of this movement is the enactment of the Right to Information Bill (2005) that has influenced and, in turn, been moulded by prior right to information legislations in a number of states in India inclusive of Rajasthan, Madhya Pradesh, Maharashtra, Goa, Tamil Nadu, Karnataka, Delhi, and Andhra Pradesh.

Caveats

However, and in spite of these welcome measures, this opportunity for popular participation in democratic governance and social change has been seriously compromised by a number of caveats and over-bureaucratised enforcement procedures that have the potential to stymie the pace and nature of change. While the 2002 variant included under its remit central, state, district and local level information and an enforceable penalty clause, the 2004 Bill has limited the right to information '...to only information available with the Central Government and Union Territories' and has diluted the effectiveness of the penalty clause for those who refuse to be transparent. The 'exceptions' listed in the schedule of the Right to Information Bill 2004, including Intelligence and Security Organizations established by the Central Government and the exclusive focus on 'Public Authority' rather than both public and private actors, is also a clear limitation.

The exercise of substantive democracy based on citizens actively exploring the meaning of democracy, making elected representatives and governments accountable, demanding transparency in the government's many public expenditures is often viewed as an irritant by the government. In other words, while governments do recognize the need for a right to information policy, they are less than enthusiastic to provide material support for a citizen's exercise of this right. It is this gap between principle and practice that remains a major issue in the practice of the right to information.

Such legislations are often accompanied by a variety of caveats that exonerate public servants and the security system from public scrutiny. In other words, a citizen who demands information on an extra-judicial murder by the military or the police may not be given this information for reasons of security. There are other ways in which governments limit the fulfilment of this right. Access to information and documentation can be routinely denied. In Australia for instance, a device called a 'compulsory certificate' can be issued to block access to information. Extortionate charges can be levied for photocopying material and delays in allowing access to information can often stifle an investigation.

Mathew Moore, the Freedom of Information reporter on the *Sydney Morning Herald* experienced this first-hand when he applied for information on the government's welfare-to-work policy in October 2005. In his words:

> In October, the *Herald* applied for a spread of documents and then refined the request to find out how many people were affected by the policy, how many expected to get jobs and what was the financial impact on those on welfare. The department replied that this information was held in 502 documents containing 3,435 pages. In a preliminary assessment it estimated 3,122 of those pages, or more than 90 per cent, were exempt from release under the various 18 pages of exemption provisions listed in the act. The cost of applying for the 313 pages is $13,055.50, of which nearly $11,000 is for 546 hours of reading documents at a rate of five minutes a page calculated at $20 an hour. Because the estimated cost is more than $100, the department has asked for a 25 per cent advance deposit, of $3,263.90. But there's a catch. Only after the deposit is paid will the department decide what documents are exempt. Once it has your money it can rule all documents exempt and provide nothing other than a bill for the outstanding 75 per cent or $9792.

Unfortunately, this response from governments is all too typical.

The RTI movement in India and social change

At local levels, the right to information as opposed to say the more abstract right to communication has become a proven, essential human right in the sense that it has become the basis for prising open possibilities to enjoy other rights and entitlements denied to people. In the context of real rises in poverty during the last decade, the right to information has become a means of survival for India's poor. Jha et al (2003: 14) in a monograph on 'Trade Liberalisation and Poverty in India' observe that studies have shown:

> ....an increase in the incidence of poverty among rural labourers. Despite healthy growth, poverty levels remained high because of the increase in inequality and the decline in agricultural wages, and, also

on account of the rise in food prices, especially in the subsidised food
prices in the PDS... the targeting and coverage of the PDS have been
inadequate and therefore the system has failed to shield the poor from
the rise in food-grain prices that has followed the rise in the price of
fertilisers and the procurement of food-grains in the aftermath of
reforms.

All available studies seem to indicate that the right to
information movement has played no small role in revitalising
participatory democracy in India:

1) The right to food security was compromised because of
corruption in the PDS system, the diversion of grain and oils
from local 'ration' shops to the open market. Social audits have
opened up employment opportunities and the establishment
of minimum wage entitlements.

2) Public hearings have played an important role in creating
the momentum for participatory democracy, through public
participation and the creation of new spaces, arenas,
environments supportive of a new politics of possibility. This
has been crucial to the re-establishment of democracy from
below and to the renewal of traditional political instruments
leading to a grassroots revitalization of democracy at state and
central levels in India that was in dire need of an overhaul. A
major outcome of the public hearings has been the
empowerment of people traditionally denied opportunities to
expression, speech, voice. The creation of opportunities to
validate 'Voice' has encouraged the education of the rural poor,
strengthened self-belief in the worth of their voice, extended
participatory democracy and helped citizen's participation, and
involvement in 'governance', and in the making and
legitimization of popular involvement in processes related to
strengthening transparency and accountability.

3) One of the outcomes of this movement is government
efforts to make e-government a reality throughout India. To
some extent government efforts at the extension of
e-government did take advantage of the software and hardware

boom that accelerated during the 1990s and continued ever since. One of the areas where there is huge corruption is access to 'land registers' and records. These are typically maintained by local government officers who often manipulate and change these records, even sell land entitlements to the rich and powerful. A recent initiative in the Southern state of Karnataka – the Bhoomi Project – has resulted in the computerisation of nearly 20 million land records. Farmers can now visit an information kiosk and use a finger-print authentication system to get a copy of their land record. The most important benefit of this project is that it has cut out the middle man and, indirectly, reduced corruption.

4) Unlike in the West and other parts of the world where the right to information is tied to freedom of expression and press freedom, the struggle in India has been inextricably linked to the basic rights to life and survival (to issues such as drought, employment, health, electoral politics) marking a distinct and in fact radical departure from other struggles around information rights. In the words of Sivakumar (2004) 'It really is this integration taking place with a wide range of issues, from food security, to displacement to communal violence that is relatively new and continues to give it life and sustenance.' This tying in to the politics of basic needs is an important statement that India today, irrespective of its emergence as a hi-tech software manufacturing centre, is still home to 350 million people who are below the poverty line, half the population who are illiterate, high infant mortality and among the highest child labour rates in the world (see Weiner: 2001).

5) The right to information movement, through its innovative struggles, has revitalised the project of participatory communication in India. The creation of the Right to Information Bill (2004) and the various state level legislations on the right to information have been unprecedented. While these legislations vary in their democratic potential, the fact remains that the impact of this particular movement cannot be compared to the impact of any other movement related to

media reform. Furthermore, this movement has demonstrated the political potential of indigenous civil society in creating an impetus for reform.

The example of the RTI movement in India reveals the many advantages of a grassroots communication rights movement that responds to local needs, local contexts, local content, local activism and empowerment. Such movements offer the global communication rights movement an opportunity for renewal.

Author's note

Mike Traber was a dear friend and colleague of mine for many years. He was an extraordinary public intellectual who has left a great impression on my own life and writings.

References

Assessing Communication Rights: A Handbook (September 2005), CRIS Campaign, New York: Ford Foundation.

Bhoomi Project, [Online] Retrieved May 15 2008 from http://www.revdept-01.kar.nic.in/Bhoomi/Home.htm. A Bhooming Success, [Online] Retrieved May 15 2008 from http://www.tve.org/ho/doc.cfm?aid =1606&lang=English.

Blanton, T (2002) 'The World's Right to Know' (50-58) *Foreign Policy*, July–August.

Calhoun, C. (ed.) (1992), *Habermas and the Public Sphere*, Cambridge, MA: MIT Press.

Fraser, N. (2003). 'Social justice in the age of identity politics: redistribution, recognition, and participation.' In Fraser, N. and Honneth, A., *Redistribution or recognition? A politico-philosophical exchange*. London: Verso, 7–109.

Gunawardena, N (2005), 'Communication Rights and Wrongs', SciDevNet, http://www.scidev.net/Opinions/index.cfm?fuseaction=readopinions &itemid=447&language=1

Hackett, R. A. & Carroll, W. K (2006), *Remaking the Media: The Struggle to Democratize Public Communication*, New York/Oxford: Routledge.

Howell, J. (2002), 'Making Civil Society from the Outside-Challenges for Donors', *The European Journal of Development Research*, 12, 1, June, (3–22).

Jha, V., Gupta, S., Nedumpra, J. & Karthikeyan, K. (2003), *Trade Liberalisation and Poverty in India*, UNCTAD, available at http://www.unctadindia.org.studies_tradeliberalisationAndPovertyinIndia:pdf

Kapoor, I. (2002). 'Capitalism, culture, agency: dependency versus postcolonial theory', *Third World Quarterly*, 23(4), pp. 647-664.

Kiely, R. (1999). 'The last refuge of the noble savage? A critical assessment of post-development theory.' *European Journal of Development Research* 11, 30-55.

Mander, H. & Joshi, A. S. 'The Movement for Right to Information in India: People's Power for the Control of Corruption' (1–29). Available at the website of the Commonwealth Human Rights Initiative http://www.humanrightsinitiative.org/programs/ai/rti/india/articles/The%20Movement%20for%20RTI%20in%20India.pdf

Muralidharan, S (2001) 'A forceful assertion', *Frontline*, Vol.18, Issue 9, April 28–May 11, http://www.flonnet.com/fl1809/18090850.htm

Pieterse, J.N. (1998) 'My Paradigm of Yours? Alternative Development, Post-Development and Reflexive Development', *Development and Change* 29: 343-373.

Sivakumar, S. K (2004), 'A battle for information', *Frontline*, Vol 21, Issue 26, December 18–31.

Special Report: Democracy Object of Desire, *Himal South Asian*, Volume 20, Number 1, January 2007, http://www.himalmag.com/2007/january/special_report1.htm

Tamang, S (2003), 'Civilising Civil Society: Donors and Democratic Space in Nepal', *Himal South Asian*, July, Accessed at: http://www.himalmag.com/2003/july/essay.htm

Taylor, C. (2002), 'Modern Social Imaginaries' (91–124), *Public Culture*, 14, 1.

Thomas, P. N. (2006), 'The Communication Rights in the Information Society (CRIS) Campaign: Applying Social Movement Theories to an Analysis of Global Media', *The International Communication Gazette*, 68, 4: (291–312).

Weiner, M (2001), 'The Struggle for Equality: Caste in Indian Politics' (pp:193–225) in Kohli, A (Ed.) Op.Cit in Kohli, A. (Ed.), *The Success of India's Democracy*, Cambridge: Cambridge University Press.

IX

Communicating Peace: The Pity (and the Absurdity) of War

Philip Lee

The First World War (or 'Great War' or '1914-18 War') was the immediate inspiration for several pacifist or 'anti-war' films in what was a relatively new but rapidly burgeoning industry. One of the most significant appeared in 1919: Abel Gance's *J'accuse* (whose title echoes the notorious Dreyfus affair of 1894). It was made with the assistance of the French army. Gance was deeply affected by his own front-line experiences as an official cinematographer and by the death in combat of many of his friends. The film includes a resurrection scene in which soldiers who have been killed return to confront those who are still alive. In 1916 Gance had written: 'How I wish that all those killed in the war would rise up one night and return to their countries, their homes, to see if their sacrifice was worth anything at all' (Brownlow, 1983: 28). The film was, of course, silent.

In the USA in the 1920s some twenty movies depicted life in the trenches, the heroic suffering of the wounded and the 'sporting' mayhem of the conflict. Then came King Vidor's *Big Parade* (1925), in which the playboy 'hero' joins the army and woos a French girl before going into battle. The film was groundbreaking for not glorifying war and its human cost, exemplified by the lead character's loss of a leg from battle wounds. It had an influence on all subsequent war films, especially *All Quiet on the Western Front* (1930).

At the beginning of the 1930s, in contrast to the 1920s and with the exception of *Big Parade*, anti-war films began to appear that were critical of the First World War and of the carnage and psychological trauma that war creates. In Europe *All Quiet on the Western Front* (Lewis Milestone, USA, 1930) *Westfront 1918* (G. W. Pabst, Germany, 1930), and *Les Croix de bois* (F. de R. Bernard, France, 1931) profoundly disturbed audiences. They depicted the mundane and horrific, underscoring the absurdities and deficiencies of political and military leadership. They also took the viewpoint of the common soldier, questioning the officer class and probing recently healed social wounds. This is in keeping with Nicholas Pronay's proposition that it takes a decade for people to begin to come to terms with the nightmare of war. He noted that:

> The experience of the inter-war period suggests that after a decade
> there comes a re-surfacing of the worst of the memories in a way
> which allows people to face them again through the recreative power
> of art ... The sudden "popularity" between 1928-32 of autobiographies,
> plays, and novels (and films); the simultaneous re-publication of earlier
> and even wartime literature... the assembling and exhibition of
> paintings or photographs of the First World War... was a striking
> phenomenon in Britain, and was paralleled in the other participating
> countries (quoted in Sorlin, 1991: 28-29).

Hundreds of war books appeared throughout Europe from 1916 onwards. Henri Barbusse's *Le Feu* was the first, winning the Prix Goncourt in 1917 and selling 300,000 copies by the end of 1918. Notable examples in English included *Undertones of War* by Edmund Blunden (1928), *Journey's End* by R. C. Sherriff (1928), *Death of a Hero* by Richard Aldington (1929), *All Quiet on the Western Front* by Erich Maria Remarque (1929),

Goodbye to All That by Robert Graves (1930), and *Memoirs of an Infantry Officer* by Siegfried Sassoon (1930). Historian A. J. P. Taylor points out that:

> By the odd sort of chance which sometimes happens with literary fashions, practically all the books on the first World war which have remained famous to the present-day… were published between 1928 and 1930. All preached the same lessons: the futility and dreariness of war, the incompetence of generals and politicians, and the ordinary men on both sides, victims of this incompetence (Taylor, 1965: 361).

Critical views about war held during the 1920s by a minority were emerging as the accepted orthodox opinion of the new decade – at least for a while.

All Quiet on the Western Front was the English title of the book *Im Westen nichts Neues* by Erich Maria Remarque, published in serial form in 1928 in the newspaper *Vossiche Zeitung* (every issue was sold out) and then in book form in German and in English in 1929. More correctly the title should be 'Nothing New on the Western Front', ironically signifying 'more of the same'. By May 1930 twenty translations were in print, including Russian and Japanese, with worldwide sales in excess of 2.5 million. In Germany copies in Braille were sent free of charge to all blind veterans. The book became the subject of more than 200 articles and essays. But times were rapidly changing. The Nazi Party labelled the book an affront to the German people and both book and film were banned. On 10 May 1933 the book went on the book-burning bonfire in Berlin's Opernplatz along with books by leading German writers such as Bertolt Brecht, Lion Feuchtwanger, and Alfred Kerr.

Remarque's humanitarian concerns were stated in a letter of November 1929 addressed to the British General Sir Ian Hamilton:

> My work… was not political, neither pacifist nor militarist, in intention, but human simply. It presents the war as seen within the

small compass of the front-line soldier, pieced together out of many
separate situations, out of minutes and hours, out of struggle, fear, dirt,
bravery, dire necessity, death and comradeship... from which the word
Patriotism is only *seemingly* absent, because the simple soldier never
spoke of it. His patriotism lay in the deed (not in the word); it
consisted simply in the fact of his presence at the front. For him that
was enough. He cursed and swore at the war; but he fought on, and
fought on even when already without hope (Kelly, 1998: 48).

Remarque left Germany in 1933, but the Nazis took bitter
revenge on him by executing his sister Elfriede in 1943 for
defeatism and for criticising the Führer. 'The fact that she was
the sister of the despised Erich Maria Remarque was not lost
on the court – at one point the president said: "Your brother,
unfortunately, got away. But you are not going to get away" '
(Kelly, 1998: 54). She was beheaded.

Lewis Milestone's film of
All Quiet on the Western Front

The film faithfully follows the novel. The few scenes that are
repositioned or omitted, and a few minor changes of detail, do
not affect the narrative. The only interpolation (the penultimate
scene in which the narrator, Paul Baumer, is killed) is a poetic
inspiration that serves to underline the overall theme of futility.
The film portrays the senselessness of war from the sympathetic
point of view of young German soldiers who learn the absurdity
of blind patriotism and the necessary camaraderie of warfare.
Among the many scenes and vignettes, the following stand out.

After a brief opening shot in which a military parade marches
through a small German town, the camera pulls back into a
classroom. Framed by the school windows, the parade can be
seen outside. This is the first of many such framings (for
example, when the soldiers are in their dug-out, the war is seen
to continue outside the makeshift doorway) that bring to mind
Dante's famous description of the gateway to hell in Canto III
of *Inferno*:

Per me si va nella città dolente,
Per me si va nell'etterno dolore,
Per me si va tra la perduta gente...
Lasciate ogni speranza, voi ch'entrate.

(Through me to the city of pain, / through me to eternal agony, / through me to the lost people. / Abandon all hope you who enter.)

In the classroom, the elderly nationalistic teacher Kantorek is advocating 'glory for the Fatherland' and underhandedly encouraging the adolescent boys to enlist. His lecture is insidious:

> I know that in one of the schools, the boys have risen up in the classroom and enlisted in mass. If such a thing should happen here, you would not blame me for a feeling of pride. Perhaps some will say that you should not be allowed to go yet – that you have homes, mothers, fathers, that you should not be torn away by your fathers so forgetful of their fatherland, by your mothers so weak that they cannot send a son to defend the land which gave them birth...There will be few losses. But if losses there must be, then let us remember the Latin phrase which must have come to the lips of many a Roman when he stood in battle in a foreign land: 'Sweet and fitting it is to die for the Fatherland'...

Kantorek concludes that 'Personal ambition must be thrown aside in the one great sacrifice for our country. Here is a glorious beginning to your lives. The field of honour calls you.'

This one speech sets the tone for the critique of war that follows. The bitter irony is that the 'glorious beginning' becomes an anonymous ending and the 'field of honour' a lethal field of self-preservation. The classroom scene also 'frames' the film, because Paul Baumer returns there on leave for a confrontation with his former teacher (see below). The allusion to the 'Latin phrase' is to Horace's *Odes* (3.2): 'Dulce et decorum est pro patria mori'. Today it is probably best known as the title of a poem in English, written by Wilfred Owen (1893-1918) and published in 1921. 'If in some smothering dreams' you too could see and hear what we do, the poem ends:

> My friend you would not tell with such high zest
> To children ardent for some desperate glory,
> The old Lie: Dulce et decorum est
> Pro patria mori.

Not all of Owen's poems can be classified as anti-war, yet in English literature, Owen and Siegfried Sassoon (1890-1967) are remembered for their powerful denunciations. In Germany, the *Duino Elegies* of Rainer Maria Rilke (1875-1926) are among the most haunting condemnations of war, despite the fact that, although called up, he never actually fought.

The boys in Kantorek's class join the army and undergo the rigours of training. Their first encounter with war is on the way to the front, where they hear the wail of enemy artillery shells for the first time. That same night they crawl out into no-man's land to string barbed wire and are caught in a bombardment. One of the boys is blinded by shell fragments and screams, 'My eyes! I'm blind!' He staggers about and is killed running into the path of machine-gunfire. One of the recruits goes to retrieve the body and the experienced and cynical Katczinsky asks 'Why did you risk your life bringing him in?' The answer is, 'But it's my friend!', to which Katczinsky replies: 'It's a corpse, no matter whose it is. Now don't any of ya ever do that again.'

In one of the famous battle scenes, often imitated in later war films, the camera moves rapidly across and in front of a French infantry charge across no-man's land. This is intercut with images of German machine-gunfire which holds the soldiers back and cuts them down. At one point a grenade explodes in front of an advancing French soldier. When the dirt and smoke clear, only his amputated hands are left gripping the barbed wire on which he has fallen.

In an interlude, the now experienced survivors discuss who should be blamed for starting the war, One soldier asks another, 'Well, how do they start a war.' Another answers, 'Well, one country offends another.' The first says, 'How could one country offend another? You mean there's a mountain over in Germany gets mad at a field over in France?' The second soldier qualifies his answer, 'Well, stupid, one people offends another.'

The argument goes back and forth as the soldiers try to decide who is benefiting from the war. 'I think maybe the Kaiser wanted a war...he never had a war before. Every full-grown Emperor needs one war to make him famous. Why, that's history.' Another soldier comments, 'Yeah, Generals too. They need war. And manufacturers. They get rich.' It is left to the pragmatic Katczinsky to explain how wars should really be fought:

> I'll tell ya how it should all be done. Whenever there's a big war comin' on, you should rope off a big field and sell tickets. Yeah, and on the big day, you should take all the kings and their cabinets and their generals, put them in the centre dressed in their underpants and let 'em fight it out with clubs. The best country wins!

In perhaps the bleakest scene in the film, Paul Baumer becomes trapped in a shell hole with a French soldier he has just stabbed in the throat. He gags the man to prevent him crying out, but cannot leave the crater because of machine-gunfire. He stays with the dying man throughout the night and, filled with remorse, tries to give him water. By morning he can no longer stand the dying man's groans. 'Stop that!', he shouts. 'I can't listen to that. Why do you take so long to die? You're going to die anyway.' Then, after realising what he has in common with the dying soldier, he begins to wish that the man will live. 'No, no. You won't die. They're only little wounds. You'll get home. You'll be all right. You'll get home long before I will.'

The French soldier is dead, his eyes wide open and almost smiling. Paul pleads with the corpse to forgive him:

You see, when you jumped in here, you were my enemy – and I was afraid of you. But you're just a man like me, and I killed you. Forgive me comrade. Say that for me. Say you forgive me! Oh, no, you're dead! Only you're better off than I am – you're through – they can't do any more to you now. Oh, God! Why did they do this to us? We only wanted to live, you and I.

There are two echoes (deliberate or unconscious) of other works here. The first is the ending of G. W. Pabst's film *Westfront 1918* (1930), where a French solider grasps the hand of a dead German soldier lying next to him in hospital and says 'Moi, camarade ... pas enemie, pas enemie' (Me comrade ... not enemy, not enemy).

The second remarkable and disturbing echo is to another poem by Wilfred Owen, *Strange Meeting*, written in 1918 but only published after the war, in which a soldier dies and finds himself among groaning sleepers. 'One sprang up, and stared with piteous recognition in fixed eyes, lifting distressed hands as if to bless.' They talk about the 'truth untold, the pity of war, the pity war distilled.' Only at the end of their conversation does the soldier find out to whom he has been speaking:

I am the enemy you killed, my friend.
I knew you in this dark; for so you frowned
Yesterday through me as you jabbed and killed.

Ironically, Wilfred Owen was killed in action on 4 November 1918 during the crossing of the Sambre-Oise Canal, exactly one week (almost to the hour) before the signing of the Armistice. His mother received a telegram informing her of his death on Armistice Day, as church bells were ringing out in celebration.

In *All Quiet on the Western Front*, Paul Baumer is wounded and sent on leave to recuperate. He returns home, where he visits his old school. The same teacher, Kantorek, is still glorifying war for the next generation of students. Seeing Paul, he urges him to address the naïve lads in the classroom: 'You must speak to them. You must tell them what it means to serve your Fatherland.' Paul is reluctant. Mistaking his reluctance for modesty, the teacher urges him 'to remember some deed of heroism, some touch of nobility'. Paul is only able to recall the trenches and the killing and he accuses the teacher of hypocrisy:

> I heard you in here reciting that same old stuff, making more iron men, more young heroes. You still think it's beautiful and sweet to die for your country, don't you? We used to think you knew. The first bombardment taught us better. It's dirty and painful to die for your country. When it comes to dying for your country, it's better not to die at all. There are millions out there dying for their country, and what good is it?

The boys turn on Paul as a coward and amid their jeers Paul decides to cut short his leave and return to the front.

In the memorable final moments of the film, just before the Armistice and with all his comrades dead, Paul is daydreaming in a trench. The day seems peaceful and through a gun-hole he sees a butterfly land next to a discarded tin. Captivated, he leans out of the trench to try to catch it, oblivious of the ever-present danger. A French sniper sees the movement and prepares to shoot. As Paul stretches towards the butterfly, the sound of a shot is heard. The hand jerks, twitches and goes limp.

This scene is not in the book. Uncomfortable with an 'anonymous' ending in which his body is discovered 'lying on the ground as if asleep', director Lewis Milestone remembered that Paul Baumer was a butterfly collector. Earlier in the film his collection is seen in his mother's house. The symbolism of dead butterflies pinned in a box and the brief life of the butterfly struck a poetic note in Milestone's mind. Unfortunately, both Lew Ayres (who played Paul Baumer) and Arthur Edeson (Milestone's cinematographer) had already completed their work and left the studio. So Karl Freund, another great cinematographer (*Metropolis*, 1926), re-set the scene and operated the camera, while Milestone's own hand appeared as Paul Baumer's.

In the film's grim epilogue, the ghosts of Paul and his comrades march through a sea of white crosses in fields strewn with corpses. The soldiers look back with sadness and bitterness in their eyes. This motif of the crosses had been seen in Abel Gance's *J'accuse* (1919) and was to be reprised by Richard Attenborough in the mesmerising shot at the end of *Oh! What a Lovely War* (1969).

Richard Attenborough's film of *Oh! What a Lovely War*

In 1961 the military historian (and later politician) Alan Clark published *The Donkeys: A History of the British Expeditionary Force in 1915,* a revisionist account of the early years of British involvement in the First World War. In 1963 Joan Littlewood, a British director famous for developing the left-wing Theatre Workshop, produced a stage musical called *Oh! What a Lovely War* based on Clark's book and on a few a scenes adapted from Czech humorist Jaroslav Hašek's *The Good Soldier Švejk.* In 1969 British director Richard Attenborough transformed that musical into a film involving many of the leading stage and film actors of the day.

The stage musical of *Oh! What a Lovely War* is traditionally performed in Pierrot costumes, using images of war and shocking statistics projected onto a backcloth to contrast starkly with the satirical comedy of the action. The stroke of genius of director Richard Attenborough and his screenplay writer Len Deighton was to recast the stage version in a cinematic *mise en scène* that combines 'reality' with end-of-the-pier burlesque. Actually filmed on West Pier, Brighton, a seaside resort on the south coast of England, and caricaturing the class distinctions between officers and 'other ranks', the statistics of war dead are presented on cricket score boards. Some critics, notably the American Pauline Kael (1971) writing for *The New Yorker*, felt that this treatment weakened the impact of the appalling numbers of deaths. But the desperate irony was not lost on other viewers, who recognized typical British understatement, and it is considerably reinforced by the film's overall tone and its powerful ending.

Oh! What a Lovely War places some 30 First World War ballads and music hall numbers within a loose but coherent historical narrative. Wartime euphoria is juxtaposed with life and death in the trenches and with the constant flow of maimed young men returning home from across the Channel. The songs are used to comment on the misery and banality of life at the front and on the horror and absurdity of war. One is sung to the tune of the hymn 'What a friend we have in Jesus' and acts as a counterpoint to the army padre's blessing of soldiers before they go into action:

> When this lousy war is over
> No more soldiering for me.
> When I get my civvy clothes on,
> Oh, how happy I shall be!
> No more church parades on Sunday,
> No more putting in for leave.
> I shall kiss the sergeant-major,
> How I'll miss him, how he'll grieve!
> Amen.

It is 1914. The film begins with a pageant of the crowned heads of Europe and their prime ministers cavorting on a giant map. Each country assures its neighbours of its peaceful intentions while simultaneously preparing for hostilities. An emcee-like character, who reappears throughout the film, gives poppies to the Archduke Franz Ferdinand of Austria and his wife to hold. The photographer's flash explodes, and they are both dead. A senile Emperor Franz Josef is tricked into signing a declaration of war and the nobility assure each other that the hostilities to come will in no way affect their personal affection.

The assassination of the Austrian Archduke, aided and abetted by a tangle of aristocratic alliances, deceit and diplomatic ineptitude, throws Europe into chaos. In England, a rousing patriotic campaign ensures widespread enlistment and optimism for a quick victory over the 'Huns'. All the conscription-age males in the Smith family – representing the common person, as does Drummer Hodge in Thomas Hardy's poem about the earlier Boer War – enthusiastically join a sea-front march by the Grenadier Guards, obtaining their entrance tickets to the pier (whose fun-fair sign reads 'World War I') at a booth run by the arrogant and career-minded Lieutenant-General Douglas Haig. The theme of an incompetent and class-ridden military leadership throwing thousands of men into battle on a daily basis for weeks, months and years recurs throughout the film.

In the music hall at the end of the pier the Smith women watch their sons, husbands and sweethearts being enticed on stage by vaudeville artiste Ella Shields (the 'Southern Nightingale', who sang the original theme song of the film, 'Oh! It's a lovely war'). Before she appears, a chorus of girls carrying lacrosse sticks perform against a backcloth that clearly represents the elitist Roedean School for Young Ladies (situated close to Brighton) – reinforcing, for those who recognize the allusion, the film's class divisions. The music hall act is the lure; reality strikes when the men step on stage to meet a garishly made-up and overlit Ella Shields who immediately hands them to the kind of recruiting-sergeant familiar from Kitchener's famous 'Your Country Needs You' poster.

Most of the songs in the film are about the miseries or daydreams of the soldiers at the front. Some are given a macabre twist: 'Hush! Here comes a whiz-bang ... and it's headed straight for you!' In another scene a group of scruffy and unruly Australians sings 'One staff officer jumped right over another staff officer's back', lampooning the officer corps that kept a safe distance from the front. At the other end of the spectrum, 'Stille Nacht' ('Silent Night') is sung during the so-called 'Christmas Truce' that took place close on the Ypres Salient in 1914 when soldiers from both sides left their trenches for a few hours to greet each other in no man's land.

The military high command conduct their campaign at one end of the stylized and sanitized pier from which only distant gunfire is audible. On a tower high above the pier, now Field Marshal Sir Douglas Haig peers at the French coast through a spyglass while, in the ballroom below, the cricket scoreboard carries the name of the current battle followed by the daily tallies: '60,000 soldiers killed. Ground gained: Zero.' Back in France, wagonloads of simple white crosses are being delivered to the front-lines and the soldiers are digging mass graves. We begin to realize that the Smith boys and their comrades are unlikely to be coming home.

Oh! What a Lovely War is not overtly anti-religious. Yet the hypocrisy of supporting the futile stalemate of trench-warfare, and the class-led connivance of officers and the established church, are underlined in a number of scenes claiming that God is on the side of the British. At New Year 1916 Haig affirms that 'God is with us' and 'Every step I take is guided by Divine Will.' But this is the stubborn, self-righteous, and inflexible 'Butcher of the Somme' speaking and should not be taken as the official view of the Church of England. The attitude of many of Haig's contemporaries, and the assumed position of many clergy serving in the army, is encapsulated in the padre's speech given in a ruined church on the eve of yet another attack:

Dearly beloved brethren, I am sure you will be glad to hear the news from the Home Front. The Archbishop of Canterbury has made it known that it is no sin to labour for war on the Sabbath. And I am sure you would also like to know that the Chief Rabbi has absolved your Jewish brethren from abstaining from pork in the trenches. Likewise His Holiness the Pope has ruled that the eating of flesh on Fridays is no longer a mortal sin. And in faraway Tibet, the Dalai Lama has placed his prayers at the disposal of the Allies. Now brethren, tomorrow being Good Friday, we hope God will look kindly on our attack.

This scene initiates a series of prayers. Haig prays: 'Oh God, show thy face to us as thou didst with thy Angels at Mons' (a reference to a supposed group of angels who protected members of the British army during the Battle of Mons at the outset of World War I). One of the Smith family, who has joined Queen Alexandra's Imperial Military Nursing Service, prays: 'Lord, I beg you, do not let this dreadful war cause all this suffering... I know you will answer my prayer!' She is answered by gunfire. Haig again: 'I thank you God. The attack was a great success. The fighting has been severe, but that was to be expected. There has been some delay along the Menin Road, but the ground is thick with enemy dead.' Scarcely pretending to question the place of religion in war, the film is, nevertheless, scathing about the British Empire's enlistment of divine providence.

At the end of the film, one of the Smith boys is the last solider to die before the Armistice. He follows a red ribbon leading from the trenches, through no-man's land, to the pier-end ballroom where a peace treaty is being signed. In this dream sequence, he runs in shirtsleeves and bare feet on green grass of England's South Downs to sit among a few of his friends. Three of the Smith women are picnicking a few yards away, but cannot see him. The moment echoes a scene earlier in the film when a soldier reads aloud the opening lines of Rupert Brooke's evocative poem *The Soldier*: 'If I should die, think only this of me: That there's some corner of a foreign field that is for ever England.' Clearly, the boys lying on the grass are all dead.

In the film's final shot, the camera pulls back from a single white cross planted on the Downs to reveal the Smith women in their white Sunday dresses moving between rank after rank of white grave markers. The screen fills with hundreds of crosses that blur into a shocking expression of the numbing reality of millions of lives wasted.

The anti-war film as a civilising influence

Cinema and warfare have changed irrevocably since the making of *All Quiet on the Western Front*. Nevertheless, the film is still revered as archetypically 'anti-war'. It pioneered a soundtrack on which the sounds of war were all too audible and it used a camera on a crane to swoop in and out of the battlefields, placing the spectator at the centre of the action. This may pale in comparison with modern cinematic techniques, but despite such apparent limitations, the film:

> ...brings together – indeed, helped establish – the classic themes of the anti-war film, book, play and poem: the enemy as comrade; the brutality of militarism; the slaughter of trench warfare; the betrayal of a nation's youth by old men revelling in glory; the incompetence of the High Command; the suffering at home, in particular by women; the dead, and the forgotten men who survived. And it did so in style, without recourse to the romanticism and glorification which marred such war films as *The Big Parade* (Kelly, 1998: 158).

Did the film really alter people's views about war? Clearly the authorities in every country where the film was shown were worried about its impact. *All Quiet* was cut, censored and banned. In Germany and Austria – under the influence of National Socialism – it was the focus of political turmoil, with violent demonstrations and government intervention:

> Few films before – or, indeed, since – have been attacked, censored and condemned in this way... by the time the film had run its initial course, there was no longer a full print available, and one would not exist for fifty-four years. Even then this was a German reconstruction; work on a complete English language version started only in 1997 (Kelly, 1998: 102).

The context in which *Oh! What a Lovely War* was released is entirely different from that of *All Quiet on the Western Front*. In Britain the anti-establishment hedonism of the 1960s, symbolized by 'flower power', formed part of the social and political revolutions sweeping the world. Examples include the American civil rights movement and the rise of feminism and gay rights which continued into the following decades. The 'Swinging Sixties' became synonymous with all the new, exciting, radical, subversive and/or dangerous (depending on the point of view) events and trends of the period. And then there was the Vietnam War which, by 1969, the year *Oh! What a Lovely War* was released, had been lost by the U.S.A. resulting in the deaths of some 50,000 U.S. service personnel and some one million Vietnamese (not including civilian casualties).

There are clearly different perceptions of the First World War in the national histories (and mythologizing) of the U.S.A. and Great Britain. American film critic Vincent Canby, writing in *The New York Times* (3 October 1969) described the film's point of view as 'focused on a dim, far-off era that now seems almost as remote as the time of the Wars of the Roses.' That was not the case in Britain, where an annual ceremony of national remembrance – with the poppy as its chief symbol – and a growing number of revisionist history books kept World War I in the public gaze. Robert Ebert, writing in the *Chicago Sun* (30 October 1969) thought that 'the deepest impact of the film comes from the realization that there have been wars even more horrible since this one' – a significant comment.

It is unrealistic to expect films about war to prevent other wars. It is a well known paradox that the great achievements of civilisation – literature, music, art, cinema, the Universal Declaration of Human Rights – are not in themselves capable of civilising humanity. Yet there is still a case to be made for the role played by cinema in providing moral guidance and critical reasoning on the great issues of life and death that affect society. Cinema has always tried to do this, but it needs to be part of a larger configuration of public education, which is why the role of the British Film Institute in media education (for example) is so vitally important.

The key question is: can societies educate people to create and maintain an environment in which the ethical imperatives of coexistence and peace are implicitly and explicitly recognized? In place of Kantorek's and Haig's jingoism, can societies educate more effectively towards recognizing and upholding the dearest values held by human beings, education that offers shared understandings of a common humanity? As Bernard Crick has pointed out, this would require nothing less than a transformation of political culture internationally, nationally and locally, so that people think of themselves as:

> ...active citizens, willing, able and equipped to have an influence in public life and with the critical capacities to weigh evidence before speaking and acting; to build on and to extend radically to young people the best in existing traditions of community involvement and public service (Crick, 2002: 114).

Public media, including cinema, could instigate and effect such a transformation. The sad fact is that, in a world in which governments flout the United Nations system, in which military and economic interests outweigh the lives and dignity of millions of human beings, in which inequality and poverty are rampant, the simple lessons of *All Quiet on the Western Front* and *Oh! What a Lovely War* have yet to be learnt.

References

Brownlow, Kevin (1983). *Napoleon: Abel Gance's Classic Film*, London: Jonathan Cape. The quotation is from *Prisme,* by Abel Gance, Paris: Gallimard, 1930.

Crick, Bernard (2002). *Democracy. A Very Short Introduction*. Oxford: Oxford University Press.

Kael, Pauline (1973). *Deeper Into Movies*. Boston: Atlantic Little Brown.

Kelly, Andrew (1998). *Filming All Quiet on the Western Front*. London: I. B. Tauris.

Sorlin, Pierre (1991). *European Cinemas, European Societies 1939-1990*. London: Routledge.

Taylor, A. J. P. (1965). *English History 1914-1945,* in the Oxford History of England series. Oxford University Press.

Part Two

X

The Holy Spirit and Communication

Michael Traber

In 1960, when I was studying communication at a university in New York, one of my fellow students submitted an outline for a thesis on 'The Holy Spirit, the Communicator'. In session after session of a seminar he was told to revise the outline. I can still hear the professor saying: 'I don't really know what that Spirit is but, surely, *something* must be *quantifiable*.' The student tried hard to 'quantify data', but the only ones he managed were biblical references to the Holy Spirit, upon completion of which he was told either to abandon the project or change the school.

I thought of this incident when the present theme was proposed [for an article in *The Ecumenical Review*], and I have wondered for a long time whether I too would have to abandon the project, because in this article also, there will be nothing to quantify, not even quotations from scripture. Nor shall I try to trace a biblical theology of the Holy Spirit and the Spirit's roles in confessing and witnessing, prophesying and truth-telling, praising and adoring, or any other aspect we associate with Christian communication. This has been done before, and in better and more systematic ways than I could do.[1]

Instead, my approach is contextual, starting with the world of communication. I shall start by showing some of the problems of communication theory, a theory which continues to grapple with the everyday reality of human communication, and yet never really succeeds in explaining it, except by the philosopher's reference to a transcendental Spirit. In this sense, communication theory itself must be seen as a parable of the Holy Spirit. Instead of looking at revelation and the Holy Spirit's role in the church and salvation, we discover the Spirit in creation, namely the uniquely human activities of creatures called men and women. These reflections will also lead us to some communication problems such as truth-telling and to the conclusion that the world of practical communication is in desperate need of the Holy Spirit.

Can a spirit communicate?

The word 'communication' first hit the headlines (as we would say today) in 1695 when the German philosopher Leibniz published a book in French with the title *Système nouveau de la nature et de la communication des substances*. One of the questions which Leibniz tried to answer was: how is it possible for humans to communicate with each other? Communication, clearly, is a matter of the mind or spirit, and so are 'ideas'. Plato had already wrestled with the same problem. His solution was that all communication and, therefore, knowledge was mediated by 'ideas', or eternal entities or concepts, which God had created and in which human beings could participate, albeit by detecting only shadows on the walls of the cave.

Leibniz's solution was similar. For him reality consisted entirely of pure mind-monads, and they have 'no windows'. In a world of pure minds there is no communication at all. Yet, commonsense shows that even monad-minds are somehow in communication with each other. Who connects them? After all, God is the origin of their being and of their apparent harmony.

This amazing reference to a transcendental Spirit is made again and again, throughout the history of philosophy about problems of communication. God is regarded as the universal communicator. God's communication happens on two levels. Firstly, as God who imparts life to all that exists – God's continuous creation. Communication is perhaps the clearest expression of the life-giving indwelling of the Holy Spirit. Secondly, God as the universal communicator is the God of salvation who establishes a relationship with human beings in a direct way, both with individuals and communities. God provides the divine logos, Christ, as 'the inner teacher', a doctrine expounded in St Augustine's *De Magistro*. In other words, the philosophical problem of communication could not be solved without recourse to theology, and thereby providing a theological answer to a philosophical question.

This leads us to another problem: the iconography of the Holy Spirit. The Spirit is not pictured as a person. The Spirit's communication is manifested through elements of nature, all of which have an almost non-corporeal quality: air, wind, tongues of fire, flowing water. As Arnold Bittlinger has rightly pointed out in an article in *The Ecumenical Review*, the fourth 'element', earth, is missing. It 'is never a symbol of the Spirit'.[2] Not even the hovering dove signalling the end of the great flood (Gen. 8:8, 12) or alighting on Jesus at his baptism (Luke 3:22) gives the Spirit that measure of corporeality which we associate with communication.

These philosophical reflections on communication are important for two reasons. Firstly, we tend to take communication for granted as an everyday reality and thus see 'no problem', or merely problems which are technical, or media-related. Yet even today's philosophers and communication theorists have not solved the basic question of how the human mind interconnects with other minds, or where and when reality differs from appearance. Human communication, as indeed the communication of the Holy Spirit, remains a mystery.

Secondly, these examples from Western philosophy point to a European cultural tradition which, willy-nilly, separates mind from body or mentality from materiality. Descartes, living only half a century before Leibniz, epitomized this tradition most clearly. His famous dictum, 'I think, therefore I am', has found its way into the above-mentioned article in *The Ecumenical Review* written by a psychotherapist and theologian.[3] The accompanying drawing shows other cultural traditions: the African, 'I dance, therefore I am', or the Asian, 'I meditate, therefore I am'.

So, can an incorporeal spirit communicate? No, say the communication theorists. But the Holy. Spirit is not human. There are other ways of communicating than those based on sense perception. African people long ago discovered this. The spirit world of their ancestors is as real to them as that of their descendants. And so is their mutual communication.

The word in the world

Human communication presupposes perception by and through our senses. It thus has an essential bodily quality. Or so it looks at first sight. In contrast to Plato and other body/ mind dualists, or separatists like Descartes and Leibniz, 'all modern communication theories have in fact been elaborated within a framework of empiricist epistemology.'[4] Marshall McLuhan's main hypothesis is that the media of mass communication are, in essence, extensions of human senses. But McLuhan and other newer and more sophisticated theoreticians of communication cannot really answer one crucial question: how does information received through the sense and processed in the brain become 'meaning'; that is, how can a message be fully 'understood'? Communication, apart from sense perception, requires that we 'assimilate', and make our own message from that received from another person. Jean-Louis Barrault, the French actor and director, described the process of finding 'meaning' as follows: 'Knowing something means having forgotten it and having found it again, inside. It is a "digested" knowledge. By study we get to the core of a thing, we know it, then we forget it; at last, we find it again inside ourselves. From that moment on, we *know* the thing.'[5]

A communicative mind is one which has reflective consciousness. Such a mind spans time and space and therefore recognizes the universality which is immanent in a particular sense perception. We call a mind constituted in this way a 'spirit', and traditionally assign as characteristics of spiritual being the two apparently contradictory but in reality mutually conditioning attributes of being-present-to-oneself and of having unlimited openness.[6] The spiritual nature of the human mind makes it possible, for us to 'link' sense perceptions and one's internal dispositions to the linguistic forms of expression or other signs and symbols.

Communication further implies a similarity of many different spiritual minds. What accounts for the similarity of these minds? Knowledge and experience are not merely mechanically 'transmitted' from outside but they become part of the spiritual consciousness itself. That consciousness exists and is shaped by a myriad interpersonal contacts in a community of life. The knowledge and experience in our minds are a result of living in a community in which knowledge and experience are built up in a similar way as in other minds, so that the same expressions or sense-perceptible signs are interpreted more and more in the same way.

These reflections show that communication is a great deal more than the mere transmission of information or 'inducement' of emotions. It is a sharing of meaning, and meaning here has to be taken in its fullest sense as ultimate relevance. Communication, therefore, is less concerned with the exchange of knowledge or information than with sharing a certain view of reality and a way of understanding the world. Or, in the words of John Macquarrie: 'Communication takes place when some aspect of the shared world is lit up and made accessible to both parties in the discourse.'[7] Yet we are far from knowing how this really happens. What is reflective consciousness or the spirit mind? Is it really an analogy of the Holy Spirit as some suggest?[8]

What we have called living-in-community essentially means using language. Learning to speak inculcates at the same time definite ways of seeing and of understanding experiences. Linguistic and any other form of communication will succeed better the more it is part of a community. Use of language means that we have to learn a language tradition which structures our experiences of the world and enables us to sort out our own personal experiences.

Language implies, as we have seen, our being-in-the-world together and refers to a world perceptible to sense. Language presupposes corporeality: vocal utterances need to be audible and word symbols carved on stone or printed on paper must be legible. But language also has its constraints. There is constantly felt linguistic inadequacy with regard to individual experiences. There are realms within the human experience which seem to lie outside linguistic objectivity. Socrates and Kierkegaard called it the 'unutterable'. Wittgenstein solemnly declared: 'What we cannot speak about we must pass over in silence'. For Wittgenstein, anything which was outside linguistic communication was 'transcendental'. Talking about God, according to Wittgenstein, was therefore impossible. 'God is not an object that could be encountered in the world or a state of affairs that could be named and pictured in a sentence.'[9]

Wittgenstein's position (which he somewhat revised later on in life) shows that language and linguistic analysis are insufficient to explain human consciousness, or indeed communication. Human consciousness knows such things as intuitions, dreams and half-dreams, feelings often expressed in metaphors and sensations which defy language. We must at least concede the possibility of extrasensory perception. Secondly, we must realize that there are human self-expressions outside language. In the words of George Santayana '... like tears, gestures may touch an observer's heart, but they do not come for that purpose. So the fund of words and phrases latent in the mind flow out under stress of emotion; they flow because they belong to the situation, because they fill out and complete a perception absorbing the mind; they do not flow primarily to be listened to.'[10] The same can be said about private prayer, in contrast to communal praying.

Language, above all, cannot fully explain the role of memory for human consciousness. Memory does not merely mean the ability to remember but, more comprehensively, a person, a community and some sort of concrete space which are all part of history involving specific personal experiences. As the French sociologist Maurice Halbwachs[11] has convincingly shown, to forget means to distance oneself from one's own physical and cultural space and to detach oneself from one's community. Even 'commemoration' is then no longer possible.

Nor can linguistic analysis say anything about 'the womb' of words: silence. Silence is essential to language. Because genuine silence is the conscious attention to oneself in relation to others, or conscious attention to others and to God in relation to oneself. When reflective and inclusive silence ceases, language transforms itself into mere noise, and communication stops. 'By communication we understand here', Walter J. Ong reminds us, 'not simply new gimmicks enabling man to "contact" his fellows but, more completely, the person's means of entering into the life and. consciousness of others and thereby into his own life. Communications in this sense obviously relate to man's sense of his own presence to himself and to other men, and to his sense of God's presence.'[12]

Language and lying

The assumption of all communication is that we tell the truth. But this elementary fact has hardly been noticed by communication theorists. Nor do lies matter if you are concerned mainly with communication as a simple linear process (sender-message-code-receiver) rather than its content and its meaning in a social context. Yet lies have a catastrophic effect on the individual and society at large.

There are two primary forms of deception. Passive deception, or concealment, is the *omission* of information in order to communicate a misleading impression. Active deception, or lying, is the presentation of *false* information, or an intentionally stated deceptive message, as if it were the truth. Ethicists argue that passive deception must be justified under certain conditions.

'Every deception, every imposture, is an assumption of power; the person deceived is reduced in stature, symbolically nullified, while the imposture is temporarily powerful,' says Alexander Klein.[13] We will return to the philosophical problem of communication and power, but before that an ethical point about today's mass media needs to be made. All centres of power and all persons in powerful positions are tempted to deceive, including the mass media. Some institutions, the most noteworthy being governments, think they have a right to deceive. President Vaclav Havel began his New Year's address (1990) to his fellow Czechoslovaks as follows:

> You have heard from the lips of my predecessors approximately the same thing for forty years: how our country is flourishing, how many tons of steel we have produced, how happy we all are, and how we trust our government, and how marvellous the prospects for the future are. I presume you have not selected me for this office so that I, too, should lie to you.

Then, speaking about the state of his country and the ruined natural environment, he continued:

> The worst aspect, however, is that we live in an environment which is morally corrupt... Because we got used to speaking what we did not think or mean... Only a few of us have had the courage to say that the mighty are not almighty.

Obviously, the spread of half-truths and lies is no prerogative of the erstwhile communist governments of Eastern Europe. It occurs in more subtle and even more dangerous ways in the West. Deliberate disinformation is now comparatively easy, thanks to the powerful combination of words, images and other symbols in modern media.

As early as 1919, the American journalist Upton Sinclair wrote: 'We define journalism in America as the business and practice of presenting the news of the day in the interests of economic privilege.'[14] One wonders how many church journalists would admit that they presented the news in the interest of their church, and how many foreign correspondents would have the honesty to say that they wrote in the interest of their own country rather than in the interest of truth. The long-term consequences of this state of affairs are serious. Truthfulness is a necessary condition for trust. Only when we are able to trust one another, trust the mass media, and trust our leaders, can we really 'live together', and live in peace, in our communities, countries and continents.

The stark imagery of the Bible serves as a useful reminder of the necessity for truthfulness in this age of mass communication. Isaiah's lament has a modern ring: 'In the public square, truth has been brought to its knees; honesty cannot enter. Truth is nowhere to be found, and whoever avoids evil is robbed' (59:14f.). The epitome of all evil, according to the New Testament, is the liar, and Satan is called liar par excellence. 'When he lies, he speaks his native tongue, for he is a liar and the father of lies' (John 8:44). Those who lie have their hearts filled with Satan (cf. Acts 5:3).

Lying, then, is the very opposite of genuine communication, first disrupting it, and after repetitions, making communication impossible, thus separating people and groups. Such separation from each other and from God is the essence of sin. It is the ultimate *ex-communication*. In contrast, truth is an attribute of God and of the Spirit of Truth; truthfulness is the mark of those who believe in God. Therefore, 'putting away falsehood, let everyone speak the truth with their neighbours, for we are members of one another' (Eph. 4:25).

Communicative actions

While language is undoubtedly a precondition for communication, communication is more than speaking or writing. Communication is an active process in which two or more communication partners negotiate the meaning of information, or of an experience. Some modern philosophers and theologians have therefore coined the term 'communicative action'.[15] Jürgen Habermas has entitled one of his most important works *A Theory of Communicative Action*.[16] His and other similar theories cannot be summarized here. Our aim is merely to highlight some aspects which are of relevance to our discussion of communication and the Holy Spirit.

The starting point in this theoretical approach is not language as a static entity. Language, in fact, is only one aspect which makes communication possible. The others are 'validity claims' which refer to the intentions of the communication partners and to the conditions of their communication. Communicative actions, therefore, imply extra-linguistic acts. One could be called credibility or reliance. Both are necessary for all engaged in communicative actions. Another characteristic is an assumed or aspired normative basis which can lead to consensus on something (the subject matter of communication).

All those dimensions of communicative actions are simultaneously present. They constitute one act. This view of communication is as much about a genuine and indeed 'ideal' human relationship as it is about the action, or communication, that brings it about. It stresses innovation and change. Those in communication strive for new qualities in life-together, which they want to achieve communally, that is, through consensus. In their communicative actions, they explore and disclose new options, new possibilities and new meanings for others and themselves.

In these speech negotiations we become the true owners of language by leaving the prison of language imposed by society to create a new language, reflecting a new and different reality. Initially, the new language is characterized by metaphors, stories and modern parables. Eventually, a 'discourse' is developed which does justice to the newly negotiated meaning of the reality to come: a new world. New meaning, however, is always constituted reciprocally and, therefore, on the basis of equality. 'The unconditional recognition of the equal standing of the communication partners excludes any attempts at force or manipulation... the refusal to revert to force or manipulation is the recognition of indisposable freedom reciprocally demanded and granted.'[17]

According to the theories of communicative action, freedom is matched by universal solidarity with others in a potentially 'unlimited community'.

> Mutual acceptance is always an essential precondition. In principle it can exclude no-one as a partner in communication, for basically its aim is an unrestricted community of communication. The moment I begin to speak I enter a universal dialogue. Rules of behaviour, that is, ethical decisions, can only be founded on, and therefore justified in terms of, this unlimited community of communication. Universal solidarity is thus the basic principle of ethics and can be shown as the normative core of all human communication.[18]

The 'ideal-speech situation' which is postulated here is not easily achieved. But it is a vision of communal praxis which could create a new society or make at least a contribution to the renewal promised by the Holy Spirit. It opens new vistas for what witnessing and confessing one's faith could mean. It is, therefore, not surprising that the concepts of communicative actions and the 'ideal-speech situation' have attracted theologians more than communication scholars. These theologians, on the basis of their analysis of Jesus' own communication, argue with great conviction that he alone brought about the 'ideal-speech situation,' that his parables were a paradigm of open, non-manipulative communication and that it was the task of his followers to re-enact Jesus' own communication through, and with the help of, the Holy Spirit.

The Spirit in meta-communication

On the first page of his book *Real Presences*, George Steiner states that his essay proposes that any coherent understanding of what language is and how language performs, that any coherent account of the capacity of human speech to communicate meaning and feeling, is, in the final analysis, underwritten by the assumption of God's presence.[19] Steiner continues:

> This study will contend that the wager on the meaning of meaning, on the potential of insight and response when one human voice addresses another, when we come face to face with the text and work of art or music, which is to say when we encounter the *other* in its condition of freedom, is a wager on the transcendence... The conjecture is that 'God' is, not because our grammar is outworn; but that grammar lives and generates worlds because there is a wager on God.[20]

Other thinkers, as we have seen, have come to similar conclusions. But Steiner, unlike them, advocating an 'ethics of reception' and a spiritual discipline of attention, tact and trust, pursues the experience of transcendence in works of communication, especially literature, music and visual art. The book's sub-title asks: 'Is there anything *in* what we say?' The answer is, yes, the presence of the Spirit of God.

This dimension of communication has also been called meta-communication. The term is variously interpreted, but common is the view of the 'a priori of the community of communication.' Meta-communication has also been called 'cosmic consciousness', it being 'the light that lightens every human being coming into the world' (John 1:9).

Meta-communication is religious in character. It refers to the other-worldly and to God. Paul Tillich distinguished two sorts of meaning in human consciousness and human action: those which are conditioned (or derivative) and those which are unconditioned (or foundational). 'Unconditioned' means here directly related to the unity and totality of consciousness. Between the conditioned and the unconditioned there is a reciprocal mediating relationship. The unconditioned or religious energizes the conditioned reference to the world of other persons and to the material environment, including nature. Tillich defines the religious as content and object, in a famous phrase, as 'that which concerns us unconditionally.'[21] Or, as Adam Heschel says: 'What we are in search of is not meaning for me, an idea to satisfy my conscience, but rather a meaning transcending me, ultimate relevance of being.'[22]

Meta-communication has also been called the common 'reservoir' of meaning, that which 'makes a communication between human beings possible at all, even if they do not speak a common language, and as what permits them to draw upon a common reservoir of meaning, and indeed guarantees them common basic logical laws.'[23]

In addition to basic common laws of logic, meta-communication also implies consensus of expectations, i.e. basic norms about expected behaviour, which are universal. Such norms then form a meta-communicative system, which is fundamental to all human behaviour. Consensus means that such behavioural expectations are arrived at in a reciprocal process of reflection, which is centred on the community, yet cannot be fully explained by either logic or human sciences.

The meta-communicative system expresses itself in a set of religious symbols. It is in these symbols that ultimate meaning is stored. They are both a model of, and a model for, reality and everyday life and 'lend a chronic character to the flow of his/ her activity and the quality of his/her experience.'[24] According to Geertz, the problem of meaning has to do with human limitations – intellectual, physiological and ethical. The apparent inevitability of human bafflement, suffering, injustice and evil threaten to annihilate order; they make life unfathomable. The experience of such crises presents radical challenges to human beings, which they try to resolve within their meta-communicative system.[25] The alternative is, in Heidegger's words, 'the clear night of the nothingness' and angst.

Ultimately, the a priori which meta-communication postulates may be the 'prior word' of which Bernard Lonergan speaks:

> Religion is the prior word [which] God speaks to us by flooding our hearts with his love. That prior word pertains, not to the world mediated by meaning, but to the world of immediacy, to the unmediated experience of the mystery of love and awe. The outwardly spoken word is historically conditioned: its meaning depends upon the human context in which it is uttered... But the prior word in its immediacy... withdraws man from the diversity of history by moving out of the world mediated by meaning and towards a world of immediacy in which image and symbol, thought and word, lose their relevance and even disappear.[26]

Lonergan's assumption of the prior or inner word as distinct from the outer, historically conditioned word, poses more questions than it answers. While philosophically it is no more than an assumption, theologically the inner word is real through the indwelling of the Holy Spirit.

The theological 'analogatum' of meta-communication and, implicitly, all communication are the work and actions of the Holy Spirit, or the Spirit's 'fellowship' (2 Cor. 13:14; Phil. 2: 1). The Holy Spirit is the a priori of communication on the deepest level. The thought that the presence of the Holy Spirit is necessary for that most genuinely human act, communication, is awe-inspiring. But reflecting on it may enhance awareness of the Holy Spirit in oneself and in others.

Adding to this what has been *revealed* about the Holy Spirit in the scriptures leaves us standing on much firmer ground. The Holy Spirit is truly the chief enabler in the communication of faith. Hearing the good news of the kingdom, being reminded of it, understanding it, witnessing to it, and proclaiming it to all creatures to the end of time – all these are ultimately the work of the Holy Spirit who, since baptism, dwells in us. 'It is this Spirit that can change the Babel of confusion into the Pentecost of genuine understanding,' the *Christian Principles of Communication* of the World Association for Christian Communication state. The Holy Spirit, the communicator, can create through us a new Pentecost.

First published in *The Ecumenical Review*, Volume 42, Numbers 3–4, July–October 1990.

Notes

1. See, for example, the rich collection of articles on the Holy Spirit in *The Ecumenical Review*, 41, 3, July 1989, especially Hans Huebner's 'The Holy Spirit in Holy Scripture' and Philip J. Rosato's 'The Mission of the Spirit within and beyond the Church', as well as *The Ecumenical Review*, 42, 2, April 1990, especially John Breck's 'The Lord is the Spirit: an Essay on Christological Pneumatology'.

2. Arnold Bittlinger, 'A Charismatic Approach to the Theme', *The Ecumenical Review*, 42, 2, April 1990. 3 Ibid., p. 108.

3. Ibid. p. 108.

4. Peter Henrici, 'Towards an Anthropological Philosophy of Communication', *Communication Resource*, No. 1, March 1983, p. 1.

5. Quoted in Ralph Ross, *Symbols and Civilisation*, New York, Harcourt, 1962, pp.218f.

6. Henrici, op. cit., p.3.

7. John Macquarrie, *God talk: an Examination of the Language and Logic of Theology*, London, SCM, 1974, p. 74.

8. Cf. H. 4. Hoehn, *Kirche und Kommunikatives Handeln*, Frankfurt am Main, Knecht, 1985, pp. 117–36.

9. Summarizing Wittgenstein's position: Helmut Peukert, *Science, Action and Fundamental Theology: Towards a Theology of Communicative Action*, Cambridge, MA, MIT Press, 1984, p.30.

10. George Santayana, *The Life of Reason, vol. III, Reason in Religion*, New York, Scribner, 1936, p.39.

11. Maurice Halbwachs, *Das kollective Gedächnis*, Frankfurt am Main, Knecht, 1985, pp. 117–36.

12. Walter J. Ong, *The Presence of the Word*, Minneapolis, University of Minnesota Press, 1981, p. 15.

13. Quoted in 'Deception', *International Encyclopedia of Communication*, New, York, Oxford University Press, 1989, p.459.

14. Quoted in *Media Development*, 1986, 3: 'Lies and Lying', p. 1.

15. Among them are Helmut Peukert, cf. note 9, Edmund Arens who has produced two seminal works, *Kommunikative Handlungen: Die paradigmatische Bedeutung der Gleichnisse Jesu für eine Handlungstheorie*, Düsseldorf, Patmos, 1983, and *Bezeugen und Bekennen: Elementare Handlungen des Glaubens*, Düsseldorf, Patmos, 1989. Other theologians in the group are Ottmar Fuchs, Kuno F. Issel, Matthew L. Lamb, Norbert Mette, Rudolf J. Siebert, etc.

16. Jürgen Habermas, *A Theory of Communicative Action*, 2 vols, Boston, Beacon, 1981.

17. Peukert, op. cit, p.213.

18. Helmut Peukert, 'Universal Solidarity as Goal of Communication', in *Media Development*, 1981, 4, p. 10.

19. George Steiner, *Real Presences*, London, Faber & Faber, 1989, p. 3.

20. Op. cit., p.4.

21. Paul Tillich, quoted by Johannes Heinrich, 'Theory of Practical Communication: a Christian Approach', 22 in *Media Development*, 1981, 4, p. 6.

22. Adam Heschel, *Who is Man?*, Stanford, University Press, 1968, p. 55.

23. Heinrichs, op. cit, p.6.

24. Clifford Geertz, 'Religion as a Cultural System', in William A. Lessa & Evon Z. Vogt eds, *Reader in Comparative Religion*, New York, Harper & Row, 1979, p. 83.

25. Op. cit, p. 85.

26. Bernard Lonergan, *Method in Theology*, London, Darton, Longmann & Todd, 1972, p. 112.

XI

Communication as a Human Need and Human Right

Michael Traber

The German communication scholar Paul Watzlawick (1967: 53) coined the axiomatic sentence: 'One cannot not communicate.' He thus echoed Plato's early definition of the human being as the 'animal which speaks' (*zoon logon echon*), which was later submerged in Aristotle's definition of the human as the animal which thinks ('rational animal'). The philosophical position of Watzlawick is that human beings are both creatures and creators of language and all other signs, symbols and rituals. As Charles Morris explains:

> Everything which is characteristically human depends on language. The human being is in a real sense the speaking animal. Speech plays the most essential but not the only role in the development and preservation of the human self and its aberrations, as it does in the development and maintenance of human society and its aberrations (Morris, 1975: 235; my translation).

The need to communicate, therefore, is intrinsic to human nature (Fisher in Fisher and Harms, 1983). Precisely because communication is such a fundamental human need, those who control communication also control people. The history of communication is a long history of silencing people, from the persecution of 'heretics' and 'freethinkers' to the transfer of 'dissidents' to psychiatric wards or solitary confinement. It is also a history of people's struggle to speak up and speak publicly. The report of the International Commission for the Study of Communication Problems (known as the MacBride Report) states:

> ...the principle of freedom of expression is one that admits of no exceptions, and that is applicable to people all over the world by virtue of their human dignity. This freedom is one of democracy's most precious acquisitions, frequently secured through arduous struggles with political and economic powers and authorities and at the cost of heavy sacrifice, even of life itself (MacBride, 1980: 18–19).

The MacBride Report encapsulates the struggle towards a New World Information and Communication Order (NWICO) which, broadly speaking, is an attempt to establish a more balanced and democratic multi-way flow of communication and information throughout the world. It proposes the establishment of free and equal communication at the national and international level. This entails the wresting of control from those who at present dominate international communications flow in the West, particularly the United States and, increasingly, the transnational corporations. Not surprisingly, those in control have resisted all calls for a NWICO. Thus the history of the right to communicate has become bound up with the fate of the NWICO.

In the following, I shall first explain the origin of the concept of communication as a right and refer, secondly, to its main articulation in the MacBride Report and through debate in UNESCO in particular. The third section is devoted to the question of control: should the State or the market control communication? The fourth part raises the issue of public responsibility for the right to communicate, and I conclude by highlighting some difficulties which need to be taken up in the debate.

The right to communicate in international human rights

The first generation of human rights, born of the French and American revolutions, emphasised individual freedom. The second generation of human rights, first formulated in the Mexican Constitution of 1917 and the Soviet Constitution of 1918, invoked the co-operation of the State in implementing human rights (see Traber, 1992).

The present generation of human rights is still evolving. It has its origins in the anti-colonial revolutions of the years after the Second World War. These rights emphasise national self-determination and non-discrimination. They are also bound up with the spirit of internationalism which emerged after 1945, and the United Nations system that enshrines it. The adoption of the Universal Declaration of Human Rights on 10 December 1948 was of special significance. It has been described as a revolutionary development, perhaps the most important development in the history of law in the twentieth century (Humphrey, 1988: 5.). Yet in spite of its Article 19 it did not formulate communication as a fundamental human right.

The present generation of human rights pertains primarily to certain planetary concerns, such as peace, people's self-determination, socio-economic development, ecological balance and communication. Their horizon is the family of nations, and their rights are, in principle, 'solidarity rights', thus carrying the French Revolution's notion of fraternity to its logical, global conclusion (see Marks, 1981). All of these rights have an individual and collective dimension. They mean, in the final analysis, that the State and all social organisations have a duty to place the common good of the people as a whole before state and individual interest.

In the debate over the concept of the right to communicate many have stressed the importance of recognising the equality of all partners in the communication process. Communications should embrace a multicultural, multi-way flow of information, including a passive as well as an active right to communicate, while promoting the highest possible degree of feedback, participation and access.

According to different political traditions and socio-economic circumstances, some will emphasise the international, others the national connotations of this right. Furthermore, it will differ depending on whether one places society or the individual at the centre of the communication process; whether it means the provision of communication resources or the protection of individuals and communities from the redundancy of information and entertainment; whether there is a primary necessity to satisfy the basic need of all people to be informed or to safeguard them against the abuses and manipulation of the mass media; or whether the universal right to communicate can also mean the right to be silent.

The right to communicate, as a fundamental human right, clearly anticipates a communication model which is democratic rather than authoritarian. As Servaes (1988: 17) has pointed out, it aims at a redistribution of communication power; its 'point of departure is not an elitist position, but development from the grassroots'. It further stipulates another role for the State than the one described in the second generation of human rights. The State is only one of several players, because the right to communicate embraces several individual rights, and institutional rights, or 'people's rights' which were the main conflict at UNESCO in the 1980s (see Roach, 1988: 19-20). The policy makers of the Reagan and Bush administrations consistently refused to accept that there are people's rights, including solidarity rights, and denigrated the demand for a free and *balanced* flow of information among nations.

The articulation of the international right to communicate

It is particularly significant in the context of the NWICO debate that the right to communicate was originally a *Western* concept (Roach 1988: 19). The Frenchman Jean D'Arcy was the first specifically to express the need for the right to communicate. He saw the need to extend Article 19 of the Universal Declaration of Human Rights (which calls for freedom of opinion and expression), in recognition of the fact that the right to communicate is more fundamental than the right to free expression (which can be justifiably restricted in exceptional circumstances). The MacBride Report in its final recommendations calls for the implementation of just such a right (Recommendation 54):

> Communication needs in a democratic society should be met by the extension of specific rights such as the right to be informed, the right to inform, the right to privacy, the right to participate in public communication – all elements of a new concept, the right to communicate (p. 265).

In particular the right to communicate is not the same as freedom of information, which is more likely to benefit those with more powerful (and profitable) means of information. One point often neglected in the crusade for a free flow of information (a standpoint which became opposed to the NWICO) is the concept, mentioned in the MacBride Report (p. 24) and elsewhere, that the freedom to communicate implies responsibility, to use such a freedom wisely and with care.

The MacBride Report describes the right to communicate as follows:

> Our conclusions are founded on the firm conviction that communication is a basic individual right, as well as a collective one required by all communities and nations. Freedom of information and, more specifically, the right to seek, receive and impart information is a fundamental human right; indeed, a prerequisite for many others. The inherent nature of communication means that its fullest possible exercise and potential depend on the surrounding political, social and economic conditions, the most vital of these being democracy within countries and equal, democratic relations between them. It is in this context that the democratization of communication

at national and international levels, as well as the larger role of communication in democratizing society, acquires utmost importance (p. 253).

Fifteen years after the publication of *Many Voices, One World* (the MacBride Report's official title) the world has changed. On the one hand, the voices are now fewer, becoming monotonous, and the world is seen merely as a global market. On the other hand, the movement in many parts of the world towards greater democracy and participation by the people has been matched by an increase in alternative, popular media, which has also affected the mass media.

State control or mass media empire?

The right to communicate has in many countries degenerated into a question of whether the State or the market place are the best guardians of a country's communication systems. The State has largely been discredited in this role. In the NWICO debate the USA took an aggressive stance against what it saw as the facilitation of the control and censorship of information by the State; though much of its criticism was based on a faulty understanding of what the State theoretically is, namely a representation of the entire body politic, its citizenry and varied institutions. As such the State has responsibility towards its citizens to allow them the right to communicate their views, facilitating both access and adequate information with which to communicate effectively.

There is no doubt that some governments do abuse their control of communications systems. But this does not mean that the State should lack any role in the elaboration of a right to communicate. The right to communicate is very much dependent upon the social structures in which it has to operate. As Kleinwachter argues (in Fisher and Harms, 1983: 104-105), the right to communicate is linked to other rights such as education: when these rights are denied, the right to communicate cannot be realised. The necessary resources must be available in order to make practical the right of every person to communicate. Such conditions require the active co-operation of the State. In national terms this means policy decisions to ensure good educational and cultural provision, and so on. Internationally, it involves the control of the powerful international media conglomerates, so that the less powerful voices are heard.

The controversy about the role of the State, with its dangerous potential for control of expression, has removed the limelight from other key players in international communi-cations: the media conglomerates. The Western demand for a 'free' flow of communications frequently means the preser-vation of media dominance by the mass media empires – which are usually Western. Kolossov (in Fisher and Harms, 1983: 116) points out that the dissemination of mass media beyond national boundaries has not been specifically codified as a right.

Western countries usually point to market-based private enterprise as a way of ensuring a free flow of information, unhindered by any form of government intervention. A free flow of communication that is purely market-based does not actually occur now, and is not likely in the future: most governments will intervene to give their media enterprises the edge in international competition. Indeed, this is one reason for the US government's intervention in the international communications debate. But in any case media controlled by private enterprise is hardly free. Commercial enterprises will only sell media and information products that are profitable. Instead of having free access to the gamut of information, we are sold information packages from a limited range:

> ...the principle of maximization of power and the principle of maximization of profit merge in the communication sphere to the detriment of that part of global society which is not governed by these principles. As a consequence, citizens are shifted away from participation in decision making and control towards strengthening their consumer function. The consequence of this process is an erosion of civil society' (Splichal, 1991: 5).

The consequence is also an erosion of the right to communicate, if such a right depends upon its profitability.

The right to communicate is a public responsibility

Neither the State nor the market can adequately uphold the right to communicate. This is the task of the people, the citizenry, although both State and market have their part to play. It is the responsibility of each citizen to participate actively in public communication, through political and social debate and action.

The public must become an active partner with the media in the maintenance of their right to communicate. In order to ensure critical media, we need a critical public, as Majid Tehranian suggests:

> ...the critical role of the media is contingent upon the existence of broad-based democratic movements. Otherwise, the decline of the public sphere under the present commercially dominated media systems spells a continuing decline of the critical functions of the media in public affairs. The ultimate threat in this process will be an imperceptible but effective evolution of democratic institutions into technostructures that are insensitive to and intolerant of public needs and interests (Tehranian, 1990: 173).

The media are dependent upon the public to act as a forum for public democratic discourse. However, the public are also dependent upon the media to provide relevant information, to place issues on the agenda for debate and to encourage people to act upon their responsibility as citizens rather than sink into an entertainment-saturated inertia. Social movements need greater access to the media at both a local and national level, to foster a truly public debate. Efforts to work out more comprehensive and profound media ethics and principles of journalism should not be confined to the media professionals. The whole community must be involved in the debate about the media's responsibilities to the public.

Active citizens' involvement in the struggle to attain and maintain a right to communicate, presupposes a change in political culture: from passive to active and responsible citizens working for the common good of the people. If we have learned any lesson from our political culture of the past ten years, it is that genuine democracy requires more than the election of representatives to a legislative assembly in a multi-party system, no matter how essential this is. Over and beyond voting and party politics, democracy requires people who can make their wishes known in public and who participate in the debate about the type of society and political process they aspire to.

The media should interact in new ways with their public, making them the principal subject, rather than objects, of their reporting. Responsible media are the champions of responsible citizens: they are orientated towards them, they seek them out, they provide access to them. Together, in mutual responsibility, media and public can develop a political culture which is participatory and free, jointly working for the common good of all.

There are already many alternative media initiatives throughout the world that seek to give the people a different voice: from independent press agencies to storytelling, from popular theatre groups to alternative computer networks. John Keane puts it thus:

> The uncoordinated and dispersed character of state power makes it more susceptible to the initiatives of social movements and citizens' groups, backed by countervailing networks of communication, which challenge prevailing codes and practise the art of *divide et impera* from below. Dispersed networks of communication can more easily penetrate the pores of civil society and build networks of meaning among various groups of citizens... they indicate ways in which new forms of social solidarity, especially among the less powerful citizenry can be developed against the atomizing effects of modern life (Keane, 1992: 3081)

Alternative or people's media are one way of securing the right to communicate, even though the mass media may ignore them.

Conclusion

Communication, both public and private, is a *fundamental* human right, and as such the precondition for other human rights, because communication is intimately bound up with what it means to be human. The freedom to speak and to publicise, and to create works of communication (cultural goods) is not only an essential component of human dignity and cultural identity, but is also necessary for any progress in other rights, such as food, clothing, shelter, education, health care, and work. The core issue is the right to be fully human both as an individual and as a member of a community and a society. It would seem that the human being is as little able to cope with the systematic suppression and control of the means and possibilities of communication as with physical degradation or material poverty.

It is one of the principle insights of the MacBride Report to have analysed communication as a human right on the international level and to have tied this to the democratisation of communication. Thus the right to communicate should exist not only within a nation but also between nations. (The latter was the primary focus of debate on the NWICO.)

There remain many questions to be taken up in the debate. The first is the problem of the nation-state, with its concomitant phenomenon of patriotism. Nationalism and patriotism have profoundly affected public communication both within and between nations. What roles can they play, or should they play, on the different levels of a new and democratic communication order? How can national sovereignty be maintained *together* with international rights?

Another unresolved problem is that of ethnicity and cultural identity. The reassertion of these cultural rights within and sometimes between nation-states presents one of the most formidable communication challenges today. It is a basic issue in most parts of Africa and in many countries of Europe. It is not sufficient to treat ethnic and cultural identity under the rubric of minority groups, as the MacBride Report tends to do (MacBride Report, 1980: 309). Each ethnic and cultural group must be seen to make a unique contribution to public communication and its national and international order.

In regard to communication technology and power, the world has changed radically since the MacBride Report first appeared. The gap has widened between the technology-rich and the technology-poor. Deregulation has increased the monopolisation of media ownership and trivialisation of media content, particularly in the electronic media. What is lacking in research is not the analysis of these trends but policy proposals in the search for alternatives. The active right to communicate, interpersonally and with spatially dispersed communities, calls for radical rethinking of technological alternatives, of which video technology and computer networking are examples.

The right to communicate is ultimately a right to democracy. The MacBride Report puts it thus:

> ...the success of measures to improve communication, in both form and content, is inextricably linked with steps to make society itself less oppressive and unequal, more just and democratic (MacBride Report, p.18).

The right to communicate cannot, therefore, be pursued in isolation, but should be seen as a vital, integral part of a wider pursuance of people's democratic rights. The right to communicate can only be realised in a context of more equitable education, culture, technology, and economic and political situations. But equally, none of these characteristics can be achieved without the right to communication. All must be worked for simultaneously, in a process that ensures the participation of all: the State, the media and, above all, the people.

First published in *Religion and Society*, Vol. XXXIX, No. 1, March 1992. Christian Institute for the Study of Religion and Society, Bangalore, India.

References

Fisher, Desmond and Harms, L. S. (1983). *The Right to Communicate: A new human right*. Dublin: Boole Press.

Humphrey, J. B. (1988). 'The greatest achievement of the United Nations - forty years on', in *Media Development* 35/4, pp.4–5.

Keane, John. (1992). 'The Crisis of the sovereign state', in Raboy, Marc and Bernard Dagenais, ed. *Media, Crisis and Democracy: mass communication and the disruption of social order*. London: Sage.

MacBride Report (1980). *Many Voices, One World: Communication and society today and tomorrow*. London: Kogan Page.

Marks, S. P. (1981). 'Emerging human rights: a new generation for the 1990s?' *Rutgers Law Review* 33/2, pp.435–452.

Morris, Charles (1975). 'Sprechen und menschliches Handeln', in Gadamer, H-G. and Vogler, S. P., eds. *Neue Antropologie*. Stuttgart.

Roach, Colleen (1988). 'US arguments on the right to communicate and people's right', in *Media Development* 35/4, pp.18–21.

Servaes, Jan (1988). 'The Right to communicate is a basic human right', in *Media Development* 35/4, pp.15–17.

Splichal, Slavko (1991). 'Are the state and civil society merging?', in *Media Development* 38/3, pp.3–5.

Tehranian, Majid (1990). *Technologies of power: information machines and democratic prospects*. Norwood NJ: Ablex.

Traber, Michael (1992). 'Changes in communication needs and rights in social revolutions', in Splichal, Slavko and Wasko, Janet, eds. *Communication and democracy*. New Jersey: Ablex.

Watzlawick, P., Beavan, J.H. and Jackson, D. D. (1967). *Menschliche Kommunikation: Formen, Stoerungen, Paradoxien*. Berne.

XII

Beyond Patriotism: Escaping the Ideological Prison

MICHAEL TRABER

K nowledge is more than information. It includes understanding and interpreting information as the basis for decisions that directly affect people's welfare. True knowledge demands access to information about issues that impact on people's lives and their ability to contribute to policymaking. Understanding the context in which knowledge moves – especially that of public communication – is vital to processes of social development, so that anything that diminishes genuine public communication must be challenged.

Patriotism permeates almost every aspect of the culture of public communication bequeathed by the 20th century. There is probably no other principle that defines mass media output and media reception as clearly as the feeling of loyalty towards one's country, which we call patriotism. I say 'probably' because we lack empirical data about this relationship. Patriotism and the related concept of nationalism have hardly figured as variables in the assessment of news and media content.[1]

What A. D. Smith said about nationalism is doubly true of patriotism:

> One can only be amazed at the comparative lack of sociological
> interest and research in this field. Sociologists from Comte and Marx
> to Parson and Dahrendorf have neglected nationalism and even today
> it has not become a major locus of sociological interest (Smith,
> 1983: 2).

It is usually in wars, often caused by nationalist hubris, and in the reporting of wars, that the phenomena of nationalism and patriotism come to the attention of communication researchers. It is as though they were then picking up the pieces of these tragedies while soon forgetting about the roles which patriotism continues to play in the life of nation-states.

What follows first addresses the concept of a culture of public communication. The second part examines the relationship between the mass media and the state. Thirdly, it shows how the ideology of patriotism imprisons public communication.

The media have created their own culture

The mass media as we know them are not some curious gift from heaven. They are what they are by virtue of specific historical processes that have been guided by specific political and economic interests. The values they enshrine and the myths they project are purposeful and part of a media culture. One such myth is the media's acclaimed objectivity. News objectivity, according to Dan Schiller, is 'a cultural form with its own set of conventions' (Schiller, 1981: 5), the purpose of which is 'the cultural configuration that permits readers to indulge in their belief' (ibid.: 6).

Johan Galtung coined the term 'social cosmology' (1986: 7), in which news and other media content are embedded. A cosmology is a doctrine and a map of the universe that tries to simplify the bewildering world we live in. A social cosmology is trying to do the same for the relationships we establish with peoples, nations and cultures on a global scale. Most importantly, the social cosmology of the mass media has a 'centre' and a 'periphery'. It thus divides the world into spaces.

North America and Europe are the world's centre, which contains the elite countries of the world, most notably the USA and a number of European countries like Britain, France, Germany and Russia. The periphery consists of places where very little happens, and when something is happening, it is usually negative. Lots of things go wrong in the centre as well, but these negative reports become part of many others which speak of positive achievements and developments. The social cosmology that guides our culture of public communication also has an ideological dimension. It used to be clear-cut: communism versus capitalism. This was more than a conflict between East and West; its scope was global; the conflict was exported to the South. It is worth recalling at least one example from that time, lest we forget.

The British newspaper *The Sunday Times* (13 May 1984) carried an exclusive report on its front page headlined 'Starving Babies' Food sold for Soviet Arms'. Below the headline was a large photograph of a naked, crying, starving baby. The reporter, Simon Winchester, wrote:

> There is mounting evidence that food sent from the West to drought-stricken northern Ethiopia is being diverted by the Ethiopian military regime to its army - and also - to an increasing extent, to the Soviet Union to help meet the regime's huge arms bill.

Winchester's sources were an anonymous Ethiopian official who had fled to Britain and a number of English public figures whose criticism of the Ethiopian government of that time was well known. The report referred to an 'emergency hearing' in the European Parliament, 'at which testimony of those who are convinced that aid is being diverted will be presented'. Yet no such hearing was planned for that time. And when Ethiopia was indeed discussed later on, an EC commissioner explicitly criticised the *Sunday Times* report.

No word about this appeared in the newspaper. The damage had been done. It was a successful attempt to fabricate a story which precisely fitted into the political cosmology and which, therefore, appeared credible: Soviet arms for Ethiopia, paid for by Western food aid, destined for babies. The story should remind us of the lies and deceptions which occurred almost daily in the media of East and West, and beyond, as a result of an ideology which had become part of the culture of public communication. It's a heritage that we have not completely expurgated. If evidence for that is needed, recall the reporting of the war in the Persian Gulf (c.f. *Media Development*, 1991).

Since the implosion of the system of state-controlled socialism in East and Central Europe and the disappearance of the Cold War, our culture of public communication is gradually changing, and this in two directions. The dominant ideology is now 'the free market economy', which basically means freedom for individual enterprise, and more freedom for financial speculators and transnational corporations.

The second direction is a new division of the world between the good and the bad, friends and enemies. Parts of the Arab world bear the brunt of this. Their leaders are demonised, regardless of what they are doing. But enemies are also created as a result of economic competition and rivalry. Japan's markets must open to US imports, though Japan adheres to the agreements of the World Trade Organisation. Reporting on Japan and its economy by US media is now fraught with problems. Among the many influences and constraints that affect our media culture, none is more penetrating and elusive than patriotism. But before this can be assessed properly the multiple linkages between mass media and the State need to be evaluated.

Mass media and the State

One of the great media myths of our time is the notion of the mass media as the 'fourth estate' viz. the 'watchdog' of government. 'The romantic image of the "adversary press" ... is a myth: "functional" for certain purposes, but wholly inaccurate as a model of what newsmen actually do or can hope to achieve' (Paul H. Weaver, quoted in Dennis and Merrill, 1991: 22). Governments are the media's most important social actors, and speak through the media as a matter of course. The assumption that the media are a guarantee against government secrecy and abuse of power, and thus assure freedom of information in the service of responsible government, is misplaced.

Timothy E. Cook goes so far as to say that the American news media are in effect governmental institutions. State and media exist in a symbiotic relationship within which the State provides information and the media decide whether or not to print or broadcast it. As Cook puts it, 'The American news media need government officials to help them accomplish their job, and American politicians are now apparently finding the media more central to getting done what they want to get done' (Cook, 1991: 18).

Frequently the media operate not only as a way of informing the public, but as a method of sharing information within the elite groups (see also Downing, 1986: 157–158). The government, in fact, relies on the media as a way of communicating within itself and with the elite establishment. The government also uses the media as part of its strategy to put its policies into effect. As Cook notes, the government can use the media to criticise another country over its policies and actions, or to place an issue on the agenda, usually an issue on which it is likely to perform better than any existing opposition groups and parties.

The media, on the other hand, rely on the government as a 'credible' source of information:

...journalists end up judging the utility of information at least as much by who says it than what it says. An 'authoritative source' is an individual given a leading role in the narrative of that newsbeat. Someone in an official role within the government hierarchy tends to

endow information with the credibility of his or her position within
the hierarchy and/or with his or her involvement in the decision-
making process; that same person outside that position saying the
same thing would be more likely to be seen as providing speculation or
hearsay (Cook, 1991: 16; see also Bennett, 1983).

Given that the media often (though not always) act as a
glorified bulletin board for the State, those outside the State
system, and those without power, are unable to make their
voices heard – unless they become the helpless victims of
disasters. Only those in public life (i.e. the politically or
economically powerful, and the stars of entertainment and
sport) have the right to articulate their views and opinions
(Scannell, 1989: 12).

Slavko Splichal argues that the State is indeed a mechanism
of control over communication and information, but that,
equally, information controls the State:

The power of the State is apparently counter-balanced, or reduced by
the growing complexity of the social systems and their environment:
more and more internal and external information is needed for the
same relative level of control in/over society. In the developed part of
the world, globalisation, which is largely based on informatisation,
reduces (at least relatively) rather than expands the State power. At the
same time the new information sector in society and the restructuring
of the economy add new functions to the State. Thus the apparatus of
government and its power to control expand due to the same process
of informatisation (Splichal, 1991: 4)

Though the State does not exercise total control over
information and media, it relies on them in order to function.
The State and the media interact with each other – but in a
manner that does not allow proper participation by the general
public.

In the last ten or so years, a great distrust of State
involvement in the media has arisen, as is demonstrated in the

crises affecting the concept of public service broadcasting. Garnham argues that the idea of public service broadcasting is in crisis as a result of the loss of faith in the State as a credible actor in social life (Garnham, 1990; see also Rowland and Tracey, 1990).

Ethically speaking, the mass media are not responsible to the State but to the public. They cannot be seen in simple terms of either government mouthpiece or government adversary. They should, instead, be understood as an essential service to the public, ensuring the provision of information and debate that is a precondition of active citizenship or civil society.

The ideology of patriotism imprisons the media

No matter how critically one views the relationship between the media and the nation, or the media and the State, the fact remains that there is a universal human need for belonging. The essentially social nature of the human being needs a family, a community, a people, a nation. Not just belonging to a nation, but being co-responsible for the nation's institutional political arrangements and structures that we call State, is one of the principal dogmas of modernity. 'Everyone has the right to a nationality' says Article 15 of the Universal Declaration of Human Rights (1948) and 'no one shall be arbitrarily deprived of his nationality nor denied the right to change his nationality.'

In his study of the history of nationalism, Ernest Gellner comes to the following conclusion:

> Nationalism – the principle of homogenous cultural units as the foundations of political life, and of the obligatory cultural unity of rules and ruled – is indeed inscribed neither in the nature of things, nor in the hearts of men, nor in the pre-condition of social life in general, and the contention that it is so inscribed is a falsehood which nationalist doctrine has succeeded in presenting as self-evident. But nationalism as a phenomenon, not as a doctrine presented by nationalists, is inherent in a certain set of social conditions; and those conditions, it

so happens, are the conditions of our time. To deny this is at least as great a mistake as to accept nationalism on its own terms (Gellner, 1983: 125).

What are those terms? The 'principal fiction' of modern nationalism is, according to Horsman and Marshall (1994: 45), that the nation-state presupposes 'ethnic, racial, linguistic and cultural homogeneity... The borders always give the lie to this construct.' If soil and blood express the darker side of nationalism, so does the demand for absolute loyalty towards the State, or the claim that any other social identity has to be submerged into the ultimately defining identity with the nation state. These claims, alas, have become part of the notion of patriotism.[2]

How patriotism affects public communication can best be demonstrated by an example. In 1975, David Astor, at that time editor of the British Sunday paper the *Observer*, wrote an article with the title 'The Unutterable'. He described the attitude of the American news media towards the war in Vietnam at the height of the conflict. It was considered their patriotic duty to provide legitimisation for that war. Astor wrote:

> What nobody of any consequence can be found to have said publicly in America throughout all this time was that the situation was entirely hopeless, that no compromise solution was likely to survive for more than months, and that the collapse of the whole South Vietnam society into the hands of the Communists... must be accepted as inevitable. The opponents of America's catastrophic war were unable publicly to admit, while the war was still on, that all the American lives had been lost for nothing. With no Congressman or journalist willing to tell the American public this truth... it is not altogether surprising that Presidents and Secretaries of State hoped against hope that some less terrible ending would be found. Successive administrations failed to reach the right conclusion partly because there was no public awareness of the totality of the catastrophe to make it easier to utter the almost unutterable (*Observer*, 27 April 1975).

Silence can be a way of deceit, a method of falsifying reality, a refusal of what Vaclav Havel (1987) calls 'living in truth'. If this is what patriotism requires of media workers, then patriotism is a major ethical problem for public communication.

In the case of another, more recent conflict, the US invasion of the Caribbean island of Grenada, Marlene Cuthbert reported that the press in each of six countries took an editorial stand which accurately reflected the attitude of their respective governments. As a result, press coverage of the invasion differed in Canada and European countries from US press coverage. Coverage in Caribbean countries depended more or less on whether a country had committed troops to the US-led invasion force. Cuthbert concluded:

> In covering the crisis in Grenada, the media of each nation or region reacted from the perspective of the perceived interests of their own national system. The journalists of each media house had to find words to report the complexity of external reality. Despite the very different pictures painted in the various regions, although there were undoubtedly individual exceptions, it seems unlikely that the journalists were deliberately distorting or slanting news. But, however committed they are to truth, the journalists' very selection of facts, and choice and organisation of words, necessarily involved interpretation, and interpretation introduced different perspectives which grew out of their ideological differences (Cuthbert, 1985: 33)

The Grenada invasion marks an interesting point in war reporting. For the first time in modern history the military took complete command of the news. This led to protests by the American media. They condemned the military's news management but, in general, justified the war. The *New York Times* (4 November 1983) said: 'Grenada was one invasion we can justify... It was the culmination of a three-year policy of confrontation that helped undermine the stability and civility of the (Grenada) government whose people we now rescue.'

When journalists actively endorse the patriotic line, they sometimes do so in defiance of public feeling. Dave Hill has observed how the Western press backed Allied action in the Persian Gulf with the claim that its 'patriotism' reflects that of the public – despite evidence of a more confused and diverse range of public opinion than the media acknowledge (Hill, 1991). The patriotic line of journalism also prevents journalists from presenting both sides of the story, and attempts to give the 'enemy's' point of view are often met with the charge of recycling enemy propaganda.

Another feature connected with the patriotic imperative is the stereotyping of the 'other', and, in cases of conflicts, the stereotyping of the enemy or, to say the least, the legitimisation and reinforcement of existing stereotypes. This became particularly evident during the war in the Persian Gulf. Circumstances led themselves to such stereotyping, because the less we know about other cultures, races and faiths, the easier it is to project the image we wish or find opportune to use.

Stereotyping during the war in the Persian Gulf, and ever since, focused on one man. Saddam Hussein became the incarnation of all evil and anything could, therefore, be said about him without any substantial proof. His vilification also implied his 'otherness', as Arab and Muslim. Stereotyping the enemy in the Gulf War extended to other Arab countries and their leaders when they did not side with the American alliance. The US media denounced them as virtual enemies. This was particularly the case with Jordan and the Palestinian leadership. If such stereotyping is deemed expedient or even necessary to uphold patriotism, then there is something basically wrong with this ideology.

The most amazing aspect about nationalism and patriotism is, however, not the deceptions, lies and stereotypes of the 'other' which are associated with them. What is truly astounding is the fact that most people are not even conscious of how patriotism manipulates the media. This is what I mean by the prison culture of public communication. By way of conclusion I would like to illustrate this with a parable.

Conclusion

Try to imagine yourself as an inmate in a prison. In fact you have been in prison all your life. You were born there and grew up there. You live there with many other prisoners. But neither they nor you really know why you are there. You catch glimpses of the outside world, and you wonder what it is like out there. But the fact that you really don't know does not worry you excessively. Because you consider the state of being a prisoner as normal, the prison is your natural habitat.

As prisoners, you don't have newspapers or radio and television sets. But there is an intercom system in your prison. The governor tells you everything that's going on outside. He should know; he is well informed. Occasionally new prisoners join you, usually for a short time. They tell you the strangest tales of what is happening outside, stories which confuse you. You are glad when they leave. Then you appreciate all the more the reassuring voice of the prison governor over the intercom.

This worldview from prison is a metaphor of our news culture. We see and hear very little of what is really going on in the world, and what we see and hear are unconnected fragments of an often distorted reality. Again, the real tragedy of this situation is that we consider it normal, that, like life prisoners, we trust the media's intercom system.

The prison is also a metaphor of the motherland, fatherland, *la patrie*, which claims our loyalty, whose 'national interest', always defined by the State rather than the people, should guide us in our actions as journalists and even as media researchers. We normally take this for granted. It is the world we live in.

Fortunately there are people and groups who from time to time are determined to break out of this prison; they start digging tunnels so that they can escape. And when they see the real world, they want to tell the real stories of all God's people, unfettered by the codes and norms of nationalism and its ideological underpinning: patriotism.

First published in *Javnost*, Vol. 2 No. 2 (1995).

Notes

1. A noteworthy exception is the issue of *Media, Culture and Society* (Vol. 9 No. 2/April 1987) devoted to the theme of nationalism. Also see *Media Development* on 'Communication and the State' (Vol. 38, 3/1991) and 'Ethno-religious conflict and the media' (Vol. 39, 3/1992).

2. An extreme manifestation of State power at times of socio-political unrest is the 'national security state', a term coined in Latin America in the 1970s. See Jose Comblin (1979), *The Church and the National Security State*, Maryknoll, NY: Orbis.

References

Bennett, W. Lance (1983). *News: the politics of illusion*. New York; Longman.

Cook, Timothy (1991). Are the American news media governmental?: re-examining the 'fourth branch' thesis. Paper delivered at the annual meeting of the International Communication Association, Chicago May 23–27.

Cuthbert, Marlene (1985). *Journalistic perspectives on the Grenada crisis: media coverage in the Caribbean, Canada, the United States and Europe*. Press Association of Jamaica.

Dennis, Everette E. and John C. Merrill (1991). *Media debates: issues in mass communication*. New York: Longman.

Downing, John (1986). 'Government secrecy and the media in the United States and Britain', in Golding, Peter, Graham Murdock and Philip Schlesinger. *Communicating politics: mass communications and the political process*. Leicester: University Press.

Galtung, Johan (1986). 'Social communication and global problems', in P. Lee, ed. *Communication for all*. Maryknoll, NY: Orbis.

Garnham, Nicholas (1990). *Capitalism and communication: global culture and the economics of information*. London: Sage.

Gellner, Ernest (1983). *Nations and nationalism*. Oxford: Blackwell.

Havel, Vaclav (1987). *Living in truth*. London: Faber.

Hill, Dave (1991). Word wars. *Marxism Today*, April, 44–45.

Horsman, Matthew and Andrew Marshall (1994). *After the nation-state: citizens, tribalism and the new world disorder*. London: Harper Collins.

Reporting the Gulf War. Media Development 1991: October special issue.

Rowland, Willard D. and Michael Tracey (1990). Worldwide challenges to public service broadcasting. *Journal of Communication* 40: 2, 8–27.

Scannell, Paddy (1989). Public service broadcasting and modern public life. *Media, Culture and Society* 11: 2, 135-166.

Schiller, Dan (1981). *Objectivity and the news: the public and the rise of commercial journalism.* Philadelphia: University of Pennsylvania Press.

Smith, A. D. (1983). *Theories of nationalism.* London: Duckworth.

Splichal, Slavko (1991). 'Are the State and civil society merging?' in *Media Development* 38: 3, 3–5.

XIII

Towards the Democratisation of Public Communication: The Need to Reconsider the Criteria for News

MICHAEL TRABER

The following reflections fall into the broad category of public philosophy of communication, or communication ethics. All philosophy and all ethics analyse phenomena, or reality, from the perspective of certain principles. The normative framework from which I proceed is the humanistic concept of the ultimate value and dignity of the human being, and therefore of the essential equality of all persons – not just before the law, but more fundamentally in their right to participate in the public realm.

The notions of human dignity, and of equality between people, do not contradict the roles, ranks and status, both ascribed and achieved, which regulate relationships in our communities and societies, and consequentially the patterns of behaviour, such as respect and social sanctions. The concept of equality in a structured community or society can, perhaps, best be explained by the attitude demanded in African societies towards two age groups, the young and the old. Both these groups may be said to be dependent, often physically, and vulnerable. They therefore demand special attention, care, and, above all, respect. But it is not just your child or our child but any child which deserves protection. Likewise, any old woman or man is worthy of special recognition, reverence and respect.

Respect for human dignity and the principle of equality – regardless of sex, education, ethnicity, wealth, status, etc. – are the foundations of democracy. Democracy is a political and social principle which extends to many spheres of life, but particularly to public communication. Communication is at the heart of the process of democratisation, and to do this it must be democratised.

What do we mean by democratisation of communication? In the words of the MacBride Report (1980: 166):

> Democratization (of communication) is the process whereby: (a) the individual becomes an active partner and not a mere object of communication; (b) the variety of messages exchanged increases; and (c) the extent and quality of social representation or participation in communication are augmented.

From the perspective of a public philosophy of communication, it is one of the roles of the media to be a catalyst in the democratic process of society. This presupposes the awareness that democracy in any society is never fully achieved. As an ideal it is never fully reached. It is therefore always a struggle. The Latin American experts' meeting in Embu, Brazil, in 1982 went a step further by saying:

> Democracy is above all a fundamental human attitude, expressed in communication by abolishing authoritarian forms and relying on the conscious, organised and collective action of the oppressed. Pluralistic participation of social sectors should manifest itself in the different levels of communication process, particularly in the production, distribution, and consumption of cultural goods (Uranga, 1985: 16).

There would be a great deal to say about the 'conscious, organised and collective' communication actions of the oppressed, or peasants and workers, or women, which have emerged in many countries of the South. My contention now is that the mass media in general are, by and large, autocratic rather than democratic. They are primarily concerned with the interests of the elite rather than with the aspirations of those whom we disparagingly call 'ordinary people', or, in the terminology of the left, 'the masses', who have no face, no name, and presumably no will of their own.

To rectify this, a new approach to journalism is needed; in fact, a change in the professional culture of journalists and broadcasters; and this has often been overlooked in the discussion on the democratisation of public communication.

The conventional criteria of news – an obstacle of democratisation

The mass media are characterised by a set of conventional 'rules' which are applied to the selection and treatment of news in a fairly uniform way. These criteria for news have been made most explicit in North American and British journalism and are part of the pattern of most news agencies. They have also been adopted by the mass media in most countries of the South. The adherence to these conventional rules of the news media is part of the acceptance of a professional journalistic culture; but it also reflects the society in which we live and the role the news media have to maintain the dominance of the dominant sectors of society.

Here then is a critique of the conventional criteria for news – from the perspective of the 'ordinary people'.

The very concept of news is tied up with that of *timeliness*: how recently has something happened? Timeliness signifies an 'event' that has taken place yesterday, or last week, or, as we sometimes write, 'recently'. 'Recently' serves us well when we report on an accident that happened some time ago in a remote rural area. But we tend to be lost when the reality we wish to describe is not an 'event' but a status quo, or, in the words of Johan Galtung, a 'permanent'. The difficulty or inability to determine the time frame of a process, or trend, or status quo, or 'permanent', makes us reject a great deal of news.

Witness the drought situation in some African countries years ago: for months it did not qualify as news, until some TV cameramen stumbled across some hunger victims and shot their pictures. Or what happens in factories, ports, railways, etc.? Unless a politician visits them and makes a speech, or unless an accident occurs, they go largely unreported. It is partly because of the rule of 'timeliness' as a criteria for news that rural reporting and people-centred industrial reporting are so difficult and take third or fifth place in the selection of news.

Another anti-democratic journalistic rule is *prominence.* How important is a person? Following this criterion of news, the mass media make people with power also socially prominent. Power, of course, is measured not only in terms of political responsibility, but also in terms of money and material possessions, in terms of the power play that goes on in politics and the economy. Add to this the prominence awarded by the mass media to the 'glamorous', the beauty queens and kings, and the heroes of our entertainment industry, and of sports, and the picture that emerges is that very few men or women truly qualify as the VIPs of the media, namely those who are either politically powerful or economically rich, or both, and those who have the looks or muscle power or a soft singing voice.

The criterion of prominence does not only apply to people, but also to countries and towns. For a long time, Britain has been one of the elite countries that figured prominently in the press of Anglophone Africa, just as France continues to be the elite country for most of the media in Francophone Africa. But the elite country *par excellence* is now the United States of America, which tends to take precedence over the countries of Europe. And there are, of course, the elite towns within our own countries, almost always the major cities. An editor seeing the word KweKwe, Zimbabwe, as dateline will scrutinise the item with special care. It is not a place on the journalistic map. However, there is a problem with some elite persons residing in our elite towns. Are they, as our elected representatives or as ministers of government, not prominent in a way that the media have a duty to cover their travel and their speeches? Of course, they are. In the South, in particular, some political leaders stand for the unity of the nation, the sovereignty of its destiny, and the integrity of leadership. The more they embody these values, the more important they are for the lives of ordinary people. Every nation needs leaders who can inspire people, and when the force of inspiration wanes or even disappears, there is a crisis of confidence and national and social identity.

But even in the best of circumstances, the prominence of the prominent should not go at the expense of the ordinary men, women and children. The powerless are not just individuals but groups of peasants, organisations of workers, associations of women, young men and women, taking initiatives to build their nation as well as their lives.

In continuing the critique of the criteria for news, I shall deal with only two more, namely, 'conflict' and the 'unusual'.

Conflict. We have become so obsessed by this news value that we capitalise on any event that contains even the slightest element of it. A certain phrase of a politician can somehow be interpreted as aimed at his political rivals, and what started as an innocent statement now becomes the opening salvo of an alleged power struggle between politicians. Are we aware of the warlike language we use in political reporting, to keep up the element of conflict, and this not only during election time? 'Minister throws back challenge'; 'Government to fight to the last drop' (meaning it will reorient its economy) – these are typical conflict headlines. Worse than that, if there are no real conflicts to report on, they are created artificially as a form of media entertainment. Sports reporting uses a war-like language.

'Giants are ready to be slain' is the headline of a cricket report (*The Independent*, 22 May 1995).

In short, there is very little space or time in our mass media that can be devoted to problems and issues and achievements which cannot easily be framed in terms of conflict. This is another reason why the lives of ordinary men, women and children are to a large extent excluded from the mass media.

The unusual. The old and utterly ridiculous story of 'man bites dog' is still traded as an example of journalistic criteria. How odd, extraordinary and bizarre must an event appear to qualify as news? It's in this category of news, however, in which ordinary people are covered by the media. If they do something particularly unusual or bizarre, like standing on their heads for four hours, or drinking twenty bottles of beer, they suddenly become news makers. If they figure otherwise in our paper or on the air, then it's usually as victims of accidents and catastrophes.

The traditional criteria for news are only one side of the problem. The other is the media's definition of an 'event', which is equally problematic, and undemocratic.

What is a news event?

When people do something significant, or if something important is happening to them, and when what they are doing or what is happening is of interest to readers or listeners, it is a news event. This is the standard description of 'event' in most textbooks of journalism. Let's examine this definition.

Firstly, we notice that the operative words 'significant', 'important' and 'of interest to readers' are already predetermined by the criteria for news, some of which have just been outlined. 'Important event' really means important person. 'Readers' interest' is to a large extent covered by the criteria of conflict and the bizarre. In practice, therefore, events mean the speeches of the prominent, the controversies of the politicians, and the rituals of public life (like cutting ribbons, opening or closing meetings, etc.).

Secondly, the more 'complete' an event is, the more likely the news media will pick it up. The classical example of a complete event is the speech. Maybe this is the reason why speech reporting is so popular in the mass media. When the speaker says 'Thank you, ladies and gentlemen' and the audience applauds, the event is over and done with. In fact it is very rare that anything really happens during or after a speech. It is usually a public ritual that is complete in itself – no follow-up needed.

Another example of a preferred event is the accident. Two men killed at a construction site – when, where and how – and the event is complete. The significant question 'why?' is sometimes asked. But the follow-up of whether or not safety procedures at the site had improved is rarely done. This type of social construction of news events is particularly prevalent on radio and television. Newspapers are more accustomed to follow-up stories and interpretation of events. Once again, the status quo or the 'permanent' almost totally eludes our definition of news event.

A third aspect of the conventional news event is its need for legitimisation. Some years ago *The New York Times* and *The Washington Post* were scrutinised with regard to their news sources. The assumption was that these two prestige papers were likely to have a more independent stance on the news than most other American papers. The analysis shows that close to half of the two papers' news content was attributed to US government officials, and another 27 percent to 'foreign officials'. Less than 17 percent came from non-government sources, and only one percent of all news stories was based on the reporters' own observation and analysis. The media's need for attribution is so great that an event becomes a news event if and when it can be attributed to a high source. This has led one researcher to construct a theory of news which he calls the 'politics of illusion' (Lance Bennett, 1983).

A fourth characteristic of 'event' lies in its repetition. News is very repetitive. The reason is that the type of things which qualify as events are already predetermined, the agenda of news is set, it's all in the news diary. New issues hardly emerge from the reality of people's lives. American researchers have pointed out that most of the problems concerning the environment, particularly the pollution of water, still do not figure on the public agenda of the American media and are therefore largely unreported.

One reason for this is what can be called the corporate journalistic culture. In spite of all the assurances of being servants of the public, most journalists don't really write for the public but what the media expect them to write about. In that you don't want to be an outsider, in spite of the high value attributed to 'scoops'. The media of information are, in many ways, one body, with few dissenting voices.

In the early months of 1980 I happened to be a part-time reporter on the Zimbabwe elections for a European radio network. One day I got a phone call from the editor, telling me that my services had been terminated. I asked why. He told me that what I was saying was entirely different from what the other media reported. I had apparently been grossly out of tune with the rest of redundant messages from Harare, hardly any of which predicted (as I had done) that Robert Mugabe would win by a large margin.

In conclusion, media events, being largely ceremonial, are also repetitive, if not entirely predictable. The result of all this is that the media inevitably create some kind of surface to the social reality we live in, which has very little to do with the real world of ordinary people. To capture that world, we need to develop alternative criteria of news and redefine the meaning of 'event'.

Alternative criteria of news

There are some newspapers, many magazines and some radio and television stations which welcome reports on the problems and issues of ordinary people. Some media managers even wish to have more reports and in-depth stories from rural areas. Such stories are increasingly acceptable to the established media, provided they are written in the conventional forms (genres) of journalism, i.e. mainly in the forms of news and feature articles. Some papers have introduced new types of features for precisely this purpose, like 'Letter from..', 'Village Voice', 'Life in the day of..', etc. In effect, the rules of journalism are changing. Alternative stories now co-exist in the media with conventional news stories.

But we need to go a step further. Alternative criteria of news should be established, and practised, and taught; and they are to a large extent a reversal of the news values of conventional journalism. What is needed, first and foremost, are *alternative social actors*, or the redefinition of the criterion of prominence. Social actors are those persons or groups of persons who, almost as a matter of right, are covered by the media and can speak through them. If the media make a conscious effort to report on, and, in fact, give preferential treatment to, the manual labourers, and their agricultural and industrial organisations, to the women and their groups, to youth and children and to the forgotten minorities, these persons and groups do in fact become social actors who can speak to the public at large and thus get a place in the public sphere. This may be at the expense of the established social actors, or at least some of them. But it's a price worth paying.

The second rule that needs to be changed is the *framework of time*, and thus the definition of the *event*. Journalists should not only deal with what happened yesterday or last week, but with what is a status quo or a development, none of which can be meaningfully measured in daily or weekly intervals. Thus most of the reports on alternative social actors can be carried by the media this week or next, or even the week after.

The third requirement is *alternative language*. Much of the journalist's training is devoted to story construction, which was developed by Anglo-American journalism and news agencies reporters. It is often referred to as the 'inverted pyramid' method. There is much value in this, particularly for providing a quick summary of the news. But it also has its limitations. It is almost useless for rural reporting. The story form seldom fits alternative social actors. A new type of narrative must therefore be developed. It is much more demanding of the journalist than our usual language of news. The wave of what some 15 years ago was called 'new journalism' soon discovered that only the best writers can do such observation and participation features. But where 'new journalism' failed, a new type of storytelling might succeed: stories from the bottom up can only be told in feature form.

A fourth criterion for democratic journalism is *empathy*, or *affinity*, which to some extent replaces the news value of 'conflict'. The journalist's empathy for, and affinity with, people and their daily lives and aspirations are at the core of alternative journalism. This, however, requires patient listening rather than quick interviewing. It has sometimes been described as 'barefoot journalism'.

When I said that empathy and affinity would to some extent replace the criterion of conflict, I did not mean that conflicts should be eliminated. What needs to be changed is conflict for conflict's sake, or for the sake of sensationalism. Naturally, the ordinary people live in situations of conflict. Their struggles should figure foremost in reporting. But they struggle to have their conflicts resolved, rather than be treated as some sort of political entertainment.

Some 15 years ago I could not have written this piece on democratisation of public communication or alternative journalism. Now I know that they can be done, and can be taught. But it is demanding. It requires, above all, a commitment. It also requires higher skills than conventional journalism, and finally presupposes the evolution of new genres and new formats of journalistic writing and broadcasting.

This approach to news is part of the new information and communication order, which the non-aligned nations of the South have long demanded. We all know that the NWICO, as proclaimed in 1980, will not be implemented for a long time on the international level. But if it were implemented on national or local levels, newspapers and news services and news broadcasts would look and sound very different from what they are today.

Yet the concept of a new order is not enough. Nor is the vision of the media as the champions of the people sufficient. What is needed, in addition, is a new type of journalism, a new professional culture and, above all, an ever new commitment to the ideas and ideals of genuine democracy.

References

Lance Bennett, W. (1983). *News, the politics of illusion*. New York: Longman.

MacBride Report (1980). *Many Voices, One World: Towards a new, more just and more efficient world information and communication order*. Paris: UNESCO.

Uranga, Washington (1985). No.26 of the Embu final document, in P. Lee, ed., *Communication for All*. New York: Orbis.

XIV

Communication Transforming Conflict

MICHAEL TRABER

A sea change is taking place, albeit gradually and quietly. As we move into the 21st century, more and more people, almost everywhere in the world, are no longer prepared to accept the violence which has dominated life and indeed world events in the 20th century. More than 130 million people have lost their lives in wars alone in the past 100 years.

Instead, people the world over are longing and working for ways in which, as a matter of principle, conflicts can be settled by peaceful means. The fashioning of such a culture of peace is the most urgent and most fundamental task before humankind at the dawn of a new millennium.

This task involves, above all, the exploration of the conditions for, and nature of conflicts. Admittedly there maybe wanton use of violence, apparently without rhyme or reason. But in general the main cause of violence lies in the urge or need to solve a conflict. The question arises whether it is possible that those engaged in acts of violence do not see, or do not wish to see, any other way of solving conflicts than by physical contestation. The tragedy is that our culture and civilisation is ready and willing not only to tolerate violence for conflict resolution but even to legitimise it.

Peace and peaceful means, therefore, are not just pious and elusive words. They are the new centres of gravity in a changing culture that tries to tackle life and life's problems in ways different from what we have been used to in the past.

Solving problems by peaceful means is tantamount to employing all means and modes of communication. Whether we call them negotiation or reconciliation or family counselling or group therapy – communication is always at the heart of these processes. There is literally only one way of overcoming violence: communication. The new culture of peace is therefore a culture of communication.

In this introductory article about the change in people's attitudes to violence and conflicts, we shall first describe the broader meaning of living with conflicts. This will be followed by an analysis of structural and cultural violence as the ground that nurtures open violence. Thirdly we shall show how communication can break the circle of violence. This principle is qualified in the final section: communication is more than 'mere words'; communication for conflict resolution includes apology and forgiveness.

Let's live like humans

This is the title of a book by Felicia Langer (1999) on the Israeli-Palestinian conflict. Its author is a Jewish lawyer who for decades defended Palestinians in Israeli courts. In 1990 she gave up her legal practice in Israel and emigrated to Germany to devote the rest of her life to peace education. 'Let's live like humans' is an apt phrase to describe the current task.

Human beings make big assumptions about each other in order to 'live like humans', that is, with dignity and in safety. The biggest assumption of all is that we expect to be safe and comfortable in the company of other human beings, even in the company of strangers. This seems to be the universal human principle. Humans do not injure, let alone kill each other, to settle their problems and rivalries. They have other means of dealing with conflicts.

Underlying this principle is the deep conviction that all life is sacred and thus worthy of respect. Cultures may differ in their application of this principle. Some, like Buddhist culture, will firmly extend it to all sentient life. Others, like western cultures, tend to limit it to human life.

All cultures, however, seem to have special provisions for the security and well being of the most vulnerable groups of society, especially the very young and the very old, who are physically defenceless and therefore most at risk. Thus they need special care and protection.

Another indication of the 'unnaturalness' of violence is the pain and embarrassment it gives to onlookers of violent actions. They are apt to close their eyes. They are tempted to flee. They feel helpless and frustrated because they cannot stop violence, except by counter violence. To solve this dilemma, humans have created institutions whose task it is to stop violence and punish its perpetrators. The government and its forces of law and order are responsible for these tasks. They hold a monopoly of force for this very purpose. This primary responsibility is to keep our country and our streets safe from violent attacks. It is an arrangement that allows us to 'live like humans'.

Conflicts are part of life

Living like humans does not mean having no conflicts but solving them in non-violent ways. Conflicts are natural. They are about life. Total non-conflict is equivalent to death. Johan Galtung sees conflicts as potentially life enhancing, as a force that should lead to the acceptance of the other or others. 'The conflict energy' can lead to 'generally loving, compassionate, accepting attitudes and positive cognitions of Others and of Self' (Galtung, 1996: 72).

When conflicts are not acknowledged for what they are and not articulated in dialogue, they cannot be overcome. Conflicts may then grow and multiply, crises may deepen, and life becomes messy and unmanageable. One of Galtung's (1996) important insights is that in many cases conflicts cannot really be 'solved' – in the sense that they disappear for good. The art of living is to live with conflicts. Instead of simply trying to 'solve' them, conflicts have to be *transformed* into new opportunities and into fresh starts. Conflicts in this sense are problems that defy solutions; they are indeed part of life.

Another danger is to minimise the complexity of conflicts. Real-life conflicts are usually rather complicated. In the heat of tensions, that complexity may easily be reduced to simple polarizations, 'leading to the nakedness of elementary conflicts, (and to) the cruel choice between this or that, we or they' (Galtung, 1996: 77). Thus conflicts can only be transformed if they are perceived in their full complexity. For the sake of understanding as well as transformation, conflicts may be analysed by splitting up actors in to sub-actors, and goals into sub-goals, and by bringing in other actors and goals. The conflict's complexity may in fact make its transformation more manageable as it discourages cheap polarizations.

Structural and cultural violence

Conflicts are human, violence is not. But the absence of violence does not equal peace. Peace, according to Galtung (1996: 9) 'is the context for conflict to unfold non-violently and creatively.' Peace is the creative power which transforms conflicts. Peacefulness, therefore, is not just an individual virtue. Peace is a social and cultural condition. It is the opposite of structural and cultural violence which often leads to open and direct violence.

Patriarchy may be a good example for what is meant by structural and cultural violence. Patriarchy is the:

> institutionalisation of male dominance in vertical structures with very high correlations between position and gender, legitimised by the culture (e.g. in religion and language), and often emerging as direct violence with males as subjects and females as objects. Patriarchy...

combines structural and cultural violence with direct violence in a vicious triangle. They reinforce each other in cycles starting from any corner. Direct violence such as rape, intimidates and represses; structural violence institutionalises; and cultural violence internalises that relationship (Galtung, 1996: 40).

The predominance of direct violence by males can only be explained by the prevailing structures and cultures of violence. It has been estimated that about 95 percent of acts of direct violence are committed by men. And the violence crime ratio between men and women is 25:1 (Galtung,1996: 41).

Structural violence always contains processes of repression and exploitation. It's about the 'relationship' between top-dog and under-dog, or the 'partnership' between horse and rider. These processes of repression and exploitation will take place within social and political structures, which make them look normal in the 'social' system. Structural violence is thus invisible. When it manifests itself in acts of direct violence, responsibility is allocated to violent individuals rather than violent structures and cultures. Violence is thus a demonstration of power. 'Its principal lesson is to show quickly and dramatically who can get away with what and against whom... It shows one's place in the societal "pecking order" ' (Gerbner, 1996: 15).

Cultural violence refers to those aspects of culture – like religion and ideology, or language and art – which can be used to justify and legitimise violence, both structural and direct violence. Cultural violence is like the topsoil from which the other two types of violence take their nutrients. Without it, neither structural nor direct violence would be allowed to continue to exist. Culture teaches and preaches that exploitation and repression are 'normal', and dulls our senses to seeing them otherwise. Societal structures based on caste, race and gender are the concrete socio-political manifestations of cultures of violence. They accommodate and tolerate acts of violence against those considered 'beneath' them.

When words replace fists

No conflict can be settled through violent means. Non-violence is the only way forward. Conflicts can only be solved by talking. Communications are the main means and strategies in the transformation of conflicts – any conflict, be it marital, familial, communal, territorial or whatever:

> In non-violence there is the assumption that what enhances me will also enhance you. Non-violence is a form of soft power, and a form of communication, with a sender and a receiver . . ...communication is predicated on the assumption of a deep communality among human beings; that Other is touched by the suffering of Self and wants to remove himself as the cause of that suffering, for instance (Galtung, 1996: 122).

Violence must be seen as the ultimate failure of acts of communication. When people in situations of conflict stop talking, they start fighting. Or when conflicts arise between groups of people and these groups are deprived of opportunities for discourse, as often the case in communal tensions, inter-group violence is almost inevitable. Before there can be strategies for dialogue, there must be opportunities for contacts and communication. Systems of 'apartheid', of separation, division and ex-communication always leads to strife and violence.

Part of the struggle for peace is, therefore, the establishment of channels of communication. Without such channels, living together in a humane and civilised way is simply not possible.

A good example for this is the women's movement-worldwide. Today it is hard to imagine a time when women were silenced almost as a matter of course, that is, cultures and social structures were such that the silencing of women appeared 'normal'. That silencing is still there, and with it the violence against women. But it is no longer taken for granted. A generation ago, women began to establish channels of communication and to challenge the structures and cultures of patriarchy. More recently they are in the process of restructuring the channels of communication with men, because an open male-female dialogue is a precondition for the transformation of gender conflicts. In some cultures women can now enter this dialogue as equal partners. Regardless, the struggle for equality in communication will have to continue in all cultures, perhaps for generations to come. Yet it is unthinkable that the wheel of time can be rolled back to when women were expected to exist in a state of silence (cf, Mananzan, M.J. et al., 1996).

Mass media and conflict

The question now arises about the role of the mass media in the peaceful solution of conflicts. Are they part of the vicious circle of violence or could they act as mediators with conflicting parties? Communication scholars have studied this question with increasing sophistication and have come to a number of conclusions.

The first is perhaps the most obvious: the mass media of communication do not operate in a vacuum, but they are part of cultural and social systems. They reflect the cultural and social structures of violence, and because they are, by definition public, they are considered to be at the apex of structural violence. The literature supporting this view is overwhelming and can only be referred to (cf Gerbner 1988, 1996; Hamelink, 1994; Tehranian, 1992, 1996).

The usual rationalisation for media violence is that the media, and television and film in particular, merely 'give the public what it wants'. Gerbner's discussion (1996: 16) of this issue can be summarised as follows:

- The most popular programmes on US television constrain rather than exacerbate violence.
- Eighty percent of the US public disapproves of the violence they see on television (1993).

- TV programmes made for home consumption in the US are considerably less violent (17 percent) than those made for export (46 percent).
- Violence dominates exports because TV and film executives believe that violence fits into any culture and needs no translation. (Gerbner quotes the producer of the film *Die Hard 2* as saying, 'If I tell you a joke, you may not get it. But if a bullet goes through a window, we all know how to hit the floor, no matter the language.')

Violence-driven cinema and television programmes, therefore, are not in response to popular request. Violence is primarily an ingredient in a global marketing formula, imposed by media executives in the US and imitated in Asia and elsewhere. For the sake of profits, screen violence in effect extends the cultural mechanisms of domination, repression and intimidation at home and abroad.

There are now literally thousands of NGOs in most countries around the globe which are trying to stem the tide of media violence. They act as the voices of huge media publics who are fed up with the violence on the screen, in the streets and in homes. There are hundreds of institutes from Japan to Cape Town and to Hawaii, specialising in the prevention of violent conflict and in the promotion of cultures of peace. The quarterly Journal of the International Peace Research Association lists most of them and describes some of their activities.

One motive for the intensification of peace efforts, mainly by NGOs, can be attributed to the recent and hardly expected catastrophes in ex-Yugoslavia and Rwanda and Burundi. As in all wars, and civil wars in particular, they demonstrated the power of public communication to incite and inflame violence.

The wars in Serbia, Croatia and later on in Bosnia started long before the first shots were fired. Most media in these countries (but less so in Bosnia) called for 'ethnic cleansing' and violent contestations to settle old and new scores. In Rwanda the infamous 'Radio Télévision Libre des Mille Colines' became the principle tool of war for the extremist cliques of Hutu fanatics who perpetrated the Rwanda genocide which started in 1990. This privately owned radio station literally directed the genocide with instructions about who should be killed next. A similar 'hate' radio station, broadcasting from neighbouring Zaire, was still fuelling the conflict in Burundi six years later (cf *Media Development*, 1996, p. 12. ff).

Chastened by the experience of the war in the Persian Gulf (1990–91), in which the American military and the US state department monopolised information about the conflict, journalists are reconsidering their roles and responsibilities in conflict situations. Firstly, some journalists now actively strive to detect 'early warning' signs, signalling potential conflicts. Secondly, they are trying more than ever to analyse conflicts as thoroughly and dispassionately as possible. By giving each side a hearing, several important steps towards conflict resolution can occur: the parties may be educated about each others point of view; stereotypes are challenged; initial perceptions can be re-evaluated and clarified (Botes, 1996: 7).

Thirdly, journalists and media commentators can assist in the mediation of conflict by informing public opinion and increasing public pressure. The British media, for example, portrayed Nelson Mandela as an outstanding public figure at a time when Prime Minister Margaret Thatcher still vowed she would never meet with this 'terrorist'. The media thus helped to change the attitude of the British public towards the African National Congress (ANC) which, in the end, became the main peace-maker in South Africa.

Not by words alone

This article has emphasised the central role which communication plays in the transformation of conflicts and the building up of a culture of peace. But words, whether spoken or written, come cheap. They can remain just that: mere words.

This concluding section therefore wants to draw attention to the underlying qualities of communication leading to genuine peace. They are forgiveness and reconciliation, qualities often forgotten in peace efforts and sadly unexplored themes in the literature on conflict resolution. Conflicts cannot really be transformed into peaceful coexistence unless there is readiness to forgive among all parties of the conflict. And for this to happen, people must have taken responsibility for all their actions, past and present. This has to happen above all, on the part of the leaders of wars or civic unrest, as well as among the ordinary people who have suffered on both sides.

If responsibility for one's actions is genuinely acknowledged, remorse, apology and ultimate forgiveness become possible. Lasting peace demands an apology, either public or private, depending on circumstances. It has been increasingly clear that public apologies lead to a healing process that makes forgiveness possible. Forgiveness is a critically important seal on the process if there is to be reconciliation and peace. Forgiveness and reconciliation reaffirm the humanity of people brutalized during conflict.

In the long run, accepting responsibility for one's actions in the past, and expressing regret and remorse, may prove to be the most important elements in the process of healing and a principal condition for reconciliation among people.

References

Botes, Johannes (1996). 'Journalism and conflict resolution', in *Media Development* 4/1996.

Galtung, Johan (1996). *Peace By Peaceful Means: Peace and Conflict, Development and Civilization.* London: Sage Publications; Oslo: PRIO.

Gerbner, George, & Signorelli, Nancy (1988). *Violence & Terror in the Media: An Annotated Bibliography.* Westport, CT: Greenview Press.

Gerbner, George (1996). 'The stories we tell', in *Media Development,* 4/1996.

Hamelink, Cees J. (1994). *The Politics of World Communication: A Human Rights Perspective*. London: Sage Publications.

Langer, Felicia (1999). *Laßt uns wie Menschen leben! Schein und Wirklichkeit in Palästina*. Göttingen: Lamuv. 1999

Mananzan, M. J., M. A. Oduyoye, M. A., Tamez, E., Clarkson, J. S., Grey, M. ., & Russell, L. M.,(eds.) (1996). *Women resisting violence: Spirituality for life*. New York: Orbis Books.

Media Development 4/1996. 'Communication and conflict'. London: WACC.

Tehranian, Katharine & Tehranian, Majid (1992). *Restructuring for World Peace: On the Threshold oft the 21st Century*. Creskill, NJ: Hampton Press.

Tehranian, Majid (1996). 'Communication and conflict', in *Media Development* 4/1996.

XV

Communication is Inscribed in Human Nature: A Philosophical Enquiry into the Right to Communicate

MICHAEL TRABER

The discourse on the right to communicate seems to be gathering a new momentum.[1] One reason for this may well be that many people, at the threshold of a new millennium, experience a sense of powerlessness about the world around them. They feel subjected to war, violence and environmental degradation. They feel manipulated in what they buy and how they vote, and feel insecure in their moral judgements. They doubt whether they can still assert themselves about the world they wish to live in and bequeath to their children. They want to speak out but cannot make themselves heard.

In this situation, the discourse on communication as a right – private and public, individual and social – needs to proceed with a high degree of clarity, concentrating on the essential grounding of communication in human nature itself.

Yes, legal frameworks for the right to communicate, and the implementations of this right, are important. So are technologies that can either militate against or enhance the chances of freedom and democracy. And so are the cultural exigencies in an era of increasingly globalised mass media. Just because the right to communicate touches upon so many and such vital facets of human life, the need to find a common ground for the discourse is crucial. This is the main aim of this essay.

Its starting point is what it means to be human. Although we may first and foremost conceive of ourselves as individual persons, our very personhood depends on others. We are both individual and social beings. We then proceed to reflect on human nature as being-with-others, conditioned and orientated towards others. The uniquely human endowment of language as our social and cultural habitat, as well as the source of individual and social empowerment, demonstrates this. Communication is, therefore, an essential human need and a fundamental social necessity. Its central core is the philosophical notion of intersubjectivity, which implies communication in freedom, equality and solidarity. Our final reflections are on communication as the life-blood of society.

Being-with-others: Intersubjectivity

One of the philosophical questions, which have occupied thinkers for centuries, is that of human authenticity. What are the essential characteristics of the human being? What distinguishes us from other mammals? What is authentically human?

Human living is different from any other in that it is essentially other-directed. We seem to be conditioned to live in a world of 'we', prior to the 'I' and 'thou'. Bernard Lonergan (1972: 57) describes this as follows:

Just as one spontaneously raises one's arm to ward off a blow against one's head, so with the same spontaneity one reaches out to save another from falling. Perception, feeling, and bodily movement are involved, but the help given another is not deliberate but spontaneous. One adverts to it not before it occurs but while it is occurring. It is as if 'we' were members of one another prior to our distinctions of each from the others.

It has often been pointed out that humans are the only mammals who are completely dependent on other humans, first and foremost their mothers, when they are born. The very survival of babies depends on others, and not just for a few weeks but for some years. Little wonder then that the first manifestation of intersubjectivity may well be a baby's smile.

We do not learn to smile as we learn to walk, to talk, to swim, to skate. Commonly we do not think of smiling and then do it. We just do it. Again, we do not learn the meaning of smiling as we learn the meaning of words. The meaning of the smile is a discovery we make on our own, and that meaning does not seem to vary from culture to culture, as does the meaning of gestures. There is something irreducible about the smile (Lonergan, 1972: 60).

The smile expresses what a mother or father means to a baby. And throughout our lives a smile indicates what one person means to another. Its meaning is intersubjective. It spontaneously signals the 'presence of the other'. It is a primordial form of self-transcendence.

Human beings become authentic in self-transcendence. That is the very core of their being social beings. Solipsism is an inhuman abyss. And the intentional 'absence of the other' is, in the words of Jean-Paul Sartre, 'hell'. In contrast, the highest form of self-transcendence is the self-surrender to another in love, which is 'the abiding imperative of what is to be human' (Lonergan, 1985: 134). Thus by transcending oneself, one becomes oneself.

Language as self-transcendence

Plato defined the human being as 'the animal that speaks' (*zoon logon echon*). There is little point in pitting Plato against his pupil Aristotle, for whom the human being is 'the animal that thinks'. Both speech and reason condition each other and are dependent on each other. Except that psychologically and in the stages of human development, language comes first.

Humans speak. We speak when we are awake and we speak in our dreams. We are always speaking, even when we do not utter a single word aloud, but merely listen or read, and even when we are not particularly listening or speaking but are attending to some work or taking a rest. We are continually speaking in one way or another. We speak because speaking is natural to us. It does not first arise out of some special volition. Humans are said to have language by nature. It is held that humans, in distinction from plants and animals, are the living being capable of speech. This statement does not mean only that, along with other faculties, humans also possess the faculty of speech. It means to say that only speech enables the human being to be the living being he or she is as a human being. It is as the one who speaks that the human being is – human (Heidegger, 1971: 189).[2]

The philosophy of language is of course much older than the writings of Heidegger, who called language 'the house of being'. Yet language as the basis for philosophical anthropology may be one of the principal philosophical insights of the 20th century. Charles Morris' seminal work, *Foundation of a Theory of Signs* (1938), was one of the first fruits of modern semiotics. Morris (1975: 235) later said:

> Everything which is characteristically human depends on language. The human being is in a real sense the speaking animal. Speech plays the most essential – but not the only – role in the development and preservation of the human self and its aberrations, as it does in the development and maintenance of society and its aberrations.

In the current philosophy of language, reason and language are co-original. One cannot develop without the other. 'Reason only advances by means of establishing communicable expressions, and language is the sole and concrete manifestation of reason' (Pasquali, 1997: 43). In the communicative act, 'language becomes the basis, form and substance of intersubjectivity' (ibid). Vaclav Havel (1990: 44) summarises the meaning of language as follows:

> Words could be said to be the very source of our being, the very substance of the cosmic life form we call people. Spirit, the human soul, our self-awareness, our ability to generalise and think in concepts, to perceive the world as the world (and not just as our locality), and, lastly, our capacity to know that we will die - and living in spite of that knowledge: surely all these are mediated or actually created by words.

Human nature itself has provided tangible evidence for this view on language. Susanne K. Langer (1974) discusses in some detail the phenomenon of 'wild children' or 'wolf children', and the experiments with chimpanzees with respect to language learning. A number of cases of 'wolf children', viz. children who grew up without human companionship, have been studied. The best attested are Peter, who was found in the fields near Hanover in 1723, Victor who was captured in Aveyron, Southern France, at the age of about 12, in 1799, and two little girls, Amala and Kamala, who were taken into human custody near Midnapur, India, in 1920. None of these children could speak in any language; instead they had imitated the sounds of the animals among which they had lived. Amala and Kamala never managed to converse with each other, and after six years in human surroundings, Kamala, (who survived her sister) had learned about forty words, managed to utter some three-word sentences, but only did so when she was spoken to. Apparently, small children have an optimum period of learning languages, which is lost in later life (see Langer, 1974: 122).

On the question of animal languages, Langer (1964: 33) comes to the following conclusion:

> Animal language is not language at all, and what is more important it never leads to language. Dogs that live with men learn to understand many verbal signals, but only as signals, in relation to their own actions. Apes that live in droves and seem to communicate fairly well, never converse. But a baby that has only half a dozen words begins to converse: 'Daddy gone.' 'Daddy come?' 'Daddy come.' Question and answer, assertion and denial, denotation and description - these are the basic uses of language. The gap between the animal and human estate is... the language line.

Language then is the common condition of the human species. We live in the house of language. No group, tribe or people has ever been found that did not have a developed language system, regardless of the linguistic differences between them. But the aural articulation of sounds for words and sentences is only one, though the most potent, type of human language. The others are so called body languages, employing mainly touch, gestures and visual symbols as signs. Therefore, being-together as human beings requires a language to form, maintain and express being-in-relation with others, just as language enables us to 'name' objects of the world around us.

In brief then, the essence of the human being as a social being is constituted and perfected by language. Being-together-in-the-world, or being intersubjective, is realised and actualised in the self-transcendence of communication. When we are deprived of this togetherness we cannot live lives worthy of human nature. Language is thus the symbolic human construct that allows the forging and maintenance of relationships.

Communication in freedom, equality and solidarity

It is fairly easy to demonstrate (as we have seen) that language is part of being human. Language in action, that is communication, is an individual human need – as basic as food, clothing and shelter. Basic needs are those that are essential for our existence and our very survival. They are the very preconditions of human life. Because of this, basic human needs become fundamental human rights. While this logic is now generally acknowledged with regard to physical human needs – food/drink, shelter, clothing, perhaps in the descending order listed – the non-material human needs like language and communications are more controversial. Most people seem to survive solitary confinement, exclusion and excommunication, partly because they somehow manage to retain some sort of intentional interpersonal communication, and maintain or renegotiate a sense of belonging even though they are silenced. Being silenced never quite succeeds, because nobody can deprive us of our relational nature.

The experience of being silenced, however, reveals another existential dimension of the human being, namely the need for freedom. What good is the house of language if we cannot converse in it freely? Language and freedom are intertwined. The gift of language is at the same time a gift of freedom. Deprivation of freedom makes genuine communication impossible, and the first sign of repression in groups and societies is the curtailment of freedom of speech. This can be very subtle. Intimidation or the inculcation of fear, the exposure to ridicule may suppress freedom, as can the building up or maintenance of authoritarian structures that allow little or no dissent. Freedom means being part of, and thus being able to participate in, life-in-common. 'The principle of freedom of expression is one that admits of no exceptions, and is applicable to people all over the world by virtue of their human dignity' (MacBride Report, 1980: 18).

'Human freedom is axiological. It needs no proof. It is part of life experience and can only be reflected on. Reflection reveals that freedom is an integral part of human nature and thus a precondition of humans to be moral beings. Freedom makes all specifically *human* actions possible, including communications... The rationale for freedom is to become more truly human and humane. Freedom is both part of being human and becoming humane... Only in the free encounter with others can genuine freedom be experienced' (Traber, 1997: 334–335). Humans, however, are not 'born free'. They are situated in existing relationships – in families and groups. Humans therefore encounter the freedom of others. True freedom accepts other freedoms unconditionally, and opens up the freedom of others. Freedom, it should be noted, is not primarily orientated towards objects but towards people. Only in the free encounter with others can genuine freedom be experienced. An intersubjective approach to the notion of freedom also establishes the rationale for the limitations of freedom, which are enshrined in the customary (and codified) laws of all societies.

These reflections lead to another dimension of communication: equality. We cannot communicate with others when we consider them 'inferior'. The master may impart information to his slave or servant, but genuine communication hardly takes place. The same is true when men consider women as 'inferior' human beings. Mere information, or the sale of and access to media products, may then become substitutes for genuine communication. Communicative freedom presupposes the recognition that all human beings are of equal worth. And the more explicit equality is and becomes in human interactions, the more easily and completely communication occurs.

Equality as a philosophical concept is unconditional, but does not deny the reality of specific social identities, loyalties or preferential interests. Equality does not mean homogeneity or uniformity. Neither does it contradict the special roles and ranks which societies confer on individuals and groups of people.

But equality also implies the right not to be discriminated against because of race, ethnicity, religion, or sex and age, etc. Commenting on the 1986 African Charter on Human and People's Rights, which emphasises the duties of the individual towards the community, and which formalises the notion of group and collective rights, Charles Husband (1998: 139) states:

> In recognising that our individuality is contingent upon those communities of identity to which we belong we recognise our connectedness, our solidarity. Consequently, individual rights cannot be fully enjoyed, or guaranteed, in the absence of respect for the dignity, integrity, equality and liberty of those communities of identities, including our ethnic community to which we belong. And in demanding the recognition of any one of our communities... we must reciprocally recognise the legitimacy of the existence, and the integrity, of other communities, including their differences from us.

The non-recognition of such identities in public communication may lead to a 'proliferation of communicative ghettos in which relatively homogenous audiences consume a narrow diet of information, entertainment and values' (Husband, 1998: 143). The inclusion into the public sphere of differentiated groups is likely to result in a heterogeneous discourse of citizens, in which social identities can be affirmed and collective interests expressed.

There is, however, another type of loyalty – often overlooked – that sustains the right to communicate, namely loyalty towards, and solidarity with, the weak and most vulnerable in society, like the physically or mentally ill, or the very young and very old. Solidarity further includes an active commitment to individuals and groups who have been relegated to the margins of society, like the refugees, the outcasts (for whatever reason), and the exploited and oppressed. It is not least a 'solidarity with those whose freedom has been taken away, rendering them less than human' (Traber, 1997: 335). Active solidarity is one of the 'inescapable claims on one another which we cannot renounce except at the cost of our humanity' (Peukert, quoted in Christians, 1997: 7). Our common being-in-the-world is ontologically inclusive, and morally transformative. Gross injustices, to say the least, upset and disgust us, and this sense of revulsion may spur us into action. Self-transcendence then acquires a new and ethical quality. Intersubjectivity implicitly strives for an equitable social order and, ultimately, for the 'good society', as one cross-cultural study on ethical proto-norms has shown (Christians & Traber, 1997). The good society is not only a utopian projection but also the subject of concrete analysis, which is both a task of social science and of social ethics. The transformative potential of communication is summarised in the following statement:

> Communication which liberates, enables people to articulate their own needs and helps them to act together to meet those needs. It enhances their sense of dignity and underlines their right to full participation in the life of society. It aims to bring about structures in society, which are more just, more egalitarian and more conducive to the fulfilment of human rights (WACC, 1997: 8).

The right to public communication for all

The human needs approach leads to the right to communicate for individuals. The right is meant to guarantee and implement the social nature of humans through interpersonal communication. Although it implies the right to public communication, an explicit confirmation is still called for, because it is on this level that the right to communicate is most contested.

The right to communicate publicly is foreign to the thinking of all those who have traditionally associated public communication with the political, social and cultural elite of society. The notion of public 'social actors' has greatly influenced the history of the press and of all other mass media of communication. The conventional criteria for news are obsessed with the news value of 'prominence': the VIPs with political and economic power, and the 'stars' of entertainment and of sports. In fact stardom is bequeathed by the media by repeated exposure; it is an invention of Hollywood that has spread from film to television and popular music. The mass media have, in the course of time, developed their own culture with its own norms. One of them is 'professionalism'. This does not necessarily mean training or education, but the elitist notion that only 'special people', with special talents, should be journalists and broadcasters. Public communication is thus the prerogative of those who can, and do, uphold the professional norms of media culture.

Another expression of elitism is the tendency (and it is no more than that) to evince mistrust towards 'common' people who may misuse the freedom and the power of public communication. This mistrust is particularly evident with respect to youth. The assumption is that political and ethical responsibility is the prerogative of members of a certain social and professional class. However, the misuses of the power of public communication in recent years have been very much in professional hands. The reporting of the war in the Persian Gulf (1991), the role radio and television played in the genocide in Rwanda (1994), and the ethnic hubris and war mongering of the media in ex-Yugoslavia (long before the conflicts erupted) are cases in point.

Advocates of the right to public information for all challenge the prerogatives of the political and professional elite. Their model of public communication is democratic rather than authoritarian. They aim at the distribution of communication power from the few to the many, from the elite to the grassroots. This right further stipulates a new role for the State, which becomes only one among several concerned parties; it embraces other institutions as well as groups and organisations – apart from individuals.

In other words, the right to communicate is very much dependent upon social structures in which public communication takes place. In brief, democracies require more than the election of representatives to a legislative assembly in a multi-party system. Over and beyond voting and party politics, democracy requires people who can make their wishes known – in public – and who participate in the debate about the type of political processes they aspire to.

The right to communicate, however, cannot stand in isolation. It is connected to other human rights, particularly the rights to education, culture and socio-economic development. Hamelink (1998: 56) stresses the entitlement to self-empowerment:

> Among the essential conditions of people's self-empowerment are access to, and use of, the resources that enable people to express themselves, to communicate these expressions to others, to exchange ideas with others, to inform themselves about events in the world, to create and control the production of knowledge and to share the world's sources of knowledge. These resources include technical infrastructures, knowledge and skills, financial means and natural systems. Their unequal distribution among the world's people obstructs the equal entitlement to the conditions of self-empowerment and should be considered a violation of human rights.

The MacBride Report (1980: 253) says that the right to communicate is a prerequisite for other human rights. There is a direct connection between communication and all those other rights that stress participation in public affairs. Society and its institutions must enable the active participation of all in the economic, political and cultural life of the community. This is not a high minded expression of benevolence, but a demand of justice. Such participation in the field of communication is of course more than 'consumer choice' or passive access to the mass media, or even the interactive chats between buddies on the Internet. The participation meant here is public dialogue about the public good. Its aim is to contribute to the debate about society, its values and priorities, and, above all, our common future. It's a dynamic and ongoing process, aimed at change and transformation.

Conclusion

So we return to the theme of intersubjectivity, or being-in-the-world-together, thus fashioning our future together. Our togetherness has a personal/private side, with its respective right, and a public responsibility, with its rights. The right to public communication pertains to public order and the public good, which are the right and responsibility of all, not just of a few.

Communication is similar to the nervous system of the human body. It is maintained by a multitude of signals originating from all parts of the body. If the nervous system or the immune system breaks down, the well being of the entire body is in jeopardy. Similarly, no modern democracy can exist, let alone flourish, without a certain level of information and participation. It is thus the very body politic that depends on the right to communicate. The roles of communication, both interpersonal and public, have been aptly described in the first paragraph of Chapter 1 of the MacBride Report (1980: 3).

> Communication maintains and animates life. It is also the motor and
> expression of social activity and civilisation; it leads people and
> peoples from instinct to inspiration, through variegated processes and
> systems of enquiry, command and control; it creates a common pool of
> ideas, strengthens the feeling of togetherness... and translates thought
> into action, reflecting every emotion and need from the humblest tasks
> of human survival to supreme manifestations of creativity – or
> destruction. Communication integrates knowledge, organisation of
> power and runs a thread linking the earliest memory of man [humans]
> to his [their] noblest aspirations through constant striving for a better
> life. As the world has advanced, the task of communication has
> become ever more complex and subtle – to contribute to the liberation
> of [hu]mankind from want, oppression and fear and to unite it in
> community and communion, solidarity and understanding. However,
> unless some basic structural changes are introduced, the potential

benefits of technological and communication development will hardly be put at the disposal of the majority of [hu] mankind.[3]

This article first appeared in *idoc internazionale*, Vol. 30, Nos. 1 & 2, January-June 1999. Rome: IDOC.

Notes

1. *The Journal of International Communication* (Sydney) devoted a double issue (Vol.5, Nos 1&2, 1989) to the debate on communication and human rights in the context of globalisation and cyberspace. It is guest-edited by Shalini Venturelli, and contains contributions from leaders in the field, such as Cees J. Hamelink, George Gerbner, Marc Raboy and others.
2. The translation of this passage by Heidegger has been altered to do justice to the inclusive term he uses for the human being, namely *Mensch*, not *Mann* (man). See also Martin Heidegger, *On the Way to Language*, (trans. Peter D. Hertz), New York: Harper and Row, 1971, in which the author marvels (pp. 47-54) at the Japanese word for language, *koto ha*, which literally means: the flower petals (*ha*) that flourish out of the lightning message of the graciousness that brings them forth (*koto*).
3. I am quoting unashamedly from *Many Voices, One World*, popularly known as the MacBride Report, which UNESCO long disowned. This blueprint for a New World Information and Communication Order (NWICO) is more pertinent today than it was in 1980, when all member States of UNESCO endorsed it (with one abstention). With the hindsight of the developments in public communications in the last 20 years, the abandoning of NWICO was an act of utter folly.

References

Christians, Clifford (1997). 'The Ethics of Being in a Communications Context,' in Clifford Christians and Michael Traber (eds.), *Communication Ethics and Universal Values*, Thousand Oaks, CAL, London, New Delhi: Sage, 3–23.
Hamelink, Cees J. (1998). 'Human Rights – The Implementation Gap,' in *Journal of International Communication*, Vol.5, No 1–2: 54–74.

Havel, Vaclav (1990). 'From Arrogance to Humility: the ambiguous power of words', in *Media Development*, Vol. 37, No. 1, 44–46.

Heidegger, Martin (1971). *Poetry, Language, Thought*, (trans. Albert Hofstadter). New York: Harper and Row.

Husband, Charles (1998). 'Differentiated Citizenship and the Multi-Ethnic Public Sphere', in *Journal of international Communication*, Vol. 5, No. 1&2, 134–148.

Langer, Susanne K. (1964). *Philosophical Sketches*, New York: New American Library.

Langer, Susanne K. (1974). *Philosophy in a New Key. A Study in the Symbolism of Reason, Rite and Art.* Cambridge, MASS: Harvard University Press.

Lonergan, Bernard J.F. (1972). *Method in Theology.* New York: Herder and Herder.

Lonergan, Bernard J.F. (1985). *A Third Collection of Papers*, edited by Frederick Crowe. New York: Paulist Press.

Morris, Charles (1938). *Foundation of the Theory of Signs.* Chicago: University of Chicago Press.

Morris, Charles (1975), 'Sprechen und menschliches Handeln', in F.I.G. Gadamer und S.T. Volger (eds.), *Neue Anthropologie.* Stuttgart.

Pasquali, Antonio (1997). 'The Moral Dimension of Communication', in Clifford Christians and Michael Traber (eds.), *Communication Ethics and Universal Values.* Thousand Oaks CA, London, New Delhi: Sage, 24–45.

Traber, Michael (1997). 'An Ethics of Communication Worthy of Human Beings', in Clifford Christians and Michael Traber (eds.), *Communication Ethics and Universal Valises.* Thousand Oaks CA, London, New Delhi: Sage, 327–343.

UNESCO (1980). (MacBride Report) *Many Voices, One World. Towards a new, more just and more efficient world information and communication order*, London: Kogan Page

World Association for Christian Communication (WACC) (1997). 'Christian Principles of Communication', in: *Statements on Communication.* London: WACC, 5–9.

Index

accountable governance, 22
Achebe, Chinua, 105
advertising, 128–9, 131–2, 133–4
Africa:
    anti-corruption laws, 38;
    cell phones, 110, 112–13;
    civil rights movements, 39–
        40;
    civil society, 22, 27–30, 40–1;
    community organizations,
        27–8;
    democratic accountability, 21;
    democracy, 103–5, 108–9;
    dependence on international
        financial institutions, 24;
    despotic rulers, 21–2;
    education, 25–6, 28–9;
    entrepreneurs, 28;
    equality, 220;
    European colonialism, 22–3,
        26;
    governing elite, 19–20, 21, 23,
        24, 32–3, 42;
    independence movements, 21,
        24;
    internet, 110–11, 113;
    journalism, 97, 98–9, 101–
        100;
    musicians, 106;
    NGOs, 27;
    postcolonial social structure,
        24–5;
    press, 21, 31–5, 37–42;
    press restrictions, 99;
    professional groups, 29–30;
    public services, 29–30;
    women's movements, 40
Africa Literature Centre, Kitwe,
    Zambia, 2
African Charter on Human and
    People's Rights, 250–1
African National Congress
    (ANC), 239
Africanity, 99–101, 107–8
Al-Jazeera, 46
Aldington, Richard, 158
All Quiet on the Western Front,
    158, 159, 160–6
alternative journalism, 226–9
AMARC, 139, 140
anti-war films, 157–72
APC, 140
Aristotle, 49, 53, 246
Article IX, 139
Astor, David, 212
Attenborough, Richard, 166

Barbusse, Henri, 158
Barrault, Jean-Louis, 180
Barron, Jerome, 94
Baudrillard, Jean, 121–3, 124, 132
Bentham, Jeremy, 81–2, 84, 91
Bernard, F. de R. 158
Bethlehem Mission Society, 1, 2
Bhoomi Project, 153
Bible, 185–6
Big Parade, 157–8
Bittlinger, Arnold, 179
Black Press Fund (BPF), 2–3
Blanton, Thomas, 144
Blunden, Edmund, 158
Boethius of Rome, 49
Bosnia: media, 238
Brazil:
    anti-racism campaigns, 115–
        18;
    NGOs, 115–16, 119–21, 129–
        30
Brecht, Bertolt, 159
Brooke, Rupert, 170
Burkina Faso:
    languages, 47

Calhoun, C. 141
Cameroon:
    radio and television, 98
Canby, Vincent, 172
capitalism, 125;
    promoters of, 88
Centre for Peace and Conflict
    Studies, 74
Centre for the Study of
    Developing Societies, 143
Cheng Hao, 49

Cheng Yi, 49
Chomsky, 55
Christianity:
    and the one-many problem,
        58
Christians, Clifford G., 14
Citizen, The, 38
Citizens' Action Against Hunger,
    119–20, 127
civil society, 85, 141, 199
Clark, Alan, 166
communication, 255;
    and nationalism, 202;
    and patriotism, 202;
    challenges, 202–3;
    definition, 186, 195–6;
    democratisation of, 220;
    ethics, 14, 46, 47–8, 52–5,
        219;
    facilitation of world affairs,
        45–6;
    history, 193–4;
    rights, 3–4, 83, 137–44, 195–
        203, 243–4, 250–4;
    roles, 255;
    systems abuse by
        governments, 198;
    theory, 178–81
Communication Rights in the
    Information Society (CRIS)
    Campaign, 138, 139–40
communicative action, 8, 186–7
conflict, 223–4, 231–3, 236, 240
conflict & communication online,
    75
consumer society, 121–6
Cook, Timothy E., 209

Coordenadoria Ecumênica de
    Serviço (CESE), 129–30
corruption, 125
Crick, Bernard, 173
Croatia: media, 238
cultural violence, 235
Cuthbert, Marlene, 213

D'Arcy, Jean, 196–7
Deighton, Len, 166
Deleuze, Gilles, 124–7, 133
democracy, 201, 220, 253–4, 255
Descartes, 59, 180
Dey, Nikhil, 147
dialogic ethics, 56–7, 60–1
Dialogues Against Racism, 115–
    17, 127, 131, 132
Dibango, Manu, 106–7
Doebler, Peter, 93
Durkheim, Emile, 89

Ebert, Robert, 172
Einstein, 55
Elsener, Joe, 6
equality, 250;
    in a structured community,
    219–20
Escobar, Arturo, 141
Ethical Journalism Initiative,
    75–6
EthicNet databank, 65

Fernandes, George, 146
Feuchtwanger, Lion, 159
Florin, Hans W., 5
Foucault, 125

France:
    Muslim immigrants, 47
Fraser, N., 141
Free Press, 139
freedom, 249–50;
    of expression, 249
Freire, Paulo, 129
Fulani, 47

Galtung, Johan, 74, 206, 222,
    233–4
Gance, Abel, 157, 166
Garnham, Nicholas, 211
Geertz, Clifford, 190
Gellner, Ernest, 211
Gerbner, George, 138, 237–8
globalization, 47–8, 61, 110, 118
God:
    and communication, 179
Grassroots, 3
Graves, Robert, 159
Gregorian University, Rome, 6
Guardian newspaper (Nigeria),
    34
Guizot, François, 91–2
Gunawardena, Nalaka, 142

Habermas, Jürgen, 7, 8, 84, 141,
    186
Hackett, Robert, 139
Halbwachs, Maurice, 183
Hamelink, Cees J., 4, 137, 138
Hamilton, Ian, 159
Hanitzsch, Thomas, 75
Hardy, Thomas, 168
Hašek, Jaroslav, 166
Havel, Vaclav, 184, 213, 247

Heidegger, Martin, 190, 246
Heraclitus, 49
Heschel, Adam, 189
Hill, Dave, 214
Hoffman, Abbie, 93
Holy Spirit, 178;
  and communication, 179–80,
  182, 188, 190–1
Howell, Jude, 141
human rights, 195, 202
Husband, Charles, 251
Hussein, Saddam, 214

IAMCR Global Media Policy
  working group, 139
ICTs, 88–9, 93, 109–10, 113
identity politics, 142
IFJ, 75
Imba Verlag, 2
India:
  corruption, 145–6, 148, 152,
    153;
  democracy, 152;
  e-government, 152–3;
  Public Distribution System,
    145, 147, 148–9, 152;
  right to information
    movement, 145–54
information and communication
  technologies (ICTs), 11
Institute for War and Peace
  Reporting, 74
Instituto Ethos, 118–19
International Commission for the
  Study of Communication
  Problems, see MacBride
  Report

International Convention on the
  Elimination of Racism, 116
International Organization of
  Journalists (IOJ), 65
International Peace Research
  Association:
  journal, 238
International Principles of
  Professional Ethics in
  Journalism, 10, 67, 68–71
Internet, 81, 84–90, 110–11, 113
intersubjectivity, 244–5, 255

J'accuse, 157, 166
Jesus, 188
Jha, V., 151
Joshi, A.S. 146
Journalism in Africa and Africa
  in Journalism (JAAJ), 97
journalists:
  and peace, 63–4, 65–6, 69–74;
  associations, 76–7;
  codes of ethics, 10, 64–74, 76

Kaelm, Pauline, 166
Kant, Immanuel, 81–2, 84, 90
Kapoor, I. 141
Keane, John, 201
Kerr, Alfred, 159
Kiely, R. 141
Kierkegaard, 182
Klein, Alexander, 184
Klein, Naomi, 123–4
Kleinwachter, 198
knowledge, 205
Kolossov, 199
Kuhn, Thomas, 55

Langer, Felicia, 232
Langer, Susanne K., 247–8
language, 182–3, 244, 247:
   and communication, 186;
   and freedom, 249;
   and lying, 183–6;
   animal, 248;
   as self-transcendence, 246–8;
   human, 248–9
Latin America:
   postcolonial social structure,
   25
Latvian Union of Journalists, 65
Lee, Philip, 139
Leibniz, 178, 180
Les Croix de bois 158
li, 49
Littlewood, Joan, 166
Lonergan, Bernard J.F., 190, 244
Lury, Celia, 128
lying, 184–6
Lynch, Jake, 75
Lyon, David, 75

MacBride, Seán, 3
MacBride Report, 3, 4 67, 68, 77
   137, 138, 194, 197, 198, 202,
   203, 220, 254, 255
MacBride Round Table on
   Communication, 4, 64, 137–8
Macquarrie, John, 181
Mambo Press, 2
Mandela, Nelson, 239
Mander, H. 146
Mannheim, Karl, 51
mass media, 87–8, 90–1, 94

Mazdoor Kisan Shakti Sangathan
   (MKSS), 147–9
McChesney, Robert, 139
McGoldrick, Annabel, 75
McLuhan, Marshall, 180
media:
   and deception, 184–5;
   and patriotism, 211–14;
   and the public, 200–1;
   and the State, 208–11;
   and US invasion of Grenada,
   213;
   autocratic nature of, 221–2;
   control of, 199;
   criteria for news, 222–8, 252–
   3;
   culture, 206, 253;
   role in conflict solution, 237–
   9
Media Development, 2, 3, 45
Melucci, Alberto, 141
meta-communication, 188–90
Microsoft: Indian information
   technicians, 47
Milestone, Lewis, 158, 160, 165
Mills, C. W., 86, 90
monism/relativism, 50–2
Moore, Mathew, 150–1
Morris, Charles, 193, 246
Moto, 2
Mouffe, Chantal, 141
Mugabe, Robert, 226
multiculturalism, 47–8

National Campaign for the
   People's Right to Information,
   149

National Conference for Media
    Reform, 139
nationalism, 211–12;
    and communication, 202;
    lack of interest in, 205–6
Navajos, 47
New World Information and
    Communication Order
    (NWICO), 3, 67, 70, 194,
    196, 197, 198, 202, 228–9
New York Times, 213, 225
newspapers, 88, 97–8
Newton, Adam, 59
NGOs, 12;
    and media violence, 238;
    Brazil, 115–16, 119–21, 129–
    30
Nigeria:
    cell phones, 112–13;
    elections, 34;
    newspapers, 38, 39;
    press, 34, 35;
    public services, 29–30;
    religious press, 35;
    super-rich, 20
Nigerian Bishops Conference, 36
Nkapa, President, 35
Nordenstreng, Kaarle, 137
NWICO, see New World
    Information and
    Communication Order
Nyerere, 21

Obasanjo, President, 34–5
Observer, 212
OECD Multilateral Agreement
    on Investment, 123

Oh! What a Lovely War, 166–72
one-and-the-many problem, 48–
    57, 60
Ong, Walter J., 183
OurMedia conferences, 139
Owen, Wilfred, 162, 164

Pabst, G.W. 158, 164
Padovani, Claudia, 139
PANOS, 140
Parmenides, 49
patriarchy, 234–5
patriotism:
    and communication, 202, 205;
    lack of interest in, 205–6
peace, 232, 234, 240
Pieterse, J.N., 141
Platform for the Democratisation
    of Communication, 138
Plato, 49, 92, 178, 180, 193, 246
Polanyi, Michael, 57
poverty:
    globalization of, 144
prayer, 183
press:
    freedom, 82, 84, 92, 93–4, 103;
    opinion, 92;
    roles, 83;
    sphere, 7–8, 81–2, 87
Pronay, Nicholas, 158
public sphere, 141
publicity:
    concepts, 82, 87, 88, 91, 92;
    dialogical, 87;
    mediated, 84, 87

Raboy, Marc, 139
Radio Télévision Libre des Mille
    Colines, 239
Rebouças, Nádia, 116
religion, 190
Remarque, Elfriede, 160
Remarque, Erich Maria, 158,
    159–60
Ricardo, Sérgio, 124
right to information, 197;
    legislation, 144–5, 149–50,
    153
Rilke, Rainer Maria, 162
Roach, Colleen, 137
Rosaldo, Renato, 59
Roy, Aruna, 147
ruling elite, 222–3
Rwanda:
    radio, 238–9

Santayana, George, 182
Sartre, Jean-Paul, 245
Sarvodaya, 143
Sassoon, Siegfried, 159, 162
Schiller, Dan, 206
Schiller, Herb, 137
Schweitzer, Albert, 53
Scottish Enlightenment, 22
self-empowerment, 254
Sen, Amartya, 7
Serbia:
    media, 238
Servaes, 196
Sherriff, R. C., 158
Sinclair, Upton, 185
Singh, Shankar, 147
Siochrú, Seán Ó, 139

Sivakumar, S.J., 153
Slovak Syndicate of Journalists,
    66
Smith, A.D., 205–6
social:
    cosmology, 206–7;
    inequalities, 89;
    opinion, 85
Socrates, 182
solidarity, 241
South African Council of
    Churches (SACC), 2
South Asia:
    democracy, 143;
    freedom, 143–4
Souza, Herbet de, 116
Soyinka, Wole, 35
Splichal, Slavko, 210
Sri Lanka:
    communication deficits, 142–
    3
St Augustine, 179
Steiner, George, 188
story-telling, 58–9
Sunday Times, The, 207–8

Tamang, Seira, 140
Tanzania:
    foreign aid, 24;
    national assembly members,
    19–20;
    newspapers, 38;
    press council, 21;
    street vendors, 20
Taylor, A.J.P., 159
Taylor, Charles, 142
tehelka.com, 146

Tehranian, Majid, 200
Tejpal, Tarun, 146
Thatcher, Margaret, 239
Tillich, Paul, 189
Tönnies, Ferdinand, 92
Toyota Motor Company, 53
Traber, Michael, 1–7, 14–15, 45, 46, 57–9, 61, 92, 118, 137; writings, 15
trade unions, 126
Transcend Peace University, 74
Transparency International, 146

UNESCO, 3, 64, 67–70, 77, 137, 196
UNESCO Mass Media Declaration, 67–8, 70
Union of Journalists in Finland, 66, 74
United Nations, 195
United Nations Millennium Declaration, 70
United Nations World Conference against Racism, Racial Discrimination, Xenophobia and Related Intolerance, 115
United States of America: elite country, 222; immigrants, 47; people's rights, 196, 199
United Theological College, Bangalore, 4, 6
Universal Declaration of Human Rights, 195, 197, 211

universal solidarity, 14–15, 187
Upanishads, 49

Vedas, 49
Vidor, King. 157
Vietnam War, 172
violemce, see conflict
Voice, The, 2

war:
    books, 158–9;
    poems, 162, 164, 168, 170
Warde, Alan, 128
Washington Post, 225
Watzlawick, Paul, 193
web communities, 86
Westfront 1918, 158, 164
White, Robert A., 4
William of Ockham, 49
Winchester, Simon, 207
Wittgenstein, 182
wolf children, 247
women's movement, 236–7
World Association for Christian Communication (WACC), 1, 2, 3, 4–5, 137, 139, 191
World Summit on the Information Society (WSIS), 13, 138, 142
World War I, 157–8, 172
Worldwatch Institute, 63
writing: introduction of, 83

Zaire: radio, 239
Znaniecki, Florian, 55

About the Authors

CLIFFORD G. CHRISTIANS (PhD) is Director, Institute of Communications Research, Charles H. Sandage Distinguished Professor, Research Professor of Communications, and Professor of Journalism and Media Studies at the University of Illinois at Urbana-Champaign, U.S.A. He is co-editor of numerous books, author of numerous chapters and articles, and recipient of many national and internal awards.

PHILIP LEE joined the staff of the World Association for Christian Communication in 1975, where he is currently Deputy Director of Programmes and Editor of the international quarterly journal *Media Development*. Publications include *The Democratisation of Communication* (ed.) (University of Wales Press, 1995); *Communication & Reconciliation: Challenges Facing the 21st Century* (ed.); and *Many Voices, One Vision: The Right to Communicate in Practice* (Southbound, 2004).

KAARLE NORDENSTRENG (PhD) is Professor of Journalism and Mass Communication, particularly electronic media, at the University of Tampere, Finland. He is a long-standing member of both the International Association for Media and Communication Research (IAMCR) and the International Communication Association (ICA). He was Coordinator of the Social Sciences, National Project for University Degree Reform (Finnish Ministry of Education) 2003-07.

FRANCIS B. NYAMNJOH (PhD) is Associate Professor and Head of Publications and Dissemination with the Council for the Development of Social Science Research in Africa (CODESRIA), Dakar, Senegal. Recent books include *Negotiating an Anglophone Identity* (Brill, 2003), *Rights and the Politics of Recognition in Africa* (Zed Books, 2004), *Africa's Media, Democracy and the Politics of Belonging* (Zed Books, 2005).

LIV SOVIK (PhD) studied English Language at Yale University (1977), obtained an MA in Latin American Studies at the University of Texas at Austin (1985) and a doctorate in Communication Sciences at the Universtiy of São Paulo (1994). She was professor in the Post-Graduate Programme on Contemporary Communication and Culture at the Federal University of Bahia (1996–2000), before joining the Federal University of Rio de Janeiro, Brazil.

SLAVKO SPLICHAL (PhD) is Professor of Communication at the Faculty of Social Sciences, University of Ljubljana, Slovenia. He is founder (1987) and convenor of the annual International Colloquium on Communication and Culture, director of the European Institute for Communication and Culture, and Editor of its journal *Javnost–The Public*. He has been member of editorial boards of *Journal of Communication, Journalism Studies, Gazette, New Media & Society, Réseaux and Zeszyty Prasoznawcze*.

PRADIP N. THOMAS (PhD) is Associate Professor, School of Journalism & Communication, University of Queensland. He has written widely on issues related to communication rights, religion and the media, the political economy of communications and communication and social change. He is the author of the forthcoming volume *Strong Religion/Zealous Media: Christian Fundamentalism and Communication in India* (Sage, 2008).

ROBERT A. WHITE (PhD) studied development sociology and the political economy of Latin America at Cornell University, New York, USA. He was Research Director of the Centre for the Study of Communication and Culture (CSCC), London (1978–89) and co-editor with Michael Traber of the long-running book series 'Communication and Human Values' published by Sage. He became Head of the Centre of Interdisciplinary Studies in Communication at the Pontifical Gregorian University, Rome, Italy (1989–2004) and is currently Professor in the Faculty of Humanities and Communications at St. Augustine University of Tanzania, Mwanza.

WORLD ASSOCIATION FOR CHRISTIAN COMMUNICATION

VISION

Our vision is a world in which communication is recognised by all as a human right and as the basis for peace and social justice.

MISSION STATEMENT

The World Association for Christian Communication (WACC) promotes communication for social change. It believes that communication is a basic human right that defines people's common humanity, strengthens cultures, enables participation, creates community, and challenges tyranny and oppression. WACC's key concerns are media diversity, equal and affordable access to communication and knowledge, media and gender justice, and the relationship between communication and power. It tackles these through advocacy, education, training, and the creation and sharing of knowledge. WACC's worldwide membership works with faith-based and secular partners at grassroots, regional and global levels, giving preference to the needs of the poor, marginalised and dispossessed. Being WACC means 'taking sides'.

World Association for Christian Communication
308 Main Street
Toronto, Ontario M4C 4X7
Canada
Tel: (+1) 416–691–1999
Fax: (+1) 416–691–1997
http://www.waccglobal.org

Who Owns the Media?

Global Trends and Local Resistances

EDITED BY PRADIP THOMAS AND ZAHAROM NAIN

The ownership of the media and issues related to the governance of global media institutions are of immense public significance. Not only are the cultural industries a major source of contemporary power — economic, political, social — they are also the primary definers of consciousness in most parts of the contemporary world.

Media ownership patterns and permutations today are a direct consequence of the globalisation of neo-liberal economics. While there are some regional variations in the ownership "mix" the trend, from South Africa to Argentina and India to East and Central Europe, is towards privatisation, deregulation, retreat from the state's public media responsibilities and the contraction of space for non-commercial, community-based media efforts.

This collection of critical writings on media ownership from different parts of the world by leading scholars, including Robert McChesney, Dan Schiller, Cees Hamelink, Sean O'Siochru, Zhao Yuezhi and others, offers a richly textured, contextual reading of the political economy of contemporary media ownership. Issues addressed include convergence, global media governance, intellectual property, telecommunications regulation and deregulation, censorship, the role of the state, with a strong accent on the need for transparency, accountability and media diversity.

Published in 2004 • ISBN: 978-983-9054-42-2 • 316 pages • 14 x 21.5 cm.

Paperback, US$20.00, available at *http://www.southbound.com.my.*

Many Voices, One Vision
The Right to Communicate in Practice

EDITED BY PHILIP LEE

W hat does the right to communicate mean to millions of people marginalised by the political and economic self-interests of the North?

- How is concentration of media ownership threatening political activism and cultural diversity?
- What needs to be done to tackle the causes of the digital divide?
- How can the right to communicate guarantee equal access and participation in democratic decision-making?
- Why is it important to place safeguards on who owns and generates information and knowledge?

These are some of the questions addressed by this book, which promotes the vision of "a new, more just and more efficient world information and communication order". Contributing authors include Cees Hamelink, Vasanth Kannabiran, Ritu Menon, Jan Servaes, Judith Vidal-Hall, and others.

Published in 2004 • ISBN: 978-983-9054-40-8 • 166 pages • 14 x 21.5 cm.

Paperback, US$18.00, available at *http://www.southbound.com.my.*